New Product Planning

MANAGEMENT
INFORMATION
GUIDE : : 38

New Product Planning

A GUIDE TO
INFORMATION SOURCES

Sarojini Balachandran

Assistant Engineering Librarian
and
Associate Professor of Library Administration
University of Illinois Library
at Urbana-Champaign

GALE RESEARCH COMPANY · BOOK TOWER · DETROIT, MICHIGAN

Library of Congress Cataloging in Publication Data

Balachandran, Sarojini.
    New product planning.

    (Management information guide ; v. 38)
    Includes indexes.
    1. New products—Bibliography. I. Title.
II. Series.
Z7164.M18B32   [HF5415.15]   016.6585'75   79-24046
ISBN 0-8103-0838-X

VITA

Sarojini Balachandran has a bachelor of science and a master of arts degree in physics from India, where she worked as a Scientific Officer (Research & Development) of the Atomic Energy Commission. She also has a master's degree in physics from Indiana State University, Terre Haute, Indiana, and an MSLS from the University of Illinois at Urbana-Champaign, where she is currently the Assistant Engineering Librarian.

Balachandran has written TECHNICAL WRITING (1977), EMPLOYEE COMMUNICATION (1976) and REFERENCE BOOK REVIEW INDEX (1979) and is a regular contributor to the REFERENCE SERVICES REVIEW and the SERIALS REVIEW.

CONTENTS

INTRODUCTION

Each year, American industry develops billions of dollars worth of new products and introduces them to consumers in an effort to satisfy their real or imaginary needs. In fact, most businesses regard new products as the life blood of the American economy. This productive preoccupation with new products is reflected in the enormous amount of time and resources channelled into research and development activities. This is also reflected in the voluminous amount of marketing literature in this area. In the past decade alone, more than one hundred doctoral dissertations dealing with the various aspects of new product development and marketing have been accepted by various universities around the country. More numerous are the books, journal articles, and reports relating to this important facet of corporate activity in this country and abroad. At one time, all that a business needed to do to be profitable and stay that way was to find a need and fill it. Now, the chief concern is creating rather than finding a need, and satisfying it effectively. In any event, whether it is finding or creating a need, it necessarily begins with scientific market research, involving a study of consumer behavior, life styles, income levels, buying and spending patterns, and other similar attributes. Depending on its size, each company has to arrive at its own decisions as to how to conduct market research, that is, whether to form its own section or hire outside professionals, and as to the type of market research most conducive, under the circumstances, to producing results. However, it is clear from a reading of the literature that the chances of success for a new product are minimal, without some kind of prior market research. Assuming that the company's market research has revealed the need for or the possibility of creating a new product, some hard and high level corporate decisions are now called for. The watchword here is planning, involving determination of potential risks, costs, and rates of return. The marketplace is full of products which are introduced without any serious planning and which consequently are destined to be withdrawn as soon as they are introduced. A look at the literature reveals a number of financial techniques and mathematical models developed to aid corporate planners to arrive at a go--no--go decision. Once this difficult decision has been taken, the corporate research and development department begins playing its role. A considerable body of new product literature is devoted to the organization and running of the research and development department in big corporations. The basic problem here seems to be to foster innovation in a corporate atmosphere without stifling individual initiative and creativity. Other problems in this area include product design and liability, and above all maintaining effective communication between the marketing and R & D departments, so that scientists and engineers are kept in tune with what the market wants. Most companies order production of new products on a limited scale before the final go-ahead is given. This is to facilitate testing the water by use of highly developed techniques in the areas of concept and product testing, most of which have been covered in this bibliography. Here, too, marketing research has a highly significant role to play in gauging the consumer reactions to the new product and in interpreting them accurately. This is one of the final stages where a decision may be made to withdraw a new product and send it back to the drawing board with suggestions for improvement.

Two other important areas of activity before the new product enters the marketing stream relate to accounting and advertising. This first one--accounting--is concerned with all stages of new product development, mainly to keep tabs on the cost of the entire project. Another important accounting function relates to the pricing of the new product, taking into consideration the rate of return on investment, the product's competitive position, and the basic economic principle of charging what the traffic will bear. No product, however attractive, is going to stay on the shelves for too long without a prior sustained promotional campaign to make the consumer aware of the product and its potential advantages to specific target groups. This bibliography contains some well-thought-out advice to those about to launch new product campaigns.

As mentioned earlier, current market literature extensively covers all the above aspects of new product planning and marketing. This annotated bibliography is a modest attempt to bring together most of the literature published in the past decade. For the sake of convenience, the citations have been classified under major subject headings. A more in-depth approach is provided through the subject index in the appendix. The author hopes that this modest contribution will help scholars in their research on new product planning, as well as practical businessmen and executives in finding the appropriate technique to solve their particular marketing problem.

In preparing this literature survey, I received help from numerous colleagues. I particularly wish to thank Jagdish Sheth and Ken Uhl of the University of Illinois College of Commerce for their critical evaluation and suggestions as to the form and content of this book. My thanks are also due to Paul Wasserman, but for whose encouragement this project would not have been completed.

Sarojini Balachandran
Urbana, Illinois

Chapter 1

PRODUCT PLANNING

Abernathy, William J. "Interfunctional Planning for New Product Introduction." SLOAN MANAGEMENT REVIEW 14 (Winter 1972-73): 25-44.

Calls for minimizing risks in new product introductions by commitment (to extensive planning) to establish a balance between inventory and back order buildup and by developing production and marketing strategies jointly.

_____. "Methodology for Planning New Product Start Ups." DECISION SCIENCES 4 (January 1973): 1-20.

Analyzes the problem of maintaining a balance between production output and demand growth during new product introductions.

Abrams, George J. HOW I MADE A MILLION DOLLARS WITH IDEAS. 1st ed. Chicago: Playboy Press, 1972. 216 p.

Adams, R.M. "Approach to New Business Ventures." RESEARCH MANAGEMENT 12 (July 1969): 255-60.

Presents the author's own experience in the corporate handling of new business ventures. Stresses need for a favorable climate, such as management enthusiasm and successful marketing prospects, and for cooperation between the technical and marketing personnel.

Ames, B. Charles. "Keys to Successful Product Planning." BUSINESS HORIZONS 9 (Summer 1966): 49-58.

Illustrates product planning, planning cycles, and control processes in both consumer and industrial product markets.

_____. "Market Planning for Industrial Products." HARVARD BUSINESS REVIEW 46 (September-October 1968): 100-11.

Reports on a survey of planning practices of fifty industrial companies to examine where market planning for new industrial products fits into the formal management process.

Angelus, Theodore L. "New Product Shops Developing in 70s." ADVERTISING AGE 40 (13 October 1969): 8.

> Predicts that new products agencies will flourish in the 1970s, and that they will offer expertise in those areas which regular agencies avoid, take the initiative by showing manufacturers where real new product opportunities exist, and create new brands to exploit these opportunities.

Association of National Advertisers. "Workshop on New Products." ADVERTISING AGE 38 (15 May 1967): 1.

> Suggests that companies should come out with similar, improved products as soon as possible after a rival company introduces its new product, so that they would all get a share of the new markets profit.

"At Pantene: Research Builds Quality." AEROSOL AGE 20 (June 1975): 32-33.

> Describes the practice at the Pantene Company where the goal in new product development is to compete with top quality items in the product category, which must conclusively prove beneficial to the user. Explains how important it is that research and development and marketing staff remain in touch with each other during production of a new product, by holding many meetings to review progress, suggest changes, and to decide on the timing of introduction into the market.

"Base New Products on Real Need." ADVERTISING AGE 46 (3 November 1975): 35.

> Claims that too many new product introductions are actually reactions to business pressures and not a result of explicit need or demand for the new product. Advises problem-beset companies that are inclined to respond with quick answers to resort to a slower new product pace.

Ben Daniel, David. "General Electric's Severed Approach." In PROCEEDINGS: AMERICAN MARKETING ASSOCIATION COMBINED CONFERENCE, edited by Ronald C. Curhan, pp. 478-80. Chicago: American Marketing Association, 1974.

> Explains how General Electric deals with new product ideas which are rejected as unpromising.

Bennet, J.B. "Total Approach to New Product Development." MANAGEMENT REVIEW 58 (June 1969): 36-39.

> Explains how new products are essential for the survival of modern industries and how their development must be a highly coordinated activity of all functions of a company--a total management task.

Discusses the total management approach which consists of: getting new product ideas, selecting the right ideas, developing these ideas into products, and making sure the results are practical. Also stresses need for constant review, constant alertness, and continued management cooperation.

Bergeron, Pierre G. "Planning for Plant Expansion." CA MAGAZINE 109 (July 1976): 18-20.

"Big-Company Product Planning is Weighted and Found Wanting." PRODUCT ENGINEERING 41 (19 January 1970): 49-50.

Discusses a study on the planning practices of large corporations which found that inadequate planning was a major problem, as is a lack of written plans for new product development.

Bogaty, Herman. "Development of New Consumer Products - Ways to Improve Your Chances of Success." RESEARCH MANAGEMENT 17 (July 1974): 26-30.

Identifies two problems in new product development: expecting too much and being unlucky. Suggests that in order to deal with the former, one ought to develop a realistic long-range plan and apply proven principles.

Brand, Gruber and Company, ed. PROFESSIONALS LOOK AT NEW PRODUCTS. Michigan Business Papers, no. 50. Ann Arbor: University of Michigan Business Research, 1969. 238 p.

"Brewing New Product Ideas." CHEMICAL ENGINEERING 80 (12 November 1973): 108.

Contains the proceedings of a meeting entitled "Ideamanship - Identifying New Opportunities," which was sponsored by the Chemical Marketing Research Association and the Commercial Development Association, including a discussion of the methods of new product idea solicitation.

Brooks, Robert W. "New Products and the Corporate Personality." In PROCEEDINGS: AMERICAN MARKETING ASSOCIATION SUMMER CONFERENCE, edited by Bernard Morin, pp. 96-98. Chicago: American Marketing Association, 1969.

Examines the common reasons used by corporate executives for deciding against high risk new product projects. Article explains how some of these reasons need to be reexamined in the light of each situation.

Brown, Charles G. "Conceptualizing New Product Opportunities." In PROCEEDINGS: AMERICAN MARKETING ASSOCIATION COMBINED CONFERENCE, edited by Boris W. Baker and Helmut Becker, pp. 284-86. Chicago: American Marketing Association, 1972.

Examines how to identify new product opportunities by using focus group interviews, mail panel folios, rough commercials, and screening.

Bruno, Albert V. "New Product Decision Making in High Technology Firms." RESEARCH MANAGEMENT 16 (September 1973): 28-31.

Deals with the poor quality of new product decision activity and suggests methods for improvement. Same article also in UNIVERSITY OF SANTA CLARA WORKING PAPER series, no. 11, 1972, p. 11.

BUSINESS STRATEGIES FOR PROBLEM PRODUCTS. Report no. 714. New York: Conference Board, 1977. 51 p.

Deals with a survey of 120 companies in terms of diagnosis, decision options, and preventive strategies.

Butrick, Frank M. "How to Spot a Market Opportunity." SALES MANAGEMENT 108 (3 April 1972): 41-44.

Advances the view that new product development takes place more or less constantly in most companies. Explains how alert sales executives can influence new product development and make profits a less chancy game by urging products which they know beforehand can be sold.

Cannon, Tom. "New Product Development." EUROPEAN JOURNAL OF MARKETING 12 (1978): entire issue.

Explores the multifarious aspects of developing a new product, and the key role played by the marketing concept with its knowledge of consumer desires and behavior. Stresses that marketing skills are very important in view of the current changing attitude toward new product development.

Cantin, Donald W. TURN YOUR IDEAS INTO MONEY. New York: Hawthorn Books, 1972. 157 p.

Carlson, K.O. "New Products - Problems and Opportunities." FOOD PRODUCT DEVELOPMENT 11 (September 1977): 34.

Cathey, P.J. "New Product Planning: It's Tougher Than Ever." IRON AGE 212 (13 December 1973): 50-51.

Explains how industrial market researcher is missing opportunities in product positioning which will place a new product in its best market segment.

Chambers, John C., et al. "Catalytic Agent for Effective Planning." HAR-
VARD BUSINESS REVIEW 49 (January-February 1971): 110-19.

> Shows how working as a diplomat and a clearinghouse can help a
> research group to press planning efforts to a successful conclusion.

"Changing Technology and the Future of Marketing." CONFERENCE BOARD
RECORD 11 (December 1974): 22-26.

> Describes the technological changes which influence the "pull"
> for new products and services.

Chenu, Pierre. "A Decision Process for New Product Selection." INDUSTRIAL
MARKETING MANAGEMENT 3 (October 1973): 33-45.

Choly, R. "Fable: Useless Product Invented to Make Use of Another Useless
Product." DRUG & COSMETIC INDUSTRY 99 (July 1966): 52-53.

Chorafas, Dimitris N. AN INTRODUCTION TO PRODUCT PLANNING AND
RELIABILITY MANAGEMENT. London: Cassell, 1967. 300 p.

Clemens J., and Thornton, C. "Evaluating Non Existent Products." ADMAP
4 (May 1968): 232.

> Outlines the gap principle, that opportunities exist in any market
> at any time if one can find them. Explains how a simple per-
> ceptual model of the market from the consumers' point of view can
> be drawn up, in order to see where unoccupied territories exist.

Conley, Patrick. EXPERIENCE CURVES AS A PLANNING TOOL: A SPECIAL
COMMENTARY. Boston: Boston Consulting Group, 1970.

> Explains how product planning strategy involves developing product
> portfolios based on market share. Describes how to use experience
> curves for this purpose.

Constandse, William J. "How To Launch New Products." MSU BUSINESS
TOPICS 19 (Winter 1971): 29-34.

> Discusses new product planning, organization, staffing, strategy,
> design, forecasting, evaluation, and promotion.

"The Continuing Search for Product Newness." NEW PRODUCTS DIGEST 3
(January 1967): 1-9.

> Examines the terms "success" and "failure" when applied to new
> product introductions. Points out some of the logical areas manu-
> facturers should consider when developing new products. Also
> discusses the copying of a competitor's product, convenience,
> variety, economy, and science.

Cooper-Jones, Dennis. BUSINESS PLANNING AND FORECASTING. New York: Wiley, 1974. 265 p.

Cotterell, L. "Why Industry Must Join the Quest for New Products." DIRECTOR 22 (September 1969): 398-400.

Coulson-Thomas, Colin J. "Checklist for the Range and Type of Matters Which Require Consideration when New Products Are Being Developed." ACCOUNTANTS DIGEST no. 60 (Winter 1977-78): entire issue.

Crawford, C. Merle. "The Trajectory Theory of Goal Setting for New Products." JOURNAL OF MARKETING RESEARCH 3 (May 1966): 117-25.

> Explains how new products are accepted or rejected faster by the marketplace, which makes it critical that research techniques be developed to provide early assessment of progress. Using an actual case study, proposes one such technique based on the astronautical theory underlying work with guided missiles.

Crisp, R.D. "Fifteen Ways to Go About Developing a New Product." ADVERTISING AGE 37 (31 October 1966): 115-16.

> Examines the view that many new products fail because of a lack of creativity during the development process. Presents fifteen areas of improvement in new product development including changes in flavor, color, size, and shape of products.

Crole-Rees, D. "You Don't Need the Whole Works for a New Product." ENGINEERING 238 (3-10 January 1974): 36-37.

Crow, Robert Thomas. ON THE DEMAND FOR NEW GOODS. Faculty Research Working paper series, no. 170. New York: State University of New York, 1973. 32 p.

Day, George S. "A Strategic Perspective for New Product Planning." JOURNAL OF CONSUMER BUSINESS 4 (Spring 1975): 1-34.

> Suggests adoption of a portfolio approach to product planning involving classification of product lines into high and low market share items.

Doblin, J. "Before It's Too Late Denovate." MACHINE DESIGN 41 (3 April 1969): 20-21.

Douglas, G., et al. SYSTEMATIC NEW PRODUCT DEVELOPMENT. New York: Wiley, 1978. 170 p.

> Analyzes the advantages of diversification to companies through new product development activity and examines how better results can be obtained through proper organization.

Dunkley, John C. CORPORATE GROWTH FROM DIVERSIFICATION AND NEW PRODUCT DEVELOPMENT. London: Industrial and Commercial Techniques, 1972. 52 p.

Dunne, Patrick M. "What Really are New Products?" JOURNAL OF BUSINESS 13 (December 1974): 20-25.

> Attempts to provide marketer with a more definitive classification of product newness, with a three dimensional matrix, each reflecting different levels of newness as seen by the producers, distributors, and consumers. Classifies products into new products, line extensions and improvements, new brands and types. Explains all the twenty-seven different ways of looking at newness.

Eastlack, J.O., Jr., ed. NEW PRODUCT DEVELOPMENT. Marketing for Executives series, no. 13. Chicago: American Marketing Association, 1968. 148 p.

> Contains articles on the development and introduction of new products in the last twenty years. Deals with the new product opportunity identification systems, advanced methods of planning new product launch efforts, and the problems associated with testing the consumer acceptability of new products.

Evans, R.H. "Assessing Introduction Factors for a New Industrial Product." INDUSTRIAL MARKETING MANAGEMENT 7 (April 1978): 128-32.

_____. "Reflections on the Politics, Philosophy and Economics of New Product Development." CHEMISTRY AND INDUSTRY, 18 October 1975, pp. 848-51.

"Finding New Products Require Initiative." IRON AGE 198 (25 August 1966): 96.

> Explains how purchasing executives should stay on top of new product developments.

Fogg, C. Davis. "Market-Directed Product Development Process." RESEARCH MANAGEMENT 20 (September 1977): 25-32.

> Deals with the planning of steps necessary before actual development work begins; and deciding whether or not a project should proceed from one stage to another.

Fond, A.B. "Persuasive Role of Product Planning." INDUSTRIAL DESIGN 13 (May 1966): 80-84.

Foss, B., and Schaefer, H.A. "Birth of a Product." CHEMICAL TECHNOLOGY 2 (July 1972): 398-401.

Foster, Douglas W. PLANNING FOR PRODUCTS AND MARKETS. London: Longman, 1972. 352 p.

Frank, Ronald E. "But the Heavy Half is Already the Heavy Half." In PROCEEDINGS: AMERICAN MARKETING ASSOCIATION SUMMER CONFERENCE, edited by Keith Cox and Ben E. Enis, pp. 172-76. Chicago: American Marketing Association, 1968.

Furst, Sidney, and Sherman, Milton. THE STRATEGY OF CHANGE FOR BUSINESS SUCCESS. New York: C.N. Potter; distributed by Crown Publishers, 1969. 186 p.

Gibson, D.P. "Creating Products for Negro Customers." SALES MANAGEMENT 102 (1 May 1969): 61-62.

> Discusses the dos and don'ts of introducing new products to the Negro market.

_____. $30 BILLION NEGRO. New York: Macmillan, 1969. 311 p.

Gisser, Philip. "Gisser On New Products as Corporate Step Children." INDUSTRIAL MARKETING 56 (April 1971): 44.

> Examines why many companies handle new products badly even though they know that more than eighty percent of the company's profits would come from products that are not on the drawing board.

Glennan, Thomas Keith, Jr. "New Product Development: Some Observations Based on the Development of Military Aircraft." Ph.D. dissertation, Stanford University, 1968. 139 p. Ann Arbor, Mich.: University Microfilms. Order no. 68-11296.

> By a case study of the development of military planes, this thesis examines the determinants of development costs in terms of the cost of engineering, special tooling, and production.

Golby, C. "New Product Development." In INDUSTRIAL SOCIETY: SOCIAL SCIENCES IN MANAGEMENT, edited by D. Pym, pp. 426-44. London: Penguin, 1968.

Gorle, Peter, and Long, James. ESSENTIALS OF PRODUCT PLANNING. McGraw-Hill Management Manuals. London; New York: McGraw-Hill, 1973. 99 p.

Goslin, Lewis N. THE PRODUCT-PLANNING SYSTEM. Irwin series in Operations Management, vol. 3. Homewood, Ill.: R.D. Irwin, 1967. 159 p.

Graf, Franklin H. NEW ITEMS: PROBLEMS AND OPPORTUNITIES. New York: Nielsen, 1967. 14 p.

Greenstein, Howard. "Licensing New Product Technology." INDUSTRIAL RESEARCH/DEVELOPMENT 20 (June 1978): 122-25.

Describes how to promote new technology for licensing, how to identify prospective licenses, ways to protect inventions and handle trade secrets.

Gross, Irwin. TOWARD A GENERAL THEORY OF PRODUCT EVOLUTION. Marketing Sciences Institute working paper. Cambridge, Mass.: Marketing Sciences Institute, September 1968.

"Growth Through New Product Development." ACCOUNTANT (England) 168 (17 May 1973): 679-81.

GUIDE TO LOCATING NEW PRODUCTS. San Mateo, Calif.: TTA Information Services, 1971. 66 p.

Develops a working tool for industrial corporations interested in acquiring new products and product lines. Provides profiles of 130 leading U.S. firms that specialize in locating and/or developing new products for corporate clients.

Haas, Raymond M. LONG-RANGE NEW PRODUCT PLANNING IN BUSINESS: A CONCEPTUAL MODEL. Morgantown: West Virginia Library, 1965. 103 p.

Outlines a conceptual model of the long-range new product planning function in business and then uses the model as a basis for examining the practical experiences of business firms in this area.

Hainer, Raymond M. UNCERTAINTY IN RESEARCH, MANAGEMENT AND NEW PRODUCT DEVELOPMENT. New York: Reinhold, 1967. 234 p.

Deals with the difficulties and complications of research, management, and new product development.

Hake, Bruno. "Strategies for Diversification." LONG RANGE PLANNING 5 (July 1972): 65-69.

Discusses the most suitable approach to the obtaining of new products by an individual firm in order to reach new market.

Hanssmann, Fred. "The Planning of Market Oriented Development Projects." INDUSTRIELLE ORGANISATION (Switzerland) 35 (March 1966): 99-108.

Harris, J.S. "The Other Side of the Coin." Paper presented at the New York Chapter of the American Marketing Association, 13 May 1971.

Hatch, Thomas E., and Urban, Glen L. NEW PRODUCTS - MINIMIZING RISK AND MAXIMIZING CREATIVITY. Working paper, Boston: M.I.T., Sloan School of Management, 1975, pp. 752-74.

Hentschel, Uwe. "On the Search for New Products." EUROPEAN JOURNAL OF MARKETING 10 (1976): 203-17.

Contains an overview of the marketing-oriented product task, which is seen as a combination of three factors: consumer information through research, systematic formation of available expert information, and adequate simulation technique. Illustrates an example taken from the beverage market to show new product development.

Herzog, Donald B. "Research in New Product Planning." MARKETING INSIGHTS 3 (20 January 1969): 8-9.

Hilton, Peter. "Growth Via the New Product Route." In his PLANNING CORPORATE GROWTH AND DIVERSIFICATION, pp. 149-61. New York: McGraw-Hill, 1970.

Hisrich, Robert D., and Peters, Michael. MARKETING A NEW PRODUCT: ITS PLANNING, DEVELOPMENT AND CONTROL. Menlo Park, Calif.: Benjamin/Cummings Publishing Co., 1978. 358 p.

Hopkins, D.S. "New Emphasis in Product Planning and Strategy Development." INDUSTRIAL MARKETING MANAGEMENT 16, no. 6 (1978): 410-19.

Appraises the role of strategic planning in product development and marketing maintenance, particularly from the viewpoint of its use to avoid problem products. Discusses the use of strategic planning for product planning, control, repositioning, and stretchout, as well as for augmenting other functional contributions to the product management.

Houlding, J.D. "Planning New Products and Technology." INDUSTRIAL CANADA 66 (July 1965): 218-20.

Hudson, R.G. "New Product Planning Decisions Under Uncertainty." INTERFACES 8, pt. 2 (November 1977): 82-96.

Describes how management science techniques have been used to assist in decision making for new product purchasing and development where the new product required significant technological innovation and was being introduced in a market where there was little previous experience.

Hulbert, Hugh M. "A Model for Corporate Growth by New Product Research Productivity." IEEE TRANSACTIONS ON ENGINEERING MANAGEMENT EM-14 (June 1967): 83-88.

Contains a highly simplified model for growth of corporate sales resulting from new product research which shows that investment of a fixed annual fraction of profits in new product research and parameter B(k+sY) exceeds unity, and annual sales grow exponentially and that for values less than unity, sales reach a steady annual value. Explains how, although too crude for quantitative prediction of individual product return, the model may have rough quantitative values for whole business or large product classes.

Hussey, D.E. "Planning for New Products." ACCOUNTANT 170 (14 February 1974): 205–6.

Stresses the importance of well-defined new product planning systems which insure proper interdepartmental coordination and help management to control what is being done.

Ingersoll, B. "Product Development Gains Speed When Planning Takes Command." PRODUCT ENGINEERING 41 (2 March 1970): 39–40.

Describes a pilot-product planning program to make a slow process more efficient. Discusses the problem areas and presents a checklist in three main areas: What kind of products will customers be asking for in the next five years or so? What characteristics must these products have? What quantities can be sold to what customers, at what prices, during what period of time?

Jolson, Marvin A. "New Product Planning in an Age of Future Consciousness." CALIFORNIA MANAGEMENT REVIEW 16 (Fall 1973): 25–33.

States that conventional methods used by new product planners give only limited consideration to the dynamics of a changing society. Describes other techniques such as scenario writing, envelope curves, credence decomposition, relevance trees, and the Delphi method.

Jones, G.W. "New Product Development." CONFERENCE BOARD RECORD 13 (September 1976): 25–28.

Discusses new product concepts, their generation, evolution of acceptability, and market testing.

Karger, D.W., and Murdick, R.G. "Art and Science of Forecasting New Product Payoff." MACHINE DESIGN 43 (30 September 1971): 38–42.

Reports on a survey which was conducted to determine the techniques currently used, decision factors companies consider important in planning, and the types of evaluation made at the following key stages of new product development; the methods of evaluation and selection of products for development, method for selecting basic research (nonproduct related) projects and formal evaluation procedures and forms utilized.

11

_____. "The Top Man Looks at New Product Problems." MACHINE DESIGN 43 (June 1971): 52-57.

> Surveys the experiences of thirty-two company presidents active in new product development.

Keegan, Warren J. "Multinational Product Planning: Strategic Alternatives." JOURNAL OF MARKETING 33 (January 1969): 58-62.

> Examines the cost of adaptation and manufacture, as well as use analysis involved in product choice decisions in international marketing.

Kelemen, Andrew L. NEW PRODUCT PLANNING AND DEVELOPMENT. Scranton, Pa.: International Correspondence School, Division of Intext, 1969. 151 p.

Kelner, H.W. "Assessment of Markets for Entirely New Products." IMRA JOURNAL 6 (November 1970): 169-80.

> Defines ways in which a new product can originate. Explains areas of application and subsequent development of "need grids" for each product, based on actual performance requirements in specific industries.

King, Stephen Harris Morley. DEVELOPING NEW BRANDS. New York: Wiley, 1973. 184 p.

_____. "Identifying Market Opportunities." In PROCEEDINGS: NATIONAL CONFERENCE ON LONG RANGE PLANNING FOR MARKETING AND DIVERSIFICATION. England: University of Bradford Management and the British Institute of Management, June 1969.

Kirk, Van. "Chemical Marketers: Change or Die." CHEMICAL TECHNOLOGY 46 (April 1973): 208-12.

> Examines the reasons for slump in the new product development in the chemical industry.

Kline, C.H. "Case of the Diversification Dilemma." HARVARD BUSINESS REVIEW 43 (May 1965): 12-14.

> Discusses a hypothetical situation which illustrates the real problems faced by companies in industrial fields which seek to diversify into other new product lines and the steps taken for a potentially successful consumer product.

Konopa, Leonard Jesse. NEW PRODUCTS: ASSESSING COMMERCIAL POTENTIAL. Management Bulletin, 88. New York: American Management Association, 1966. 29 p.

Konson, A. "The Forecasting of Demand for New Products." PROBLEMS OF ECONOMICS 11 (June 1968): 16-24.

> Stresses the importance of accurately forecasting the demand for new products and discusses the factors determining new product demand.

Koontz, H. "Making Strategic Play Work." BUSINESS HORIZONS 19 (April 1976): 37-47.

> Discusses one of the major strategies of a business which relates to the development and marketing of new products. Provides guidelines for the effective implementation of strategic planning.

Kraushar, Peter Maximilian. NEW PRODUCTS AND DIVERSIFICATION. London: Business Books, 1969. 213 p.

Lang, John B. FINDING A NEW PRODUCT FOR YOUR COMPANY. Management Aids for Small Manufacturers, no. 216. Washington: U.S. Small Business Administration, 1972. 8 p.

Lauro, G.J. "New Product Development: To Flush Out Winners You Must Have a Working New Product Plumbing System." FOOD TECHNOLOGY 26 (April 1972): 22-26.

Lawrence, W.D. "Selecting and Developing New Products." ELECTRONICS AND POWER 17 (July 1971): 260-64.

> Suggests a six-phase process to identify and fulfill an existing consumer need, which should be the combined effort of marketing, sales, and engineering departments.

Lawson, William H. "Financial Concepts in New Product Development." FINANCIAL EXECUTIVE 33 (March 1965): 38.

> Explains the factors which are essential to a new product planning program, namely, resource allocation, project selection, and periodic review. Discusses the financial information needed for setting up a scheme to cover these situations.

Leiter, L.I. "Developing Product Ideas." INDUSTRIAL DESIGN 24 (November 1977): 60-61; 25 (January 1978): 62-63.

Lenz, R.C., and Lanford, H.W. "The Substitution Phenomenon." BUSINESS HORIZONS 15 (February 1972): 63-68.

> Examines the substitution forecast theory which is helpful in deciding whether or not to invest in a new technology, based on the idea that a product which exhibits better performance over an older, established or conventional product will eventually substitute the latter.

Linsky, Barry R. "Which Way to Move With New Products." ADVERTISING AGE 45 (22 July 1974): 45-46.

> Indicates some of the sources of new product myopia, namely, narrow corporate self image, budgetary myopia, and concept screening myopia. Defines five guidelines for combating new product myopia. Gives two examples of successful diversification.

Little, Blair. "New Focus on New Product Ideas." BUSINESS QUARTERLY 39 (Summer 1974): 62-69.

> Reveals the view that for too long, in too many firms, new product managers have accepted ideas which happen by chance. Suggests that they should take control of the system generating new product ideas and give it direction.

Locander, William B., and Scamell, R.W. "Conceptual Approach to Planning New Product Introductions in Sets." ACADEMY OF MARKETING SCIENCE JOURNAL 3 (Summer-Fall 1975): 355-68.

> Suggest that external pressures such as energy crisis, raw material scarcity, and price control have created the need for better planning methods to support decisions in new product introduction. Discusses an approach which would enable planner to allocate scarce resources over a number of products and to plan within and/or across product lines while taking such factors into account as advertising expenses, and so forth.

Lynn, J.E. "Pioneer or Guinea Pig in Adapting Really New Techniques." AMERICAN DYE STUFF REPORTER 58 (21 April 1969): 46-47.

MacDonald, Morgan B. APPRAISING THE MARKET FOR NEW INDUSTRIAL PRODUCTS. Business Policy study, no. 123. New York: National Industrial Conference Board, 1967. 112 p.

> Examines current practices of industrial product companies in appraising the market for their new products, based on the experiences of more than 100 U.S. and Canadian manufacturers. Study reviews some of the causes underlying new product failures in the industrial goods field. Shows how companies are using market planning and research to reduce failure and the high risks involved in new product ventures.

McGuire, E. Patrick. SOURCES OF CORPORATE GROWTH. New York: Conference Board, 1974. 28 p.

> Contains the results of a survey of opinions from the panel of senior marketing executives on new products as a source and obstacle to corporate health.

"Managing the Product Planning Function." In MARKETING IN A COMPETITIVE ECONOMY, edited by L.W. Rodger, pp. 100-128. 3d ed. London: Hutchinson, 1972.

Marvin, Philip Roger. PRODUCT PLANNING SIMPLIFIED. New York: American Management Association, 1972. 221 p.

Mathey, C.J. "New Approaches to Management of Product Planning." RESEARCH MANAGEMENT 19 (November 1976): 13-18.

Proposes that mere financial techniques for analysis of product proposals are insufficient. Explains that while such numeric techniques are necessary, they really are only the result of more fundamental underlying causes. Describes new tools for strategic (nonfinancial) planning and they include force field analysis, experience curves, technological forecasting, and visual screening.

Megathlin, Donald E., and Schaeffer, Winnifred E. A BIBLIOGRAPHY ON NEW PRODUCT PLANNING. AMA Bibliography Series, no. 5. Chicago: American Marketing Association, 1966. 62 p.

Mockler, Robert J. "Systematic Management Planning Aids a New Product: A Case Study." MARQUETTE BUSINESS REVIEW 9 (Winter 1965): 1-9.

More, Roger Allan. "Primary and Secondary Market Information for New Industrial Products." INDUSTRIAL MARKETING MANAGEMENT 7 (June 1978): 153-60.

"Much New Product Work is Wastefull." ADVERTISING AGE 43 (20 November 1972): 110.

Explains reasons why most new product work is wasteful. It is nearly impossible for corporate managers to "experience the ups and downs, the social and economic problems of everyday people." A second reason corporations are at fault is that most of them are organized to sell existing products, not new ones.

Mueller, Robert K. "Venture Vogue: Boneyard or Bonanza?" COLUMBIA JOURNAL OF WORLD BUSINESS 8 (Spring 1973): 78-82.

Discusses the rationale for new venturing in terms of the process by which the sponsor couples to the new venture management process itself and the different style required as the new venture evolves.

Mullick, Satinder K., and Haussener, Donald P. "Product Decisions for New Products." MANAGEMENT ACCOUNTING 56 (August 1974): 27-32.

Discusses a simulation model which either can compute risk directly or rapidly evaluate the effects of errors in estimates. Includes a case study of a project in which the costs of several production plans have been accurately predicted under varying conditions to provide a strong basis for decision making.

Murdick, R.G., and Steiner, G.A. "Hazard Analysis for New Product Development." BUSINESS REVIEW 38 (October 1974): 2-5.

Myers, James H. "Benefit Structure Analysis: A New Tool for Product Planning." JOURNAL OF MARKETING 40 (October 1976): 23-32.

Develops a benefit structure analysis especially for finding new product opportunities in very broad product service categories. Determines consumer reaction to a large number of relatively specific benefits desired from a type of product service and provides relatively complete information to ambient conditions surrounding the use of the product.

"New Approaches to New Products." INDUSTRY WEEK 184 (3 February 1975): 24-26.

"New Product Concepts Diminishing." ADVERTISING AGE 44 (23 April 1973): 30.

Cites reasons for trend of companies preferring low risk, low investment new product ideas.

"New Product Development." ACCOUNTANT (England) 167 (6 July 1972): 14-15.

"New Product Development." FOOD TECHNOLOGY 21 (November 1967): 1442-45.

"New Product Development." In PROCEEDINGS: CONFERENCE ON NEW PRODUCT DEVELOPMENT. University of Strathclyde, Glasgow, 1965.

"New Product Development: Goliath or Tom Thumb?" BUSINESS MANAGEMENT 37 (December 1969): 35-36.

Puts forward the view that the best breeding ground for new products is the newer, smaller, and undercapitalized company, since it does not suffer from rigid management thinking.

"New Product Development: Symposium." FOOD TECHNOLOGY 23 (July 1969): 885-88.

"New Product Development in New England Mills." Joint TAPPI-PIMA meeting, 8-9 October, Manchester, Vt., abstract of papers. AMERICAN PAPER INDUSTRY 48 (March 1966): 21-22.

"New Product Planning for Changing Markets." In NEW PRODUCTS MARKET-ING CONFERENCE, 7th, Detroit, 1967, edited by Martin R. Warshaw, and Gerard P. Murphy, Michigan business papers, no. 47, Ann Arbor: Bureau of Business Research, University of Michigan, 1968.

"New Products: Concepts, Development, and Strategy." In NEW PRODUCT MARKETING CONFERENCE, 6th, Detroit, 1966, edited by Robert R. Scrase, Michigan business papers, no. 43, Ann Arbor: Bureau of Business Research, University of Michigan, 1967.

"New Products Are Risky But Necessary." PRODUCT ENGINEERING 42 (September 1971): 16.

> Cites the findings of a survey conducted by the Conference Board, New York. Reports that more than twenty percent of the major new products introduced over the past five years have failed. Discusses the reasons for the failure. Among industrial product manufacturers sixty-seven percent said that the risk was worth it "more often than not," thirty percent said it was "nearly always" worth it, and three percent said it was seldom worth it.

NEW PRODUCTS, NEW MARKETS. Edited by Blair Little. London, Ontario: University of Western Ontario, School of Business Administration, Research and Publications Division, 1973. 88 p.

"New Products Seen as Key to Increasing Competitive Struggle." MANAGE-MENT SERVICES 4 (May 1967): 9.

Novak, J. "Production Planning on Paper." MANAGEMENT REVIEW 60 (January 1971): 11-16.

> Discusses the product chart as a highly useful tool for the manufacturing team for controlling and reviewing complex production processes. Same article also in INDUSTRIAL ENGINEERING 2 (October 1970): 18-24.

Null, Gary, and Simonson, Richard. HOW TO TURN IDEAS INTO DOLLARS. New York: Pilot Books, 1969. 55 p.

Nye, Bernard C., and Dorr, E.L. PRODUCT PLANNING. Occupational manuals and projects in marketing. Marketing activities, no. 2. New York: Gregg Division, McGraw-Hill, 1970. 124 p.

O'Meara, John T. "Selecting Profitable Products." HARVARD BUSINESS RE-VIEW (January-February 1961): 80-88.

> Discusses a study made by Ross Federal Research Corporation for Peter Hilton, Inc., entitled, "The Introduction of New Products."

Pearl, D.R. "New Products Called Risky But Necessary." MACHINE DESIGN 38 (22 December 1966): 16.

> Explains why the introduction of products is still considered a risky business, although growth in sales volume comes from new products. Odds against the success of new product ventures are so formidable that unless the calculated probability of success is high, it is usually better to desist.

Pearson, Arthur S. "How to Compare New Product Programs." JOURNAL OF MARKETING RESEARCH 2 (June 1971): 3-8.

> Examines the need to improve the productivity of new product programs and the issue of resource allocation. Discusses how most companies make decisions on new products, and outlines a specific case, using a special computer program. Illustrates the use of probability estimates integrated with the financial parameters of the marketing plans which makes a choice among projects quite clear.

"Permissible Period of Time During Which New Products May Be Described As New." FEDERAL TRADE COMMISSION ADVISORY OPINION DIGEST, No. 120 (15 April 1967).

Pessemier, Edgar A. NEW PRODUCT DECISION. New York: McGraw-Hill, 1966. 214 p.

> Studies the formulation of sound product policy from research and development to marketing strategy. Viewing product policy as a central factor in overall corporate strategy, outlines the objectives and structural elements of a dynamic new product program, with particular attention to problems of timing and scheduling. Includes a discussion of PERT network analysis and planning procedures that can be used effectively for controlling new product development.

Pessemier, Edgar A.; and Root, H. Paul. "The Dimensions of New Product Planning." JOURNAL OF MARKETING 37 (January 1973): 10-18.

> Reviews models employed in the analysis and planning of four critical areas of new product management: (1) the search process that affects the rate and character of new product proposals, (2) the screening process that determines the modifications and refinements of a given proposal, (3) the demand analysis process that evaluates the competitive structure of the market, and (4) the investment analysis process that influences the amount and timing of financial resources committed to a well-defined new product proposal.

"Plan Ahead or Risk Extinction." ADVERTISING AGE 39 (6 May 1968): 52.

> Suggests that since constant changes are brought about by science,

business, and industry, marketers should plan ahead to stay on top of the risk of competitors' new products.

"Poor Product Planning Handicaps Their Companies." MANAGEMENT ADVISER 10 (March 1973): 10.

Contains the results of a survey of leading marketing managers' experiences in new product launchings which reveals that lack of proper planning was a major cause of many failures.

Posner, Frederick. "New Products: Before You Build a System." MARKETING REVIEW 10 (December 1971): 18-19.

Pressley, Milton. "A Revised Look at New Product Development Process." NORTH CAROLINA REVIEW OF BUSINESS AND ECONOMICS 2 (April 1975): 12-13.

Updates a study done in 1964 about the time taken from the conception of the idea to the time of achievement of initial distribution objectives. Products involved are grocery products. Study indicates that some successful large firms seemingly wait for their competitors to innovate.

"Product Planning Helps Firms to Suit the Market." ENGINEER 230 (12 February 1970): 63.

"Product Planning Must be Founded on Definition." PRODUCT ENGINEERING 38 (23 October 1967): 91.

Discusses the corporate philosophy of product planning based on five questions: what are we providing to our customers from their viewpoint, why do our customers buy from us rather than from our competitors, why have we suceeded in certain areas, why have we failed in other areas, and what does our competition do better than we are doing?

THE PROFESSIONALS LOOK AT NEW PRODUCTS. Edited by Brand Gruber and Company. Michigan Business Papers, no. 50. Ann Arbor: University of Michigan, 1969. 238 p.

"The Professionals Look at New Products." In NEW PRODUCTS CONFERENCE, 8th, Detroit, 14-15 March 1968. Edited by Brand Gruber. Michigan Business Papers, no. 50. Ann Arbor: Bureau of Business Research, University of Michigan, 1969.

"Question Tree Leads to Better New Product Decisions." PRODUCT ENGINEERING 46 (September 1975): 15.

Raddant, R. "Filling the New Product Gap." IRON AGE 200 (7 September 1967): 50-52.

Examines the proposition that companies should concentrate on searching for and filling the need for new industrial products.

Raviolo, V. "Planning of a Product." SAE JOURNAL (Society of Automotive Engineers) 77 (May 1969): 28-34.

Explains how the application of engineering methods facilitates new product planning.

Ringbakk, Kjell-Arne. "Big Company Product Planning is Weighed and Found Wanting." PRODUCT ENGINEERING 41 (January 1970): 49-52.

Describes a survey of forty large companies which revealed that product planning and marketing functions are the most important priorities.

Rockley, Lawrence E. CAPITAL INVESTMENT DECISIONS. London: Business Books, 1968. 260 p.

Rodgers, William N. "Intuitive Leap of Faith Essential to New Venture Planning." In PROCEEDINGS: AMERICAN MARKETING ASSOCIATION SPRING-FALL CONFERENCE, edited by Fred C. Allvine, pp. 132-37. Chicago: American Marketing Association, 1971.

Suggests operational synergy to identify and overcome organizational constraints to a venture function built into every corporation.

Root, H. Paul. "New Product Investment Decisions: the Process and Procedures." In PROCEEDINGS: AMERICAN MARKETING ASSOCIATION SPRING-FALL CONFERENCE, edited by Fred C. Allvine, pp. 147-50. Chicago: American Marketing Association, 1971.

Examines the relationships between procedures and the structure of the organization in the new product development process.

Rothberg, Robert R. CORPORATE STRATEGY AND PRODUCT INNOVATION. New York: Free Press, 1976. 518 p.

Deals with product innovation, strategy formulation, product management planning, organizing for new product development, product life cycle, and barriers to successful innovation.

_____. "Playing It Safe in New Product Decisions." ADVANCED MANAGEMENT JOURNAL 40 (Autumn 1975): 11-19.

Discusses how a major obstacle in the path of finding a new successful product can be the very people in charge of each project. Suggests ways in which this problem can be avoided.

Rothberg, Robert R., and Mellott, Douglas W. NEW PRODUCT PLANNING: MANAGEMENT OF THE MARKETING/R & D INTERFACE. Chicago: American Marketing Association, 1977. 44 p.

Roxburgh, Douglas, ed. "New Product Development." In PROCEEDINGS OF A CONFERENCE, held at the University of Strathclyde on 11-12 September 1965. Glasgow: University of Strathclyde, 1966. 154 p.

Sandkull, Bengt. ON PRODUCT CHANGES AND PRODUCT PLANNING. Utg. av: Swedish Institute of Administrative Research, SiAR Lund, Studentlitteratur, 1968. 191 p.

Schon, Donald A. "The Fear of Innovation." INTERNATIONAL SCIENCE AND TECHNOLOGY 60 (14 November 1966): 70-78.

> Because new products affect stability of corporations, some may oppose their introduction. Tells how to overcome this attitude.

Scott, W.R. NEW PRODUCTS THROUGH ACQUISITION. American Society of Mechanical Engineers, Paper 75-WA/mgt 3. New York: American Society of Mechanical Engineers, 1977. 8 p.

> Acquisition method eliminates much of the time and expense of internal new product development. A meaningful analysis of potential firms can provide management of the quantitative information required to accept or reject such an acquisition. Such analysis must evaluate the existing product, the major product competition, the general financial suitability of the firm, and the firm's management capability.

Scrase, Robert R., ed. NEW PRODUCTS: CONCEPTS DEVELOPMENT AND STRATEGY. Michigan Business papers, no. 43. Ann Arbor: University of Michigan Business Research Bureau, 1970. 91 p.

Sellstedt, Bo, and Naslund, Bertil. "Product Development Plans." OPERATIONAL RESEARCH QUARTERLY 23 (December 1972): 497-510.

> Identifies two kinds of uncertainty associated with the development of new products: (1) uncertainty during the technical phase when the product is developed, i.e., about its quality and time required for development, (2) uncertainty associated with the commercial phase during which the product is produced and hopefully sold, i.e., about consumer tastes and actions taken by competitors.

SEMINAR ON RESEARCH FOR NEW PRODUCT DEVELOPMENT, Neu Isenburg, Germany, 4-7 November 1970, papers. Amsterdam: European Society for Opinion Surveys and Market Research, 1970. 125 p.

Smith, Alan A. TECHNOLOGY AND YOUR NEW PRODUCTS. Small Business Management Series, no. 19. 2d ed. Washington, D.C.: U.S. Government Printing Office, 1967. 61 p.

Studies the various aspects of new product technology. Discusses the importance and uses of research, the problems related to generating, assessing, and evaluating ideas for new products, which are factors to consider in the application of technology in new product development.

"Solve New Products Problems at the Top." Booz Allen Company study. IRON AGE 196 (16 December 1965): 61.

Spitz, A. Edward, ed. PRODUCT PLANNING. Rev. ed. New York: Petrocelli, Charter, 1976. 320 p.

Starbuck, W.H., and Bass, F.M. "An Experimental Study of Risk-Taking and the Value of Information in a New Product Context." JOURNAL OF BUSINESS 40 (April 1967): 155-65.

Analyzes the responses from 785 nonrandomly selected persons concerning a specific risk-oriented problem of introducing a new product. Seeks to determine the ability of decision makers to process information and reach good decisions according to some objective criterion.

Starczewski, J. "How to See New Ventures." HYDROCARBON PROCESS 48 (December 1969): 163-64.

Starkey, E.A. "Business Development: A New Concept." In PROCEEDINGS: AMERICAN MARKETING ASSOCIATION SUMMER CONFERENCE, edited by Bernard Morin, pp. 91-95. Chicago: American Marketing Association, 1969.

Explains how new products would not be successful if they do not relate to the market place. Article tells how businesses can develop long-range plans to obtain this result.

Stone, Merlin. PRODUCT PLANNING. New York: Wiley, 1976. 142 p.

Product planning decisions are usually heavily influenced by the constraints of a firm's existing resources and markets. Author argues that these self-imposed restrictions limit the effectiveness of product research and development and planning. To base planning on projections of future demand in all markets open to a company is a better approach.

Stumpe, Warren R. "Who Pays for New Product Development." RESEARCH MANAGEMENT 21 (September 1978): 17-19.

Describes how a company uses a pay-back method for funding research and development projects which provides incentive and establishes a commitment to accomplish a stated task.

Summers, Edward L. "How Learning Curve Models Can Be Applied to Profit Planning." MANAGEMENT SERVICES 7 (March-April 1970): 45-50.

Talley, Walter J. THE PROFITABLE PRODUCT: ITS PLANNING, LAUNCHING AND MANAGEMENT. Englewood Cliffs, N.J.: Prentice-Hall, 1965. 200 p.

Tauber, Edward M. "Discovering New Product Opportunities with Problem Inventory Analysis." JOURNAL OF MARKETING 39 (January 1975): 67-70.

Search for a new product is supposed to begin with the search for a customer need or problem. This is easier said than done. Problem inventory analysis helps identify how products can improve the quality of life. Applied samples are given.

_____. "Profiles of Future: The Emerging New Product Development Industry." BUSINESS HORIZONS 16 (April 1973): 5-6.

Presents an analysis of the emerging "new product development industry." Included are the results of a survey of a sample of those firms covering the nature of their services, clients, free structure, and track record. Gives an in-depth look at the advantages and difficulties of employing external new product development (NPD) sources.

Taylor, Stanford H. "Keys to Success in Product Introduction." In PROCEEDINGS: AMERICAN MARKETING ASSOCIATION SUMMER CONFERENCE, edited by John S. Wright and Jack L. Goldstucker, pp. 229-37. Chicago: American Marketing Association, 1966.

Examines the areas where corporate new product planning theory and practice are weak and offers suggestions to remedy the situation.

A TECHNOLOGY MANAGEMENT SEMINAR ON STRATEGIES FOR PRODUCT DEVELOPMENT, edited by Noreen Mooney. Innovation Transcript, no. 2. New York: Published for members of the Innovation Group by Technology Communication, 1970. 37 p.

"There's More to Product Planning Than the Generation of New Ideas." ELECTRONICS 43 (30 March 1970): 86-93.

Describes the view that product planning is the job of both the marketing executive as well as the technologist. Neither can do without the other.

Twedt, Dik Warren. "How to Plan New Products, Improve Old Ones and Create Better Advertising." JOURNAL OF MARKETING 33 (January 1969): 53-57.

> Presents a three-step method for planning a new product, planning product improvement, and evaluating the relative strength of copy claims. The first step involves systematic exploration of all conceivable product variations. The second step assigns differentiation ratings, and the third evaluates three primary factors of product attributes, namely, desirability, exclusiveness, and believability. The resulting charts provide diagnostic profiles that suggest ways in which particular copy claims may be strengthened.

Ullmann, John, ed. BUSINESS AND TECHNICAL DETERMINANTS OF PRODUCT CHANGE. Hofstra University Yearbook of Business, series 9, vol. 4. Hempstead, N.Y.: Hofstra University, 1974. 504 p.

Uman, David B. NEW PRODUCT PROGRAMS: THEIR PLANNING AND CONTROL. New York: American Management Association, 1969. 159 p.

U.S. Agricultural Research Service. NEW PRODUCT DEVELOPMENT FOR ECONOMIC GROWTH IN RURAL AREAS. U.S. Dept. of Agriculture. Miscellaneous Publication, no. 1013. Washington, D.C.: U.S. Government Printing Office, 1965. 11 p.

Van Horne, James. "Analysis of Uncertainty Resolution in Capital Budgeting for New Products." MANAGEMENT SCIENCE 15 (April 1969): B376-86.

> Develops a method for analyzing the resolution of uncertainty over time for the individual new product and for combinations of existing and new products or firms overall product mix. Probability concepts are employed.

Varble, Dale L. "Social and Environmental Considerations in New Product Development." JOURNAL OF MARKETING 36 (October 1972): 11-15.

> Discusses whether new product analysis should include environmental and societal factors, as well as the traditional economic factors of profitability, sales volume, and product line compatibility. Examines the drawbacks resulting from including these factors in the new product evaluation process, such as the probable increase in product development costs and time.

Verma, Dharmendra Tekchand. "New Product Planning and Development: Utah Manufacturers." Ph.D. dissertation, University of Utah, 1969. 232 p. Ann Arbor, Mich.: University Microfilms. Order no. 69-03511.

> Identifies some of the problems and decision processes involved in the development and marketing of new products.

Villani, K.E.A., and Morrison, D.G. "Method for Analyzing New Formulation Decisions." JOURNAL OF MARKETING RESEARCH 13 (August 1976): 284-88.

Inflation and shortages have forced management to resort to product reformulation as a means of keeping costs down and prices competitive. Article suggests how to estimate the market size for current and proposed new formulation of a product.

Vinson, Donald E., et al. "A Pragmatic Approach to New Product Planning." JOURNAL OF SMALL BUSINESS MANAGEMENT 13 (April 1975): 37-44.

Wallace, Irving Hold. "New Product Planning Procedure." Ph.D. dissertation, University of Minnesota, 1967. 243 p. Ann Arbor, Mich.: University Microfilms. Order no. 67-10446.

By surveying the new product experiences of several manufacturers, this study attempts to arrive at a generalized new product planning procedure which may be applied in most situations.

Wallenstein, Gerd D. CONCEPT AND PRACTICE OF PRODUCT PLANNING. New York: American Management Association, 1968. 127 p.

Ward, Edward Peter. THE DYNAMICS OF PLANNING. New York: Pergamon Press, 1970. 347 p.

_____. "Planning Tomorrow Today through Successive Focussing." JOURNAL OF MARKETING 31 (July 1967): 23-27.

Article addresses how to plan an integrated method for product planning. It attempts this by introducing the concept of the dynamic product area, and the idea of stages of successive focussing, which are analysis, exploration, search, acquisition, evaluation, and action.

Watton, Harry B. NEW-PRODUCT PLANNING; A PRACTICAL GUIDE FOR DIVERSIFICATION. Englewood Cliffs, N.J.: Prentice-Hall, 1969. 176 p.

Weinberger, M. "Six Ways to New Product Ideas." ADVERTISING AGE 42 (6 December 1971): 41.

Explains how to simplify some of the complexities involved in devising new product ideas.

Weiss, E.B. "So, What About the New Product Policy and Practice?" STORES 49 (November 1967): 23-29.

West, A.C. "How to Doom New Product Planning." IRON AGE 195 (6 May 1965): 69.

Describes how to avoid the so-called shortcuts to new product development which result in failure.

West, Raymond. "How to Plan for New Product Development." BUSINESS MANAGEMENT 38 (September 1970): 24-27.

Explains how it is better to have an entrepreneurial new product project manager rather than a new product committee.

White, Roderick. CONSUMER PRODUCT DEVELOPMENT. London: Longman, 1973. 267 p.

Wilemon, David L., and Hulett, P.L. "A Systems Approach to Corporate Development." LONG RANGE PLANNING 5 (March 1972): 46-51.

Examines the processes involved in developing new products in a large corporation calling for long-range planning, product line audits, and creation of special venture groups.

Wolff, Ernst. "Is Technology Transfer a Good Source of New Products?" In DESIGN ENGINEERING TECHNICAL CONFERENCE, 1st, New York, 5-9 October 1974, pp. 35-37. Available from American Society of Mechanical Engineers, Design Engineering Division, New York, 1974.

Wood, J.F. "New Product Development." ADMAP 3 (1967): 1-10.

Zoppoth, Raymond C. "The Use of Systems Analysis in New Product Development." LONG RANGE PLANNING 5 (March 1972): 23-36.

Discusses some of the leading techniques used in new product development including modelling, program planning, and requirement estimation in terms of resources, personnel, and technology needed.

Chapter 2

PRODUCT MANAGEMENT

Ames, B. Charles. "Dilemma of Product/Market Management." HARVARD
BUSINESS REVIEW 49 (March-April 1971): 66-74.

Introduction of new industrial products results in organizational
changes. Article examines how product growth should be han-
dled, i.e., by adding to product management staff or market
management staff.

APPLICATION OF AN EXISTING TECHNOLOGY FOR THE DEVELOPMENT
OF A NEW PRODUCT LINE. Proceedings of an annual forum on Developing
and Marketing New Products for Business and Industry. Princeton, N.J.:
Marketing Communications Research Center, 20 January 1970.

Asokan, E. "Economics of Product Development and Design." MANAGEMENT
ACCOUNTANT (India) 1 (October 1966): 520-23.

Auber, R.P. "New Products: Beware of Outside Ideas." MANAGEMENT
REVIEW 54 (August 1965): 22-26.

Considers the patent problems that may occur when an outside
individual or agency discloses ideas for a new product to a manufacturer. Discusses various protective measures that should be
used by a firm receiving unsolicited ideas.

Ball, L.W. "Using the Critical Activity Concept." QUALITY PROGRESS 8
(October 1975): 16-19.

Identifies the new product activities, such as program management
and contracting, engineering and test, manufacturing and quality
control, and support and operations. This identification and index-
ing system helps in preparing a checklist in a form suitable for
integration and achieving this integration by using them to make
inputs into the basic function program plans.

Baloff, N., and McKersie, R. "Motivating Startups." JOURNAL OF BUSI-
NESS 39 (October 1966): 473-84.

Introduction of a new product, or a new production process, can frequently pose important problems of adaptation and motivation for the personnel of a manufacturing firm. Such innovations can result in a distinct "learning" or "startup" period during which personnel strive to improve the low level of output usually experienced at the outset of manufacture. This paper explores the two issues that are central to the effective motivation and control of many start-ups.

Baumann, H.D. "Designing Multinational Products." INSTRUMENTS AND CONTROL SYSTEMS 47 (November 1974): 61-63.

Discusses the problems of product design for international use, such as: whether to use metric or English dimensions, how to meet diverse international standards, and how to meet diverse safety codes with one design.

Beattie, J.M. "Managing Ideas Into Profits." IRON AGE 211 (25 January 1973): 45-47.

Only a few of the many new ideas for products will be successful. This article discusses how to determine which products they will be.

Bell, D.E. "New Product Development Function in the Corrugated Industry." TAPPI 50 (March 1967): 87A-92A.

Discusses the structure of and policies relating to new product development in the corrugated industry.

Bennett, K.W. "Product Development Mystery Vitamin for Growth." IRON AGE 214 (21 October 1974): 29-31.

Individual case study is used to analyze the roles of the product manager, chief engineer, and key figures in the new product development process.

Bensahel, J.G. "How to Bury an Ill-Fated Project." INTERNATIONAL MANAGEMENT 29 (April 1974): 47.

Describes the common feelings and reactions to the scrapping of a failing product. Outlines questions of who to consult about the shutdown and how to tell them about it.

Benson, George. "Improving the Effectiveness of New Product Development." MARQUETTE BUSINESS REVIEW 14 (Winter 1970): 217-27.

Describes four basic areas of consideration important for new product development and success, namely, role of top management, role of the functional departments (i.e., marketing, research and development, production, finance), role of corporate formal procedures and role of the marketing concept. Lack of concern in one of these areas during development will probably result in failure.

Berow, S. William. "The Functions of Product Management, Past, Present and Future." In PROCEEDINGS: AMERICAN MARKETING ASSOCIATION SUMMER CONFERENCE, edited by John S. Wright and Jack L. Goldstucker, pp. 563-70. Chicago: American Marketing Association, 1966.

Outlines the evolution of the job of product management. Describes its functions and examines its future.

Betts, D.J. "Designing for Production." BUSINESS MANAGEMENT (London) 98 (December 1968): 38-41.

One problem for small companies is how to produce a new product without expensive "debugging" delays and costs. The solution lies, in part, with the elimination of some things used in larger companies, such as marketing surveys. As the market for a small company will also be small, it is possible to do several steps of the development simultaneously.

Bickford, J.J. "How to Fit in With the Product-Planning Committee." MACHINE DESIGN 44 (16 November 1972): 120-24.

Describes the general characteristics of the engineering, marketing, and financial personnel who make up a product planning committee. Discusses the chief product planner's responsibilities. Same article also in MANAGEMENT REVIEW 62 (February 1973): 68-70.

Binkered, E.F. "Luxury of New Products Development." FOOD TECHNOLOGY 29 (September 1975): 26-27.

"New products" are not really new all the time; more often they are just improvements of existing products. A great deal of the money spent on new product development is actually in the marketing phase. Author estimates only five to ten percent of the total expenditures goes to research and development costs. Also examines product failures which result from marketing causes rather than technical inadequacies.

Bolz, Roger W. PRODUCTION PROCESSES. Winston-Salem, N.C.: Conquest Publications, 1978. 1,089 p.

Provides a complete guide to the design of new products, components, and redesign of currently produced products. Discusses the design of individual parts, emphasizing those features that insure simple economic processing.

Booz, Allen and Hamilton, Inc. MANAGEMENT OF NEW PRODUCTS. Chicago, 1968. 31 p.

> Describes with the use of charts and tables how corporate growth can be supported by developing and acquiring new products and how this process should be managed.

Buddenhagen, F.L. "Internal Entrepreneurship As a Corporate Strategy for New Product Development." S.M. dissertation, M.I.T., 1967.

Buell, Victor P. "The Changing Role of Product Manager in Consumer Goods Companies." JOURNAL OF MARKETING 39 (July 1975): 3-11.

> Examines how product managers have no more direct decision making authority. Instead they are more involved with gathering data, planning, and evaluating performance.

Bujake, John E. "Ten Myths About New Product Development." RESEARCH MANAGEMENT 12 (January 1972): 33-42.

> Identifies and suggests remedies for common false generalizations about the process of new product development.

Bull, John S. "The Product Management System: Plague or Panacea?" BUSINESS QUARTERLY 33 (September 1968): 76-80.

> Presents an analysis of the product manager system as it relates to new product development. Expresses the view that product managers are necessary for corporate growth and that when product managers are no longer used, the company can no longer grow.

Bursk, E.C. "Case of the Product Priority; Excerpts from Cases in Marketing Management." HARVARD BUSINESS REVIEW 44 (March 1966): 6-8.

> Deals with the management decision-making process concerning product priorities. Steps that are undertaken to assure themselves of their decisions are discussed. Includes a segment of dialog between top executives as they discuss two products that they must choose between.

Butrick, Frank M. HOW TO DEVELOP NEW PRODUCTS FOR SALE TO INDUSTRY. Englewood Cliffs, N.J.: Prentice-Hall, 1971. 208 p.

_____. "Your Best New Product May Be in Your Catalog." INDUSTRIAL MARKETING 54 (December 1969): 36-39.

> Article is concerned with new product development. Companies often have products that were not developed completely at first and, therefore, do not sell well. By redeveloping these products, they can be made more profitable without involving much risk to the company.

Campbell, Gary J. "Organizing for New Product Development." MACHINE DESIGN 46 (16 May 1974): 116-19.

Case, H.M. "Designed Decay." HARVARD BUSINESS REVIEW 44 (January-February 1966): 126-31.

Discusses the concept of designed decay, or the designed factor that limits the life cycle of products in order to prepare for new innovations. Several practical examples of the designed decay process are discussed. Design parameters are identified as time, quality, reliability, safety, operability, maintainability, expandability, state of the art, and cost.

Chamblin, Mathew D. "Making Product Managers into Marketers." MAR-QUETTE BUSINESS REVIEW 11 (Summer 1967): 59-64.

Clayton, Henry L. "Pruning of Sick Products." MANAGEMENT ACCOUNT-ING 47 (June 1966): 17-18.

Article deals with the problem of products that are beginning to fail and how to go about removing them from the market. A survival score system is devised where products are scored on areas of financial security, financial opportunity, marketing strategy, social responsibility, and organized intervention.

Cleland, David I. "Understanding Project Authority." BUSINESS HORIZONS 10 (Spring 1967): 63-70.

Discusses project management concept that has been developed to deal with situations where production and marketing strategies for new products do not fit a purely functional type of organization. Examines the authority patterns of the project manager, a subject incompletely dealt with in the contemporary literature.

Clewett, Richard M., and Stasch, S.F. "Shifting Role of Product Manager." HARVARD BUSINESS REVIEW 53 (January-February 1975): 65-73.

Examines the new role of the product manager resulting from shifting business environments.

Collons, Rodger Duane. "Criteria for Aiding Administrations to Determine the Level of Creativity Embodied in a Product." Ph.D. dissertation, Georgia State University, 1967. 790 p. Ann Arbor, Mich.: University Microfilms. Order no. 68-05934.

Proposes and tests certain criteria to enable administrators to test the level of creativity in a product with a view, among other things, to establish patentability.

THE COMMERCIALIZATION OF INTERNALLY SUPPORTED RESOURCES. Report no. 695. New York: Conference Board, 1976. 32 p.

Deals with corporate experience with internally developed products or services originally intended for in-house use now being sold commercially.

Constable, G.E.P. "Ten Ways Not to Design for Production." ENGINEERING 215 (November 1975): 900-902. Discussion of this article appears in ENGINEERING 216 (January 1976): 22.

Constandse, William J. "Why New Product Management Fails." BUSINESS MANAGEMENT 40 (June 1971): 16-17.

Discusses the criteria for proving the financial success for a new idea, namely, return on investment, profitability-payoff risk ratio, and the experience and acumen of people who are responsible for developing new products.

Conway, H.G. "Design Organization; Past, Present and Future." AERONAUTICAL JOURNAL 80 (May 1976): 205-8.

Cook, Frederick W. "Venture Management Organizations." In PROCEEDINGS: AMERICAN MARKETING ASSOCIATION SPRING-FALL CONFERENCE, edited by Fred C. Allvine, pp. 129-31. Chicago: American Marketing Association, 1971.

Explains the technique for launching and building new businesses that are dissimilar from existing ones.

Cooper, Arnold C. "Small Companies Can Pioneer New Products." HARVARD BUSINESS REVIEW 11 (September-October 1966): 162-79.

While the development of technically advanced new products entails elements of risk which some small manufacturers may well decide to leave to others, many of these barriers can be overcome. This article, based on a survey of five small companies and supplemented by interviews with executives of eighteen other organizations, provides a basis for judging the extent to which major problems might be barriers to small companies, and considers ways in which these can be overcome or minimized.

Cooper, Robert G. "Introducing Successful New Industrial Products." EUROPEAN JOURNAL OF MARKETING 10 (1976): Entire issue.

Presents the results of a two-phase empirical study on new product development. Phase I focusses on a large sample of new product failures, and reveals that industrial product firms suffer from an inward orientation. Phase II presents three Canadian case histories of exceptionally successful and well-executed industrial new product ventures.

Crawford, C. Merle. "Product Development: Today's Most Common Mistakes." UNIVERSITY OF MICHIGAN BUSINESS REVIEW 29 (January 1977): 1-6.

Discusses the lack of an overall product strategy, good communication lines, product modification contingency plans, and coordination between research and development and marketing as some of the factors why some new products fail.

_____. "Strategies for New Product Development." BUSINESS HORIZONS 15 (December 1972): 49-58.

Discusses the advantages and disadvantages of alternative strategies for new product development.

_____. "Unsolicited Product Ideas - Handle With Care." RESEARCH MANAGEMENT 18 (January 1975): 19-24.

Surveys how companies deal with many unsolicited new product ideas without getting into trouble with trade secret laws.

Daniel, David Ben. "General Electric's Severed Approach." In PROCEEDINGS: AMERICAN MARKETING ASSOCIATION COMBINED CONFERENCE, edited by Ronald C. Curhan, pp. 478-80. Chicago: American Marketing Association, 1974.

Discusses a procedure for dealing with new product projects which fail to live up to initial expectations and are therefore spun off, with the company retaining an equity in the new venture.

Danielenko, T. "Those New Product Wizards: How Good are They?" PRODUCT MANAGEMENT 5 (September 1976): 40-44.

DeVries, Marvin G. A DYNAMIC MODEL FOR PRODUCT STRATEGY SELECTION. Ann Arbor: University of Michigan, Industrial Development Research Program, Institute of Science and Technology, 1963. 100 p.

Dominguez, George S. PRODUCT MANAGEMENT. New York: American Management Association, 1971. 404 p.

Dunn, Dan T., Jr. "The Rise and Fall of Ten Venture Groups." BUSINESS HORIZONS 20 (October 1977): 32-40.

Discusses the experiences of ten companies in implementing an entrepreneurial type of development group, the demise of these groups and the apparent causes, evolving organizational approaches which are replacing the venture group concept, and lessons drawn from the experiences of the sample companies.

DUPONT GUIDE TO VENTURE ANALYSIS. Wilmington, Del.: E.I. DuPont
Nemours and Company, 1971, pp. 15-45.

> Presents some useful guides to the market analysis of new product
> projects.

"DuPont's Answer Machine." BUSINESS WEEK (20 December 1969): 68-70.

> Defines venture analysis as "a systematic and quantitative disci-
> pline for organizing and processing information to guide business
> decisions." Explains how DuPont's marketers use venture analysis
> as a fast way of finding the information needed to make new prod-
> uct decisions.

Eckles, Robert W. "The Deletion of Products--A Necessary Evil." COLO-
RADO BUSINESS REVIEW 44 (September 1971): 2-4.

> Analyzes data collected in the veterinary ethical drug industry
> and the small electrical goods manufacturing industry, to illustrate
> common features which provide the foundation for the develop-
> ment of a product deletion decisions system.

_____. "Product Line Deletion and Simplification." BUSINESS HORIZONS
14 (October 1971): 71-74.

> Examines product line deletion in terms of periodic review of the
> entire line and appropriate time for the deletion decision.

Eggleston, David. "New Product Development." MANAGEMENT CONTROLS
20 (September 1973): 214-15.

Egloff, William F. "Product Management - Today and Tomorrow." In PRO-
CEEDINGS: AMERICAN MARKETING ASSOCIATION SPRING-FALL CON-
FERENCE, edited by Fred C. Allvine, pp. 120-23. Chicago: American Mar-
keting Association, 1971.

> Explores new organizational approaches directed towards the new
> product problem.

"The Emerging New Product Development Industry." BUSINESS HORIZONS
16 (April 1973): 5.

> Discusses in detail concepts and benefits of a new product develop-
> ment division in a firm. Explains the overall advantage.

Fendrich, C. Welles. THE INDUSTRIAL PRODUCT MANAGEMENT SYSTEM.
Management Bulletin, no. 80. New York: American Management Association,
Marketing Division, 1966. 24 p.

Fulmer, Robert M. "Does the Product Manager Manage?" SOUTHERN ILLI-
NOIS UNIVERSITY BUSINESS PERSPECTIVES 4 (Winter 1968): 11-16.

_____. "Organizational Constraints on New Product Success." UNIVERSITY OF WASHINGTON BUSINESS REVIEW 26 (Summer 1967): 57-67.

Success of a company's new product program is to a large degree contingent upon its skill and ingenuity in providing the optimum organization approach for the particular needs of the firm under consideration. Various organization forms for planning and controlling the development of new products are explored.

_____. "Panorama of Product Management." UNIVERSITY OF HOUSTON. CENTER FOR RESEARCH IN BUSINESS AND ECONOMICS. BUSINESS REVIEW, Spring 1967, pp. 11-12; Spring 1968, pp. 76-80.

_____. "Product Managers and New Product Development." JOURNAL OF BUSINESS 6 (December 1967): 6-12.

Discusses the use of a product manager as an organizational alternative to accomplish new product development. Outlines the roles, responsibilities, and specialities of product managers, and points out how they differ from company to company, according to the nature of the business and to the factor of "people resources."

_____. "Theoretical and Operational Implications of the Product Manager System in the Consumer Goods Industry." Ph.D. dissertation, University of California, Los Angeles, 1966. 262 p. Ann Arbor, Mich.: University Microfilms. Order no. 66-00213.

Contains the results of a survey of product managers relating to the historical development of, need for, and advantages and disadvantages of establishing a product manager system in consumer goods industries. Also looks at their duties and authority in the organization.

Galliver, G.B. "Economic and Production Problems in the Development of New Protein Sources." NUTRITION SOCIETY PROCEEDINGS 28 (March 1969): 97-102.

Gemmill, Gary A., and Wilemon, David A. "The Product Manager As an Influence Agent." JOURNAL OF MARKETING 36 (January 1972): 26-30.

Explains how the limited written authority of the product manager can be extended by using various indirect devices.

Gerlach, John T., and Wainwright, Charles Anthony. SUCCESSFUL MANAGEMENT OF NEW PRODUCTS. Communication Arts book. New York: Hastings House, 1968. 221 p.

Giese, Goetz. "Product Policy and Profitability." MANAGEMENT ACCOUNTING 49 (May 1968): 40-41.

Describes how to strike a balance and arrive at an optimal level between the number of products in a line and requirement of profit since products manufacturered in small quantities turn out small profits.

Gluck, Frederick W., and Foster, Richard N. "Managing Technological Change." HARVARD BUSINESS REVIEW 53 (September-October 1975): 139-50.

Stresses the importance of top management in decisions as to which technological opportunity to pursue.

Grayson, Robert A. "The Effect of Formal Organizational Structure on New Product Development for Branded Consumer Packaged Goods Marketers." Ph.D. dissertation, New York University, 1968. 130 p. Ann Arbor, Mich.: University Microfilms. Order no. 68-14052.

Examines which type of corporate organizational structure is most helpful in new product development, that is, whether it is a full-time product manager system or a part-time product management system or a no-product manager system.

_____. "If You Want New Products, You Better Organize to Get Them." In PROCEEDINGS: AMERICAN MARKETING ASSOCIATION SUMMER CONFERENCE, edited by Bernard Morin, pp. 75-79. Chicago: American Marketing Association, 1969.

Analyzes the results of a survey of major consumer goods companies as to the advisability and economic advantages of corporations having a full-time new product development department against part-time efforts.

Gronseth, J.R. "Putting a New Product On Stream." MACHINE DESIGN 49 (24 November 1977): 103.

Explains the need for and the ways to coordinate new product operations between manufacturing, engineering, and marketing departments.

Gumucio, Fernando. "Product and Management Today and Tomorrow." In PROCEEDINGS: AMERICAN MARKETING ASSOCIATION SPRING-FALL CONFERENCE, edited by Fred C. Allvine, pp. 117-19. Chicago: American Marketing Association, 1971.

Hanan, Mack. "Corporate Growth Through Venture Management." HARVARD BUSINESS REVIEW 47 (January-February 1969): 41-61.

Explains uses of intracorporate, intercorporate, and supracorporate venture teams for developing major new products.

_____. VENTURE MANAGEMENT. New York: McGraw-Hill, 1977. 392 p.

Covers the process of launching a new product or service in a corporate environment. Discusses in detail the various steps in the complicated new venture process. Case histories are included.

Hill, R.M., and Hlavacek, J.D. "Learning from Failure: Ten Guidelines for Venture Management." CALIFORNIA MANAGEMENT REVIEW 19 (Summer 1977): 5-16.

_____. "Product Development Through Venture Teams." In PROCEEDINGS: AMERICAN MARKETING ASSOCIATION SPRING-FALL CONFERENCE, edited by Fred C. Allvine, pp. 138-42. Chicago: American Marketing Association, 1971.

_____. "The Venture Team: A New Concept in Marketing Organization." JOURNAL OF MARKETING 36 (July 1972): 44-50.

Explains and compares the advantages of establishing venture teams as distinguished from the established methods of managing new products.

Hilton, Peter. KEEPING OLD PRODUCTS NEW. Englewood Cliffs, N.J.: Prentice-Hall, 1967. 230 p.

Demonstrates how a number of firms in a wide range of business and industry succeeded in making their standard items contemporary and competitive. Uses case histories to illustrate ideas and suggestions concerning slight product modification, searching for new markets and new uses, packaging changes, fresh promotion approaches, industrial marketing concepts, price changes, and the use of premiums.

Hippel, Erich Von. "Successful and Failing Corporate Ventures: An Empirical Analysis." INDUSTRIAL MARKETING MANAGEMENT 6, no. 3 (1977): 163-74.

New venture involves developing a new product, bringing it to market, and carrying it through the initial phases of market activity. By comparing successful and unsuccessful ventures, the author identifies factors which lead to the success of a given venture.

Hise, Richard T. PRODUCT/SERVICE STRATEGY. New York: Petrocelli, Charter, 1976. 225 p.

Hise, Richard T., and Mcginnis, M.A. "Product Elimination: Practices Policies, Ethics." BUSINESS HORIZONS 18 (June 1975): 25-32.

Reports the results of a comprehensive analysis of the product elimination practices of ninety-six large manufacturing firms. Study reveals that most firms lack a sophisticated program for product elimination. Many fail to do an effective job and tend to overlook the consumer in making decisions.

Hlavacek, James D. "Alternatives in Venture Management." In PROCEEDINGS: AMERICAN MARKETING ASSOCIATION COMBINED CONFERENCE, edited by Ronald C. Curhan, p. 481. Chicago: American Marketing Association, 1974.

_____. "Toward More Successful Venture Management." JOURNAL OF MARKETING 38 (October 1974): 56-60.

By an examination of twenty-one new product failures, the article draws lessons for successful organization and conduct of venture management schemes.

Hlavacek, James D., et al. "Tie Small Business Technology to Marketing Power." HARVARD BUSINESS REVIEW 55 (January-February 1977): 106-16.

New joint ventures between a small and big company can take advantage of small company enthusiasm and useful technology tied to the marketing power of a large company. Cites examples and notes pitfalls to avoid.

Hoge, W.H. "Four Fables of Failure-Pitfalls in Product Development." PULP AND PAPER 42 (25 March 1968): 29-31.

Holt, K. "Managerial Aspects of Product Development in Norwegian Companies." MANAGEMENT INTERNATIONAL REVIEW 8, nos. 2-3 (1968): 37-47.

Hopkins, David S. OPTIONS IN NEW PRODUCT ORGANIZATION. New York: Conference Board, 1974. 55 p.

Considers the relative merits of different ways of organizing the new product activities of a company. Presents several approaches and opinions about management style and philosophy for organization of new product planning and development.

_____. "The Roles of Project Teams and Venture Groups in New Product Development." RESEARCH MANAGEMENT 18 (January 1975): 7-12.

Discusses the advantages and disadvantages of project and venture teams in management of complex projects.

Horowitz, Tamar. "The Man in the Middle." JOURNAL OF MARKET RESEARCH SOCIETY 17 (January 1975): 26-40.

"How To Shrink Lead Time in New Product Production." BUSINESS MANAGEMENT 29 (May 1966): 81-90.

Deals with the problem of shortening the lead time between new product conception and introduction. Describes how a leading manufacturer of dry copy reproduction machines shaved eighteen months from a new product lead time with a modified program evaluation and review technique system.

Jackson, David H. "New Product Management." MANAGEMENT ACCOUNTING 56 (July 1974): 54-56.

Examines new product development in terms of a managerial process and its related information system. Discusses organizing, staffing and directing, initial planning, information system, control. Stresses that each review of the new product should be as completely documented as possible so that future evaluations can be made in terms of the original considerations.

Jackson, Myles. NEW PRODUCT DEVELOPMENT AS A NORMAL PART OF GENERAL MANAGEMENT ACTIVITY. Presidents Special Study, no. 28. New York: Presidents Association, 1966. 28 p.

Johnson, Howard Edward. "Production and Inventory Control of New Products from Initial Production to Establishment in the Market." Ph.D. dissertation, Washington University, 1967. 387 p. Ann Arbor, Mich.: University Microfilms. Order no. 67-09410.

Examines how companies carrying lines where there is need for frequent change in styles, handle the problem of production and inventory functions associated with the introduction of newly designed products.

Johnson, Paul Robert. "A Normative Model for the Determination of an Optimal New Product Mix." Ph.D. dissertation, Stanford University, 1968. 209 p. Ann Arbor, Mich.: University Microfilms. Order no. 69-08202.

One of the critical managerial decisions relates to the determination of an optimal new product mix. This thesis examines some of the mathematical techniques, such as linear programming algorithm which may make such decisions easier.

Jones, Kenneth, and Wilemon, David. "Emerging Patterns in New Venture Management." MANAGEMENT REVIEW 27 (February 1973): 59-61.

Article summarizes the results of a survey of 500 companies on their use of venture management teams and their experiences.

Jones, Wayne Paul. "The Development of New Grocery Products." Ph.D. dissertation, University of Louisville, 1971.

Karger, D.W. "How Top Management Looks at New Product Problems." MANAGEMENT REVIEW 60 (September 1971): 52-54.

Presents the conclusion of survey conducted to determine the problems associated with new product venture management. Most companies had new product committees which had the control of the
development and marketing of new products.

Karger, D.W., and Murdick, Robert G. NEW PRODUCT VENTURE MANAGE-
MENT. New York: Gordon and Breach, 1972. 280 p.

Covers new product risks and opportunities, product planning, and
organizing for new products, tapping sources for new product
ideas, research and engineering, evaluation, costing, pricing,
and promotion. Discusses the roles played by various specialists
like the researcher, lawyer, and engineer in the venture process.

_____. "Product Design, Marketing and Manufacturing Innovation." CALI-
FORNIA MANAGEMENT REVIEW 9 (Winter 1966): 33-42.

Discusses integrated product differentiation through design, marketing, and manufacturing. Presents a matrix to help companies identify the combinations of innovation which they are best equipped
to pursue.

Kellogg, Marion S. "Do You Manage Interfaces?" HYDROCARBON PRO-
CESSING 54 (January 1975): 163+.

Examines the formal and informal communications mechanisms in
large organizations for creating interface between marketing, engineering, and research and development departments.

Killick, R.W. "Product Development: An Organized Approach." AMERICAN
PERFUMER 85 (June 1970): 57-60.

Kolb, J. "Shepherding a New Product From Brainwave to Hardware." PROD-
UCT ENGINEERING 38 (16 June 1967): 38-41.

Discusses some commonsense criteria to avoid pitfalls of product
development. Among the important criteria before you even begin
are: Is this a real innovation you have in mind, or merely a variation? Can you profit by others' mistakes?

Koontz, H., and Bradspies, R.W. "Managing Through Feed Forward Control."
BUSINESS HORIZONS 15 (June 1972): 25-36.

Describes the use of feed forward control in cash planning, inven-
tories, and new product development. Offers seven guidelines for
its application.

Kotler, Philip. "Phasing out Weak Products." HARVARD BUSINESS REVIEW
43 (March-April 1965): 107-18.

Product pruning is just as important as product improvement and

new product development, yet most firms have no systematic procedure for pruning weak products. Discusses a control system which
will help drop "superannuated" products from weakening product mix.

Kratchman, S.H. "Management Decisions to Discontinue a Product." JOUR-
NAL OF ACCOUNTANCY 139 (June 1975): 50-54.

Discusses how management accounting can help decide the product
discontinuance function by forcing the accounting and marketing
areas of the firm to interact and cooperate with each other.

Kunstler, Donald A. "Corporate Venture Groups: The Need, the Responsibility
the Organizations, the Leadership." In PROCEEDINGS: AMERICAN MARKET-
ING ASSOCIATION FALL CONFERENCE, edited by Robert L. King, pp. 449-
54. Chicago: American Marketing Association, 1968.

Article examines how professional venture groups are formed to
develop new products and commercialize them. Also how to prevent waste of money on ineffective product development efforts.

Latham, Richard S. "The Role of the Industrial Designer in Product and Package Development." In HANDBOOK OF MODERN MARKETING, edited by
V.P. Buell, pp. 89-98. New York: McGraw-Hill, 1970.

Discusses packaging, display, and exhibition of a new industrial
product.

Lee, A.W. "The Design Process--The Birth of a New Product." ELECTRONICS
AND POWER 14 (November 1968): 442-44; discussion of this article appears
in ELECTRONICS AND POWER 15 (January 1969): 25.

Explains how a product engineer designing a new product has to take
into account, among other factors, market research, policymaking,
budgetary control, critical path scheduling, value analysis, decision making by committee, personal responsibility, teamwork, step
stressing, and failure analysis. Suggests that use of modern design
techniques leads to greater control and purpose and prevents waste
of money and effort.

Lee, J. "Communication the Key to Successful Designing." ENGINEERING
216 (February 1976): 104-8.

Explains how communications can be developed to improve total
product design. The creation of new products which meet users'
real needs and can be manufactured reliably, efficiently, and at
acceptable cost needs the cooperation of all departments in a company.

Lesley, Kenneth L. "Subcontracting New Product Development." MANAGE-
MENT REVIEW 62 (March 1973): 13-21.

When a promising idea for a new product occurs and the company manpower is fully committed to another project, it is possible to subcontract outside the company. Article discusses how this can be done.

Libien, Myron A. "Product Design is Everybody's Business." MANAGERIAL PLANNING 25 (January-February 1977): 30-33.

Luck, David J. "Interfaces of a Product Manager." JOURNAL OF MARKETING 33 (October 1969): 32-36.

Explains how intercompany and intracompany functions may create obstacles to the smooth performance of the product management functions and how to avoid pitfalls in the various interfaces.

_____. PRODUCT POLICY AND STRATEGY. Englewood Cliffs, N.J.: Prentice-Hall, 1972. 118 p.

Provides an overview of all major aspects in management of product policies and strategies.

Luck, T.J., and Nowak, T. "Product Management: Vision Unfulfilled." HARVARD BUSINESS REVIEW 43 (May 1965): 143-50.

Examines the corporate constraints which hamper a firm's orderly expansion into new products and new markets. Suggests remedies for overcoming these marketing problems.

McCarthy, J. "How a Product Finds Its Place." INDUSTRIAL MANAGEMENT 4 (September 1974): 20-22.

McDonald, D.J. "Human Factors: The Forgotten Element in Design." MACHINE DESIGN 48 (9 September 1976): 108-15.

Many promising new products fail because of inadequate attention given to the ultimate consumer. Article tells how to take into account human factors in designing a new product.

McDonald, Philip R., and Eastlack, Joseph O. "Top Management Involvement With New Products." BUSINESS HORIZONS 14 (December 1971): 23-31.

Discusses the present nature and extent of top management's involvement in new product activities.

MacFarlane, Iain. "The Place of Research in New Product Marketing Today and in the Seventies." AUSTRALIAN JOURNAL OF MARKETING RESEARCH (August-November 1972): 80-84.

Looks at new product development as an "action function" rather than a "staff" or "line" function. Emphasizes the "resourcing concept" in view of the diminishing natural resources.

"Managerial Assembly Line Now Creates New Wares." ADVERTISING AGE 41 (26 January 1970): 3.

> Explains how a common denominator in all successful new product programs is a carefully structured communication process which involves committee and line activities.

MANAGING ADVANCING TECHNOLOGY. Edited by the Staff of Innovation. New York: American Management Association, 1972. 2 vols. 245 p.; 177 p.

MANAGING PRODUCT RECALLS. Report no. 632. New York: Conference Board, 1974. 95 p.

> Examines the policies and programs, organization and operation of product recall programs, the reason for recalls, and the methods to identify faulty products.

Marsden, B.A. "Problems in Product Design." MANAGEMENT ACCOUNTING 44 (March 1966): 105-6.

Melville, Donald R. "Product Management - A Portfolio of Business." In PROCEEDINGS: AMERICAN MARKETING ASSOCIATION COMBINED CONFERENCE, edited by Edward M. Mazze, p. 359. Chicago: American Marketing Association, 1975.

Miller, H.M.S. "New Product Development Management." IRISH MANAGEMENT INSTITUTE 17 (April 1970): 31-33.

Moore, K.K. "Behind the Scences at Flavor Secrets." FOOD PRODUCT DEVELOPMENT 11 (July-August 1977): 42 .

National Industrial Conference Board. ORGANIZATION FOR NEW PRODUCT DEVELOPMENT: A SYMPOSIUM. Experiences in Marketing Management, no. 11. New York, 1966. 83 p.

> Examines the problems of new product management, and discusses the merits of alternative organizational approaches in overcoming them. Discusses the need for coordination, factors influencing new product organization, and various specific approaches. Includes selected organization charts.

National Industrial Conference Board. PRODUCT MANAGER SYSTEM: A Symposium. Experience in Marketing Management, no. 8. New York, 1965. 126 p.

Nelsen, A.B., et al. "Life Insurance Product Development." BEST'S REVIEW (LIFE ed.) 73 (July 1972): 14.

Offord, Ray Hamilton. PRODUCT MANAGEMENT IN ACTION. London: Business Publications, 1967. 165 p.

Pagano, Dominic F. "New Cookie Development." MANAGEMENT ACCOUNTING 56 (August 1974): 37-39.

Describes how the new products manager selects and scheduled the planning, manufacturing, and testing of new products. Discusses the estimating of raw material costs, raw material cost per package, formulation of kitchen test trials in order to develop a cookie which is acceptable for appearance, texture, taste, and quality, production test run, and the final decision.

Payne, Richard A. THE MEN WHO MANAGE THE BRANDS YOU BUY: A CANDID REPORT ON THE PRODUCT MANAGEMENT SYSTEM, ITS FUNCTIONS AND FRUSTRATIONS. Chicago: Crain Communications, 1971. 130 p.

Pedraglio, Gerard. "Getting into Shape to Manage New Products." EUROPEAN BUSINESS 28 (Summer 1971): 38-47.

Pessemier, Edgar A. "The Practice of Business-New Product Venture." BUSINESS HORIZONS 11 (August 1968): 5-19.

Strong product line and the capacity to develop new improved products are the hallmarks of a well-managed company. Discusses the importance of currently appraising the emerging social and scientific environment to discover new needs and means to satisfy them. Discusses factors involved in development.

Petrini, Bart F., and Grub, Phillip D. "Product Management in High Technology Defense Industry Marketing." CALIFORNIA MANAGEMENT REVIEW 15 (Spring 1973): 138-46.

Explains how to use the product management approach in supplying technology products for the defense industry.

Phelps, Ernest D. "Improving the Product Development Process." INDUSTRIAL MARKETING MANAGEMENT 6, no. 1 (1977): 47-51.

Focuses on "people activity" as the key element in the successful development of a new product, such as identification of the capabilities of the firm, a mutual understanding among the chief operating executive and the various functional heads involved in new product development and assignment of responsibilities, and the successful informal relationships at all levels.

Pilditch, J., and Scott, D. "Organization and Product Planning." DESIGN (BRITAIN) no. 206 (February 1966): 38-40.

Plant, A.F. "Maximizing New Product Dollars." INDUSTRIAL RESEARCH 13 (January 1971): 44-47.

Describes what is involved in control, guidance, and periodic re-evaluation of new products in order to get maximum value from investment in new products.

"Plotting a New Product Line: Tek Tactics." EE/SYSTEMS ENGINEERING TODAY 33 (April 1974): 78-81.

Primak, G.J. "Effect of Patents, Licenses and Trade Marks on New Product Development." CANADIAN MINING AND METALLURGY BULLETIN 66 (May 1973): 43-47.

"Product Development Checklist." FOOD ENGINEERING 42 (May 1970): 96-98.

PRODUCT MANAGER SYSTEM. New York: Conference Board, 1965. 126 p.

Discussion of their responsibilities, working relationships, training, organizational problems, and conflicts, with organizational charts and position guides.

"Prune Product Line for Profitability." TMS Survey Report. ADVERTISING AGE 38 (13 November 1967): 20.

Discusses the merit of traditional product deletion decisions versus the "readily usable numerical point scale" deletion decision system.

"Purchasing Catalyst for Ideas." PURCHASING 72 (20 June 1972): 111-13.

Suggests that new product design can be enhanced by soliciting ideas from suppliers as early as possible. Explains how purchasing can play a key role in encouraging vendors to work as members of the design team. Gives an evaluation of the functions of the engineer, salesman, and purchasing manager.

Rae, Alan J. "Product Manager - A New Concept." CANADIAN CHARTER-ED ACCOUNTANT 88 (March 1966): 204-7.

Randall, J.S. "Prepare the Company for the Product." IRON AGE 195 (7 January 1965): 153-56.

Since new products can have drastic organizational effects and their correction is time-consuming, the article suggests that man-agement must face up to these effects ahead of time.

"Rescue Those White Elephants." INDUSTRIAL RESEARCH 12 (December 1970): 32.

Discusses the role of new products versus new uses for existing products.

Riegel, W.M. "How Line Executives Can Eliminate Road Blocks to New Product Success." PAPER TRADE JOURNAL 150 (7 November 1966): 51-52.

Riggio, C.A. "Taking the Tossup Out of New-Product Development." MACHINE DESIGN 48 (10 June 1976): 82-85.

Explains a reliable method for choosing the most promising out of a number of available new product candidates. The method involves weighing the risks against probable benefits before company's resources are committed.

Rondeau, Herbert F. "New Products." INDUSTRIAL RESEARCH 14 (February 1972): 53-56.

Discusses the reasons why the new products department method of product innovation will not work. Describes a constructive alternative for such a function.

Rothe, J.M. Harvey, and Phines, W. "New Product Development Under Conditions of Scarcity and Inflation." MICHIGAN BUSINESS REVIEW 29 (May 1977): 7.

Suggests that through the reexamination of the classical product development cycle, in light of a scarcity-inflation marketing environment, a method will evolve to explore and develop new product opportunities.

Rudkin, J. "From Bright Idea to Plant Production." CHEMICAL ENGINEERING 82 (3 February 1975): 69-71.

Discusses a phased approach to new product development and introduction. By breaking down the process into key stages, managers would be able to identify and avert potential problems.

Rutenberg, David P., and Shaftel, Timothy L. "Product Design: Subassemblies for Multiple Markets." MANAGEMENT SCIENCE 18 (December 1971): B220-31.

Deals with the problem of finding the best standard modules for a multiproduct, multimarket corporation. Parts are grouped in subassembly modules.

Scheuing, Eberhard Eugen. NEW PRODUCT MANAGEMENT. Hinsdale, Ill.: Dryden Press, 1974. 307 p.

Shames, William H. VENTURE MANAGEMENT: THE BUSINESS OF THE INVENTOR, ENTREPRENEUR, VENTURE CAPITALIST AND ESTABLISHED COMPANY. New York: Free Press, 1974. 289 p.

"Shaping of Things to Come: New Product Development." FOOD TECHNOLOGY 23 (July 1969): 885-88.

"Short-Cut Formula May Predict Products' Chance of Success." PRODUCT ENGINEERING 40 (27 January 1969): 80.

Discusses a new shortcut method to help planning staff predict whether or not a proposed new product will be successful enough to justify investing chronically short, even more costly engineering manpower. The short cut is based on a formula that uses as its principal component the ratio of engineering development labor costs to total development costs, as indicated by prior comparative product-development experience.

Sims, John Taylor. "On Measuring the Long-Run Effects of Product-Line Extensions." Ph.D. dissertation, University of Illinois, Urbana-Champaign, 1970. 109 p.

By analyzing the case history of an addition of a new flavor to an existing grocery brand line, author attempts to analyze the long-run marketing effect of such product line extensions.

Slocum, Donald H. NEW VENTURE METHODOLOGY. New York: American Management Association, 1972. 208 p.

"Spin-Offs Spurned." SALES & MARKETING MANAGEMENT 117 (11 October 1976): 16-21.

Special products made for firm's own use are later sold to outsiders, sometimes profitably. Deals with why many companies miss such possibilities completely.

Staudt, T.A. "Higher Management Risks in Product Strategy." JOURNAL OF MARKETING 37 (January 1973): 4-9.

Discusses the new complexities of the business environment that account for higher risks in product management and strategy. Both risks and penalties for product failure are increasing. Therefore, improving the effectiveness and profitability in product policy and strategy represents new management imperatives.

Steel, Roy G. "Phasing Out Weak Products." CANADIAN CHARTERED ACCOUNTANT 98 (February 1971): 111-14.

Stefflre, Valnoy. "Market Structure Studies. New Products for Old Markets." In APPLICATIONS OF THE SCIENCES IN MARKETING MANAGEMENT, edited by F. Bass, et al., pp. 251-68. New York: Wiley, 1968.

Stewart, John M. "Making Project Management Work." BUSINESS HORIZONS 8 (Fall 1965): 54-68.

Provides guidelines for the installation of a project management system to undertake large complex tasks.

"Still Too Many Failures." MANAGEMENT REVIEW 66 (May 1977): 3-4.

> Article says too many new products fail needlessly and shows some of the areas of management weaknesses.

Stoll, W.F. "New Product Development: Industry Approach." JOURNAL OF MILK AND FOOD TECHNOLOGY 33 (October 1970): 464-66.

Swager, W.L., and Lipinsky, E.S. "Structuring Ideas for Product Development With Relevance Trees." AMERICAN COSMETICS AND PERFUMERY 87 (May 1972): 47-50.

Talley, Walter J., Jr. "Product Line Planning-Industrial Goods." In HANDBOOK OF MODERN MARKETING, edited by V.P. Buell, pp. 41-51. New York: McGraw-Hill, 1970.

> Explains product planning in terms of developing and marketing new products and where mergers and acquisitions fit into this process.

Terry, H., and Nagy, S.F. "Effective Product Development: A Closely Managed Activity." INDUSTRIAL RESEARCH 16 (August 1974): 38-41.

> Suggests that creativity should be encouraged and channeled towards a defined business goal and tight controls be applied to implementation of the elements of the development process.

Turner, R.E. "Product Priorities Within a Multiple Marketing Organization." JOURNAL OF MARKETING RESEARCH 11 (May 1974): 143-50.

> Examines organizational problems in the allocation of marketing budget to individual products in a multiproduct company regarding the above. Describes the priorities of product managers, salesmen, and other managerial roles.

Tyler, Ralph. "The Care and Feeding of New Products." TELEVISION 22 (November 1965): 25-29, 49-56.

> Describes how important the creation of new products has become to American industry, and by extension, to television, the major national advertising medium. Comments by both advertising and marketing experts are included.

Urban, Glen L. "Product Interdepending in New Product Decisions." In PROCEEDINGS: AMERICAN MARKETING ASSOCIATION FALL CONFERENCE, edited by Raymond M. Haas, pp. 653-56. Chicago: American Marketing Association, 1966.

> Suggests looking at the new product as part of a total product line. Article says that until now the interdependence of the new product in a product line has been ignored in acceptance decisions.

Vancil, Richard V. "Better Management of Corporate Development." HAR-
VARD BUSINESS REVIEW 50 (September-October 1972): 53-62.

Describes a new way to approach the process of managing internally generated growth, including a new type of planning and
control systems for executives.

"The Venture Adventure." SALES MANAGEMENT 98 (15 January 1967): 35-
40.

Discusses how venture groups, small teams of marketing and technical groups, are making profits for their companies by keeping
them one step ahead of tomorrow.

Vesper, K.H., and Holmdahl, T.G. "How Venture Management Fares in Innovative Companies." RESEARCH MANAGEMENT 16 (May 1973): 30-32.

Reports on how a significant number of large firms with demonstrated ability to innovate use the venture management approach.

Wallace, Robert T. "New Venture Management at Owens-Illinois." RESEARCH
MANAGEMENT 12 (July 1969): 261-70.

Describes the different philosophies of the various companies of
Owens-Illinois, Inc., whose common goals were to seek ideas for
new business opportunities, relate these to corporate resources in
meaningful ways and organize to develop the few most promising
ones into viable businesses by the meticulous capabilities of planning and entrepreneurship.

Wasson, Chester P. PRODUCT MANAGEMENT: PRODUCT LIFE CYCLES
AND COMPETITIVE MARKETING STRATEGY. St. Charles, Ill.: Challenge
Books, 1971. 252 p.

Weiss, E.B. "Expanded Product Lines Make Contract Production Vital." AD-
VERTISING AGE 40 (16 June 1969): 68.

Wilemon, David L. "Managing Product Development Systems: A Project Management Approach." BUSINESS AND ECONOMIC DIMENSIONS 6 (May
1970): 14-19.

Willets, W.E. "Product Improvement Never Ends." PURCHASING 70 (4
March 1971): 57-62.

Explains how, in order to improve product design and production
profits, purchasing and production must work together. Stresses
that suppliers must be sought out with ideas for better materials,
better components, and better techniques.

_____. "Supplier Know-How Improves Design." PURCHASING 70 (18 February 1971): 47-49.

> Describes how a company using the program management concept makes sure that suppliers have the opportunity to suggest product improvements. Purchasing department, as the representative of all suppliers, sits in on design review sessions with engineering, quality assurance, and production.

Wind, Yoram. "Product Portfolio Analysis: A New Approach to the Product Mix Decision." In PROCEEDINGS: AMERICAN MARKETING ASSOCIATION COMBINED CONFERENCE, edited by Ronald C. Curhan, pp. 460-64. Chicago: American Marketing Association, 1974.

> Suggests the desirability of treating product mix decision as a portfolio decision and outlines an operational approach for implementing the portfolio approach in the context of the product mix decision.

Wortuba, Thomas Robert. "Procedure for Product Line Diversification." Ph.D. dissertation, University of Wisconsin, 1965. 290 p. Ann Arbor, Mich.: University Microfilms. Order no. 65-04856.

> Prescribes a procedure which would help management select appropriate product lines for diversification by taking into account the objectives of the firms, as well as its marketing policies.

Wrist, P.E. "Production Goals Can Block New Products." PULP AND PAPER 40 (31 October 1966): 33.

Young, Jerry Delano. "An Analysis of the Role of the Product Manager in Industrial Goods Firms." Ph.D. dissertation, University of Washington, 1970. 223 p. Ann Arbor, Mich.: University Microfilms. Order no. 70-02345.

> Looks at the role of product managers in industrial goods companies from the point of view of what he does and what he is capable of, given sufficient authority.

Yousoufian, H.H. "The New Product Development Process: Analyzing Market Needs." BUILDING SYSTEMS DESIGNS 67 (July 1970): 39-40.

> Explains how market needs, as well as the capabilities and long-range objectives of the company, are logical starting points in the redesign of an existing product line or inauguration of a new product to complement existing product lines. Examines the functional aspects of top management development of a new product in the air conditioning industry.

Chapter 3

QUANTITATIVE TECHNIQUES AND MATHEMATICAL MODELS

Abrams, A.S., and Shadek, W.H. "Drug Manufacturer PERTs New Product Development Program." DATA SYSTEMS 9 (10-24 June 1968): 8-9.

Discusses the use of program evaluation and review technique (PERT) as an aid in the commercial development of new products. It is first used at the time of preclinical studies and also when full scale production of the product commences. The computerization process associated with PERT is also explained.

American Institute of Certified Public Accountants. TECHNIQUES FOR FORECASTING PRODUCT DEMAND. Management Services Technical Study, no. 7. New York: 1968. 88 p.

Amstutz, Arnold E. COMPUTER SIMULATION OF COMPETITIVE MARKET RESPONSE. Cambridge, Mass.: M.I.T. Press, 1967. 457 p.

_____. "Simulated Behavioral Models for Product Development from Conception through National Introduction." In PROCEEDINGS: AMERICAN MARKETING ASSOCIATION SPRING CONFERENCE, edited by David L. Sparks. Chicago: American Marketing Association, 1970.

Explains the use of microanalytic market simulation techniques for dealing with uncertainties related to development and marketing of a new product.

Assmus, Gert. "NEWPROD: The Design and Implementation of a New Product Model." JOURNAL OF MARKETING 39 (January 1975): 16-23.

Urges companies to make a larger use than is done now of models designed to help marketing managers decide whether or not to continue the introduction of a new product. Discusses the characteristics of new product introduction models, whose benefits are the following: application to prediction problems before test marketing helps in the determination of market share, and uses data that are readily available or estimated. Stresses that the models have to be supplemented by human judgment.

Averink, G.J. "Marketing Models for Consumer Durable Products." EURO-PEAN SOCIETY FOR OPINION SURVEYS AND MARKET RESEARCH (ESOMAR) CONGRESS, Barcelona, 6-10 September 1970, pp. 155-80.

Ayal, Igal. MODEL BASED INFORMATION SYSTEMS FOR MARKETING NEW PRODUCTS. Cambridge, Mass.: Harvard University, 1972. 41 p.

_____. "Simple Models for Monitoring New Product Performance." DECISION SCIENCE 6 (April 1975): 221-36.

Discusses a disaggregate model, which gives separate consideration to trials of new product and repeaters, and which is shown to perform better in predictive ability than a widely used single equation aggregate model.

Balachandran, V. "A Predictive Model for Monitoring Product Life Cycles." In PROCEEDINGS: AMERICAN MARKETING ASSOCIATION SPRING-FALL CONFERENCE, edited by Fred C. Allvine, pp. 543-46. Chicago: American Marketing Association, 1971.

Suggests that new product life cycles can be predicted through fitting a fourth degree polynomial and its derivatives to the data of a retired product belonging to the same family.

Bass, Frank Myron. A NEW PRODUCT GROWTH MODEL FOR CONSUMER DURABLES. Institute for Research in the Behavioral, Economic, and Management Sciences. Paper no. 175. Lafayette, Ind.: Purdue University, Krannert Graduate School of Industrial Administration, 1967. 33 p.

_____. "A New Product Growth Model for Consumer Durables." MANAGE-MENT SCIENCE 15 (January 1969): 215-27.

Develops and tests a growth model for the timing of initial purchase of new products against data for eleven consumer durables. Basic assumption of the model is that the timing of a consumer's initial purchase is related to the number of previous buyers. Model yields good predictions of the sales peak and the timing of the peak when applied to historical data.

Bass, Frank Myron, and King, C.W. "The Theory of First Purchase of New Products." In PROCEEDINGS: AMERICAN MARKETING ASSOCIATION SUMMER CONFERENCE, edited by Keith Cox and Ben E. Enis, pp. 263-72. Chicago: American Marketing Association, 1968.

Presents a model to predict the new product initial purchase peaks and the timing of the peak.

Beardsley, G., and Mansfield, Edwin. "Note On the Accuracy of Industrial Forecasts of the Profitability of New Products and Processes." JOURNAL OF BUSINESS 51 (January 1978): 127-35.

Bellas, Carl J., and Samli, A. Coksun. "Improving New Product Planning With GERT Simulation." CALIFORNIA MANAGEMENT REVIEW 15 (Summer 1973): 14-21.

> Contains a review of existing planning and control models. Illustrates GERTS (Graphical Evaluation and Review Technique Simulation) as an effective simulation technique for planning and controlling projects, such as new product introductions.

Bernhardt, Irwin, and Mackenzie, Kenneth D. "Some Problems in Using Diffusion Models for New Products." MANAGEMENT SCIENCE 19 (October 1972): 187-99.

> Examines six diffusion models in terms of uncertainty, the kind and source of information necessary for adoption which determine the form of the diffusion process, and the effectiveness of information which depends upon several factors including the efforts of the seller agent, his relation to potential adopters, the social system of the potential adopters, and the social structure linking them.

Berning, Carol A. Kohn, and Jacoby, Jacob. "Patterns of Information Acquisition in New Product Purchases." JOURNAL OF CONSUMER RESEARCH 1 (September 1974): 18-23.

> Develops a paradigm capable of capturing and studying new product purchase decisions as a dynamic ongoing process. By using this paradigm, article examines how patterns of information acquisition vary for new versus established purchase alternatives, and for innovators versus noninnovators.

Blattberg, R., and Golanty, J. "Tracker: An Early Test Market Forecasting and Diagnostic Model for New Product Planning." JOURNAL OF MARKETING RESEARCH 15 (May 1978): 192-202.

Braden, John H.C. "A System Approach to the Introduction of a New Product." BUSINESS QUARTERLY 36 (Autumn 1971): 58-64.

> Using a computer simulation model, article discusses the total systems approach in assessing the marketing and financial viability of a new product.

"Can You Do It by the Numbers." PRINTERS INK 290 (25 June 1965): 55.

> Discusses the decision mapping via go-no-go networks' mathematical model for new product planning.

Cardoza, Richard N., and Ross, Ivan. "A Computer Based Study of New Product Decision." In PROCEEDINGS: AMERICAN MARKETING ASSOCIATION FALL CONFERENCE, edited by David L. Sparks, p. 125. Chicago: American Marketing Association, 1970.

Explains the potential of computer-based research techniques in new product decisions.

Cardoza, Richard N., et al. "New Product Decisions by Marketing Executives: A Computer Controlled Experiment." JOURNAL OF MARKETING 36 (January 1972): 10-16.

Describes a computer controlled experiment in which marketing managers and researchers from consumer product firms were given an actual new product situation and asked to decide whether or not to introduce the product. The experiment involved a dialogue between marketers and a computer.

Carr, Richard Pendleton, Jr. "A Proposed Technology for Validation of Sales-Forecasting Models of New Products with Applications for Validation of Marketing Simulations." Ph.D. dissertation, Northwestern University, 1972. 437 p. Ann Arbor, Mich.: University Microfilms. Order no. 72-32398.

Attempts to develop a validation technology for use in new product sales forecasting models, whose criteria are predictive validity, convergent validity, and discriminant validity.

Carter, E. Eugene. "A Simulation Approach to Investment Decisions." CALIFORNIA MANAGEMENT REVIEW 14 (Summer 1971): 18.

Discusses the use of computer simulation in investment decision making, in terms of interdependencies and multiple goals. Shows how such simulation models can be used for product planning and control.

Chacko, George Kuttickal. TODAY'S INFORMATION FOR TOMORROW'S PRODUCTS: AN OPERATIONS RESEARCH APPROACH. Washington, D.C.: Thompson Book, 1966. 225 p.

Chambers, John C., et al. "How to Choose the Right Forecasting Technique." HARVARD BUSINESS REVIEW 49 (July-August 1971): 45-74.

With the use of charts and tables, article explains how techniques like time series analysis and causal modeling are used in new product planning and development and other managerial decisions.

_____. "Strategic New Product Planning Models for Dynamic Situations." Paper presented at the 13th International Meeting of the Institute of Management Sciences, 6 September 1966, Philadelphia, Pa.

Chang, R.C., and Ehrenfeld, E. "Sequential Stopping Rules for Fixed Sample Acceptance." OPERATIONS RESEARCH 22 (January 1974): 100-07.

Discusses optimal stopping rules for fixed-sample acceptance tests where the observations with time delays are obtained sequentially.

Studies two cases, one with a known prior distribution and the other without a prior distribution.

Charnes, A. "Demon: Decision Mapping Via Optimum Go No-Go Networks: A Model for Marketing New Products." MANAGEMENT SCIENCE 12 (July 1966): 865-87.

Interprets a dynamic adaptive model, called DEMON, in terms of a network, which is employed to reduce the problem of selecting optimal decision procedures so that these can be interpreted in terms of a conditional sequential designation of links from such a network. In the DEMON application to new product marketing, it is necessary to comprehend additional chance and deterministic constraints, such as payback conditions, minimum expected level of profits required, and study budget limits.

Charnes, A., et al. "DEMON: A Management Model for Marketing New Products." CALIFORNIA MANAGEMENT REVIEW 11 (Fall 1968): 31-46.

New product marketing has become an area of major importance and concern to business management in response to consumer demand and also in response to expanding research and development activities. Authors explain how the DEMON model operates when applied to marketing a new product.

_____. "Demon, Mark II: An Extremal Equation Approach to New Product Marketing." MANAGEMENT SCIENCE 14 (May 1968): 513-24.

DEMON model is given a new formulation in terms of an extremal equation. A general analytic characterization is achieved and then replaced by more special ones. Means for effecting study and decisions and inferences are discussed. A chart is provided for interpreting aspects of policy which bear on the problems of marketing a new product.

_____. "Demon, Mark II: Extremal Equations Solutions and Approximations." MANAGEMENT SCIENCE 14 (July 1968): 682-91.

Develops a new method for the solution of DEMON—type functional equations. Methods of approximation and bounding are also developed and interpreted for the general case.

Clark, John J. MANAGEMENT OF FORECASTING. New York: St. Johns University Press, 1969. 424 p.

Claycamp, Henry J., and Liddy, L.E. "Prediction of New Product Performance: An Analytic Approach." JOURNAL OF MARKETING RESEARCH 6 (November 1969): 414.

Few attempts have been made to build analytical models for predicting product performance before market introduction. Article applies a model for predicting consumer trials and repeat purchases as a function of controllable and uncontrollable marketing variables.

Claycamp, Henry J., and Massy, William F. "A Theory of Market Segmentation." JOURNAL OF MARKETING RESEARCH 5 (November 1968): 388-94.

Presents a multistage mathematical model of the full range of segmentation possibilities from the perfectly discriminating monopolist to the mass marketer.

Conrath, David W. "From Statistical Decision Theory to Practice: Some Problems with Transition." MANAGEMENT SCIENCE 19 (April 1973): 873-83.

Presents a new product decision model using decision theory. Discusses the advantages and disadvantages of the use of this technique by managers in this and other situations.

Cook, Victor J., and Herniter, Jerome D. "Performance Measurement in a New Product Demand Simulation." In PROCEEDINGS: AMERICAN MARKETING ASSOCIATION FALL CONFERENCE, edited by Robert L. King, pp. 316-22. Chicago: American Marketing Association, 1968.

Deals with the use of historical data on consumer preferences in simulation of a model to identify consumer demand for a new product.

Cooke, Ernest F., and Edmondson, B.C. "Computer Aided Product Life Cycle Forecasts for New Product Investment Decision." In PROCEEDINGS: AMERICAN MARKETING ASSOCIATION COMBINED CONFERENCE, edited by Thomas V. Greer, pp. 373-77. Chicago: American Marketing Association, 1973.

Presents a computer program entitled LIFER (Life Cycle Forecaster) which utilizes the product life cycle concept for forecasting. Contains explicit mathematical definitions of the boundaries between phases.

Copulsky, William. "Models of Product Development and Promotion." EUROPEAN RESEARCH 5 (May 1977): 106-11.

Examines existing models of product development, their limitations, advantages, and disadvantages. Also analyzes the uniqueness of the consumer and the pitfalls of segmentation. Suggests that the proper way to use advertising and promotion is as a way of building and maintaining differentiation to a product, that is, getting consumers to perceive a product as unique.

Cravens, David W., and Cotham, J.C. "Identifying Segments Using Canonical Correlation Analysis." In PROCEEDINGS: AMERICAN MARKETING ASSOCIATION FALL CONFERENCE, edited by David L. Sparks, p. 60. Chicago: American Marketing Association, 1970.

Examines relationships between key marketing action variables and potentially sensitive customer classification characteristics.

Day, George S. "Using Attitude Change Measures to Evaluate New Product Introductions." JOURNAL OF MARKETING RESEARCH 7 (November 1970): 474-82.

Complexity and cost of new product introductions have spawned a number of techniques for describing and forecasting the performance of a brand during the introductory stage. Explores the diagnostic value of statistical measures of brand attitude change as obtained from "three-wave reinterview panel" data. Primary focus is on the problem of evaluating the effectiveness of introductory advertising and promotion.

De Jong, P.L.F. "Market Forecast Models for Consumer Durables." EUROPEAN SOCIETY FOR OPINION SURVEYS AND MARKET RESEARCH (ESOMAR) CONGRESS, Barcelona, 6-10 September, 1970, pp. 125-53.

Dodds, Wellesley. "An Application of the Bass Model in Long-Term New Product Forecasting." JOURNAL OF MARKETING RESEARCH 10 (August 1973): 308-11.

Bass has developed a model for first purchases activity which portrays the growth patterns for a large number of new products, such as durables in which repeat purchasing is not a major factor in early years of the product life cycle. In this paper the framework of the model is used to develop a long-term forecast of cable television adoption.

Dodson, John W. "Long range Forecasting and Planning Technique." MANAGEMENT ACCOUNTING 49 (December 1967): 9-18.

Describes a computer-based forecasting model which takes into account average expense patterns, product life cycle, and total expense. Model will be useful in new product evaluations.

Dowst, S. "How VA/VE Improves Product Acceptance." PURCHASING 70 (24 June 1971): 62-63.

Explains how the value analysis-value engineering team can study consumers and bring fresh ideas to new product problems. Suggests that improvements can be singled out and the product can be made more acceptable to the market.

Dusenbury, Warren. "Applying Advanced Science to Marketing and Ad Plans." PRINTERS INK 291 (24 September 1965): 15-21.

Reports how by using the critical path method, a company forced the new product innovators to think through the entire program, squeeze the program into a narrow time period, and control the progress of the program.

_____. "CPM for New Product Introductions." HARVARD BUSINESS REVIEW 45 (July–August 1967): 124–39.

Describes a new and promising approach to market planning, in particular, programs for the introduction of new products, by use of the critical path method (CPM). A CPM diagram of the successful introduction of a new food product and the scheduling involved illustrate its applicability to marketing new products.

Ehrenberg, A.S.C. "Predicting the Performance of New Brands." JOURNAL OF ADVERTISING RESEARCH 11 (December 1971): 3–10.

Examines whether a new product brand's ultimate market performance can be accurately predicted. Illustrates how such predictions can be used as targets by which initial planning, test market, and launch evaluations can be guided.

Enrick, Norbert Lloyd. "Qualitative Values into Quantitative Measures: Marketing Decisions Applications." JOURNAL OF THE ACADEMY OF MARKETING SCIENCE 1 (Fall 1973): 90–99.

Eskin, Gerald J. "Causal Structures in Dynamic Trial Repeat Forecasting Models." In PROCEEDINGS: AMERICAN MARKETING ASSOCIATION COMBINED CONFERENCE, edited by Ronald C. Curhan, pp. 198–201. Chicago: American Marketing Association, 1974.

Describes a method for forecasting alternative marketing plans for new products in which the time and level of trial is affected by marketing expenditures. Estimates are obtained for new product introduction and forecasts are made for various expenditure patterns via simulation.

_____. "Dynamic Forecasts of New Product Demand Using a Depth of Repeat Model." JOURNAL OF MARKETING RESEARCH 10 (May 1973): 115–29.

Presents a depth of repeat model for forecasting the demand for new consumer products. Also discusses data analysis, estimation procedures, and the observed accuracy of forecasts. Gives an illustrative example of the use of the model by presenting data on a new product.

Eskin, Gerald J., and Malec, John. "A Model for Estimating Sales Potential Prior to the Test Market." In PROCEEDINGS: 1976 FALL EDUCATORS' CONFERENCE, SERIES No. 39, edited by W. Locander, pp. 230–33. Chicago: American Marketing Association, 1976.

Fisher, Rupert, and Hirst, Melvyn. "Model Building in Marketing: A Review of the British Literature." EUROPEAN JOURNAL OF MARKETING 6 (Autumn 1972): 170–81.

Surveys British literature on marketing models including new product models.

Frank, Ronald E. "The Interface Between Market Segmentation and Market Modelling." In PROCEEDINGS: AMERICAN MARKETING ASSOCIATION FALL CONFERENCE, edited by Robert L. King, pp. 119-23. Chicago: American Marketing Association, 1968.

_____. "Predicting New Product Segments." JOURNAL OF ADVERTISING RESEARCH 12 (June 1972): 9-13.

> Develops a segmentation scheme, based on both household pattern of product use and on demographic characteristics and tracks and analyzes purchasing behavior of the new product given the a priori segmentation scheme developed.

Gatty, Ronald. "Adapting Attitude Measurement to Computer Processing." COMPUTER OPERATIONS 2 (April-May 1968): 12-16.

Gerstenfeld, Arthur. "Technological Forecasting." JOURNAL OF BUSINESS 44 (January 1971): 10-18.

> Analyzes current techniques of forecasting employed by businesses to predict time for developing a product or when it will be a commercial success.

Gibson, R.E. "Performance Space Analysis for an Industrial Product." OPERATIONAL RESEARCH QUARTERLY 23 (June 1972): 125-38.

Godfrey, J.T. "Production and Marketing Planning with Parametric Programming." INTERNATIONAL MANAGEMENT REVIEW 10 (Fall 1968): 61-75.

Gorenstein, S. "Planning Tire Production." MANAGEMENT SCIENCE 17 (October 1970): 1372-82.

> Gives a planning model and its application to tire production both long and short term.

Green, Paul E. "Marketing Applications of MDS (Multidimensional Scaling): Assessment and Outlook." JOURNAL OF MARKETING 39 (January 1975): 24-31.

> Examines the usefulness of MDS techniques in new product design decisions. Discusses methodology and other applications.

Green, Paul E., and Carmone, F.J. MULTIDIMENSIONAL SCALING AND RELATED TECHNIQUES IN MARKETING ANALYSIS. Boston, Mass.: Allyn and Bacon, 1970. 203 p.

Green, Paul E., et al. ANALYSIS OF MARKETING BEHAVIOR USING NON-METRIC SCALING AND RELATED TECHNIQUES. Cambridge, Mass.: Marketing Science Institute, 1968.

_____. "Cluster Analysis in Test Market Selection." MANAGEMENT SCI-ENCE 13 (April 1967): B387-B400.

Explains the use of cluster analysis technique in which geographical test areas can be matched on multiple dimensions at the same time or can be given differential weightage.

Greene, Jerome D. "Projecting Test Market Trial-Repeat of a New Brand in Time." In PROCEEDINGS: AMERICAN MARKETING ASSOCIATION COMBINED CONFERENCE, edited by Ronald C. Curhan, pp. 419-22. Chicago: American Marketing Association, 1974.

Suggests a method for predicting from panel data how many people will try a new brand, how many will buy again, and how often they will repeat.

Hamburg, Morris, and Aikins, Robert J. "Computer Model for New Product Demand." HARVARD BUSINESS REVIEW 45 (March-April 1967): 107-15.

Describes a large pharmaceutical company's successful development to guide marketing decisions during the early life of a new product, including the estimation of future sales levels of new products.

Hamelman, Paul W., and Mazze, Edward M. "Improving Product Abandonment Decisions." JOURNAL OF MARKETING 36 (April 1972): 20-26.

Proposes a model to enable evaluation of the product line which will make use of available marketing and cost information in abandonment decisions.

Heeler, Roger M., et al. "Modelling Supermarket Product Selection." JOURNAL OF MARKETING RESEARCH 10 (February 1973): 34-37.

Models supermarket chains' selection process to reduce management appraisal time and obtain a greater understanding of the variables and decision rules used. Three alternative decision models evaluated include compensatory, conjunctive, and disjunctive. These are described in detail and the results obtained are examined.

Heffernan, K. "Quasi-Quantitative Techniques in Cosmetic New Product Planning." DRUG AND COSMETIC INDUSTRY 107 (November 1970): 58.

Hillcrest Products, Inc. "New Product Sales Forecast." In FUNDAMENTALS OF MARKETING, edited by William J. Stanton, pp. 698-99. New York: McGraw-Hill, 1967.

Hodges, S.D., and Moore, P.G. "Product Mix Problem Under Stochastic Seasonal Demand." MANAGEMENT SCIENCE 17 (October 1970): B107-B114.

Deals with the problem of how to determine the best quantity of each product to manufacture over a complete range of products competing for limited resources, especially when uncertainty of demand is a major problem.

Hugh, McSurely. "A Product Evaluation Improvement and Removal Model." INDUSTRIAL MARKETING MANAGEMENT 2 (August 1973): 319.

Presents a model dealing with product lines rather than specific products, known by the acronym PEIR which stands for Product Evaluation and Removal Model.

Johansson, John K. "Product Positioning with Competitive Reaction: An Iterative Clustering Model." In PROCEEDINGS: AMERICAN MARKETING ASSOCIATION COMBINED CONFERENCE, edited by Ronald C. Curhan, pp. 202-5. Chicago: American Marketing Association, 1974.

Develops a decision model for new product positioning in the face of potential competitive response. Model is used for evaluating the best entry position for an illustrative case with alternative objective functions for the entrant as well as for the existing firms.

King, William R. "Early Prediction of New Product Success." JOURNAL OF ADVERTISING RESEARCH 6 (June 1966): 8-13.

Presents a technique for making predictions of eventual sales success in a newly entered market area using only early performance data. The feasibility of using variations of this technique in solving the selection and reevaluation problems involved in controlling an expansion program are also discussed.

Klompmaker, Jay. "Sales Forecasting For New Industrial Products." Ph.D. dissertation, University of Michigan, 1973. 238 p. Ann Arbor: University Microfilms. Order no. 74-3659.

Studies the new product development process in firms, specifically their use of new product sales forecasting techniques. Unstructured interview technique was used in collecting the data. Includes conclusion drawn from the survey.

Kotler, Philip. "Competitive Strategies for New Product Marketing Over the Life Cycle." MANAGEMENT SCIENCE 12 (December 1965): B104-B119.

Presents how to formulate a long run competitive marketing strategy for a new product introduced into a market with classic growth, seasonal, and merchandising characteristics. Develops market and accounting models to compute profits.

_____. MARKETING DECISION MAKING: A MODEL BUILDING APPROACH. New York: Holt, Rinehart and Winston, 1971. 720 p.

Examines a wide variety of problem oriented marketing models including sales models for new products.

_____. "Sales Models for New Products." In his MARKETING DECISION MAKING: A MODEL BUILDING APPROACH, pp. 519-63. New York: Holt, Rinehart and Winston, 1971.

Kotler, Philip, and Schultz, R.L. "Marketing Simulations: Reviews and Prospects." JOURNAL OF BUSINESS 43 (July 1970): 237-45.

Describes, among other things, some new product simulation models and examines their effectiveness.

Kovac, F.J., and Dague, M.F. "Forecasting by Product Life Cycle Analysis." RESEARCH MANAGEMENT 15 (July 1972): 66-72.

Lifespan (in terms of demand) of many products, from their birth in the research and development department until their decline years later in the marketplace, takes the form of an S-curve. Using tires as an example, the authors describe how future projections can be made based on this principle.

Learner, David B. "DEMON New Product Planning: A Case History." In PROCEEDINGS: AMERICAN MARKETING ASSOCIATION CONFERENCE, edited by Frederick E. Webster, pp. 489-508. Chicago: American Marketing Association, 1965.

_____. "Recommends DEMON Plan at BBDO for Market Testing." ADVERTISING AGE 37 (24 January 1966): 10.

Recommends new goals for new products be established to reduce the number of failures. Outlines the use of DEMON and gives a few statistics to indicate its success.

Lerviks, Alf-Erik. "Forecasting New Consumer Durables by Market Segmentation." EUROPEAN JOURNAL OF MARKETING 10 (1976): 257-65.

Presents a forecasting and simulation model called SIMDEK which predicts the pattern of growth and stabilization in demand for new durables, especially household goods after their introduction.

Levine, Philip. "Pinpointing New Product Target Markets Through Discriminant Analysis." In PROCEEDINGS: AMERICAN MARKETING ASSOCIATION SPRING CONFERENCE, edited by David L. Sparks, p. 32. Chicago: American Marketing Association, 1970.

Explains how the application of discriminant analysis would help sharpen marketing targets for new products and facilitate better planning in evaluation, media scheduling, and test marketing.

Lipstein, Benjamin. "Marketing Models and Their Strategy Implications." EUROPEAN RESEARCH 4 (September 1976): 216-23.

Reviews a new product birth process model which enables brand switching matrices to be monitored. An index of the stability of the brand switching matrices is drawn up and its pattern traced during a new product introduction.

_____. "Modeling and New Product Birth." JOURNAL OF ADVERTISING RESEARCH 10 (October 1970): 3-11.

Examines the nature and content of a marketing model. Discusses some of the criteria which should be applied to these models to judge their value in business decisions. Presents two marketing models which describe the birth process of a new product. The application of the models to a new product introduction is also examined.

Little, Blair, and More, Roger Allan. "Sales Forecast Errors for New Product Projects." INDUSTRIAL MARKETING MANAGEMENT 7 (February 1978): 49-53.

Develops major indicators of sales forecast error from an analysis of 185 new product projects, which would help alert product managers to special development problems.

Little, J.D.C. BRANDAID, AN ON LINE MARKETING MIX MODEL. Working paper. Cambridge, Mass.: M.I.T., Sloan School of Management, February 1972.

Lodish, L.M. "Decision Models for Marketing Management." WHARTON QUARTERLY 7 (Fall 1972): 53-56.

Longbottom, D.A. "The Application of Decision Analysis to a New Product Planning Decision." OPERATIONAL RESEARCH QUARTERLY 24 (March 1973): 9-17.

Describes techniques of decision analysis used to evaluate the profitability of acquiring resources to manufacture refrigerator container units on a regular basis. Presents guidelines to management for planning production capacities in terms of manpower and factory floor space over an eleven-year period and for indicating optimum price levels for the container units.

Marks, E.S., et al. "A Model of Purchase Intervals for New Product Introduction." In PROCEEDINGS: BUSINESS ECONOMIC STATISTICS, SECTION OF THE AMERICAN STATISTICAL ASSOCIATION CONFERENCE, 1972, pp. 373-35.

Deals with predicting time curve of consumer response in order to plan for better promotional campaign for product introduction.

Martin, Albert Joseph, Jr. "An Exponential Model for Predicting Trial of a New Consumer Product." Ph.D. dissertation, Ohio State University, 1969. 98 p. Ann Arbor, Mich.: University Microfilms. Order no. 69-22174.

Examines the kinds of awareness measures used to determine advertising effectiveness in a new consumer product introduction. Also looks at the relationship between advertising media weight, brand awareness, and trial by consumers.

Massy, W(illiam).F. EXTENSIONS TO STEAM. Working paper, no. 4. Pittsburgh: Carnegie Graduate School of Industrial Administration, Institute of Technology, January 1967.

_____. "Forecasting the Demand for New Convenience Products." JOURNAL OF MARKETING RESEARCH 6 (November 1969): 405.

Author's stochastic evolutionary adoption model (STEAM) is described. Methods for estimating its parameters from panel data covering the first part of the introductory period are outlined. Method by which the future purchase history of each panel household can be simulated and the results projected into a total market forecast is reported.

_____. "A Stochastic Evolutionary Model for Evaluating New Products." Paper presented at the Meeting of Institute of Management Science, 4-6 April 1967, Boston.

_____. "Stochastic Models for Monitoring New Product Adoptions." In APPLICATIONS OF THE SCIENCES IN MARKETING MANAGEMENT, edited by F. Bass, et al., pp. 85-111. New York: Wiley, 1968.

Millgram, Joseph B. "How PERT and Critical Path Can Contribute to the New Product Program." In PROCEEDINGS: AMERICAN MARKETING ASSOCIATION SUMMER CONFERENCE, edited by R.E. Vosburgh and M.S. Moyer, pp. 37-48. Chicago: American Marketing Association, 1967.

By controlling and minimizing marketing costs, the time for getting back the return on original investment is shortened. Article analyzes how the application of PERT and CPM can help in this area.

Modig, Jan-Erik. "Models for New Product Decisions: A Review of Recent U.S. Developments." EUROPEAN REVIEW 2 (September 1974): 188-93, 224.

Discusses new product models, including PERCEPTOR which incorporates a mapping procedure, as well as forecasting modelling of the likely trial and repeat purchase process, multi-attribute attitude models, COMP, SPRINGER, NEWS, Time series prediction models of sales, models with marketing decision variables, i.e., SPRINTER MOD III, NOMMAD, and models of retail trial of new products.

Montgomery, David B., and Urban, Glen L. APPLICATIONS OF MANAGEMENT SCIENCES IN MARKETING. Englewood Cliffs, N.J.: Prentice-Hall, 1970. 481 p.

_____. MANAGEMENT SCIENCE AND MARKETING. Englewood Cliffs, N.J.: Prentice-Hall, 1969. 376 p.

More, Roger Allan. "Sales Forecast Uncertainty in the Screening of New Industrial Products: A Descriptive Model With Predictive Implications." Ph.D. dissertation, University of Western Ontario, 1974.

Morgan, N., and Purnell, J.M. "Isolating Openings for New Products in a Multidimensional Space." JOURNAL OF MARKET RESEARCH SOCIETY 11 (July 1966): 245–66.

Myers, John G. "New Uses of Mathematical Models in Test Marketing." In PROCEEDINGS: AMERICAN MARKETING ASSOCIATION SPRING-FALL CONFERENCE, edited by Fred C. Allvine, pp. 531–37. Chicago: American Marketing Association, 1971.

> Discusses models in use in the area of test marketing of new products.

Nagi, M. "A Bayesian Decision Model for Test Marketing." OPERATIONAL RESEARCH QUARTERLY 6 (November 1968): 140–45.

Nakanishi, Masao. "Advertising and Promotion Effects on Consumer Research to New Products." JOURNAL OF MARKETING RESEARCH 10 (August 1973): 242–49.

> Develops a stochastic model of consumer response to new products which incorporates the effects of overtime variations in advertising and promotion. Explains its usefulness in terms of its ability to generate conditional forecasts of product sales to evaluate alternative marketing programs for new product introduction.

_____. "A Model of Market Reaction to New Products." Ph.D. dissertation, University of California, Los Angeles, 1968. 251 p. Ann Arbor, Mich.: University Microfilms. Order no. 68-16563.

> Develops a quantitative model for finding the reactions of consumers to new products which lead to their ultimate acceptance or rejection.

_____. "A Model of Market Reactions to New Products. "In PROCEEDINGS: AMERICAN MARKETING ASSOCIATION FALL CONFERENCE, edited by Keith Cox and Ben E. Enis, p. 593. Chicago: American Marketing Association, 1968.

> By analysis of the process of consumer acceptance of new products, this article develops a quantitative behavioral model of how consumers would react to new products.

Naples, M.J. "Using Marketing Models in New Product Forecasting." FOOD PRODUCT DEVELOPMENT 10 (December 1976): 21-22.

"National Analysts Offer New Panel to Test New Products." ADVERTISING AGE 36 (24 May 1965): 154.

> Describes a new mathematical index of stability which captures the rate of change in brand loyalties during test marketing.

Neidell, Lester A. "The Use of Nonmetric Multidimensional Scaling in Marketing Analysis." JOURNAL OF MARKETING 33 (October 1969): 37-43.

> Discusses a new analytical marketing tool called nonmetric multidimensional scaling and its application to marketing problems including new product introductions.

Norek, Bernard Jean-Marie. "Simulation Models of New Product Introduction and Market Evolution." Ph.D. dissertation, University of Pennsylvania, 1970. 255 p. Ann Arbor, Mich.: University Microfilms. Order no. 71-07839.

> Develops probabilistic models for application in the estimation of consumer demand for products. Consumer panels are used to obtain data.

Ohsol, E.O. "Evaluation of Research Projects; Marketing Cost Estimation." CHEMICAL ENGINEERING PROGRESS 67 (April 1971): 19-24.

> Describes some quantitative approaches to identify the probability of commercial success of new product.

Pader, M. "Model to Assess New Product Development." COSMETICS AND TOILETRIES 92 (November 1977): 45-46.

Pengilly, P.J., and Moss, A.J. "Choice of a New Product, Its Selling Pattern and Price." OPERATIONAL RESEARCH QUARTERLY 20 (June 1969): 179-85.

> Describes the development of a decision theory model which takes into account the competitive reaction to the introduction of new brands into an existing market.

Perreault, C.M., and Darden, William R. "Unequal Cell Sizes in Marketing Experiments; Use of the General Linear Hypothesis." JOURNAL OF MARKETING RESEARCH 12 (August 1975): 333-42.

> Discusses the advantages and problems of using the general linear hypothesis approach to the analysis of marketing data and illustrates the hypothesis in the context of a new product experiment.

Pessemier, Edgar A. "Market Structure Analysis of New Product and Market Opportunities." JOURNAL OF CONSUMER BUSINESS 4 (Spring 1975): 35-67.

Discusses the technique of market structure analysis and illustrates its methodology and limitations in its application to new product planning.

_____. MODELS FOR NEW-PRODUCT DECISIONS. Paper no. 247. Lafayette, Ind.: Purdue University, Institute for Research in the Behavioral, Economic and Management Sciences, Krannert Graduate School of Industrial Administration, 1969. 44 p.

_____. STRATOP: A MODEL FOR DESIGNING EFFECTIVE PRODUCT AND COMMUNICATION STRATEGIES. Paper no. 470. Lafayette, Ind.: Purdue University, Institute for Research in the Behavioral, Economic and Management Sciences, Krannert Graduate School of Industrial Administration, 1974. 19 p.

Piersol, Robert James. THE ACCURACY OF METHODS OF ESTIMATING GEOGRAPHIC MARKETS FOR INDUSTRIAL PRODUCTS. Cambridge, Mass.: Harvard University, 1967. 30 p.

Quinn, James Brian. "Technological Forecasting." HARVARD BUSINESS RE-VIEW 45 (March-April 1967): 89-106.

Discusses the methodology and applications of technological forecasting in new product planning.

Raun, Donald L. "Product-Mix Analysis by Linear Programming." MANAGE-MENT ACCOUNTING 47 (January 1966): 3-13.

Deals with the problem of determining the optimal product mix combination of products sold that will maximize profits with given costs and sales prices and subject to given physical and financial limitations.

"A Ready-Made PERT Network for Launching New Products: Is It Practical?" MARKETING FORUM 2 (September 1966): 23-27.

Program Evaluation and Review Technique (PERT) is used more often for new product introductions than for any other marketing purposes. Article presents a standard planning and control format designed and tested by a marketing man for launching new nondurable industrial goods. His findings and conclusions are also included.

Reinmuth, J.E. "Forecasting the Impact of a New Product Introduction." JOURNAL OF THE ACADEMY OF MARKETING SCIENCE 2 (Spring 1974): 391-400.

In the absence of a historical base data used in regular forecasting models, long- and short-term forecasting in the area of new product introduction has to depend on panel concensus, Delphi technique, historical analogy, and marketing research. Each of these methods are evaluated from the point of view of accuracy.

Reynolds, William H. "Heuristics for the Businessman." MSU BUSINESS TOP-
ICS 16 (Winter 1968): 14-22.

Ricketts, Donald E., and Zimmer, Robert K. "A Dynamic Optimization Model
for Planning in a Multiproduct Environment." DECISION SCIENCES 6 (April
1975): 274-83.

Robertson, J.A. "Analyzing Field Failure." QUALITY PROGRESS 2 (January
1969): 12-13.

> Discusses how to estimate the amount or rate of failure claims of
> a new product. Computer programs are available to compare the
> limited information and any number of assumptions as to the pat-
> tern of failure that will occur during the warranty period. A
> simple manual method is also described.

Robertson, Thomas S., and Kennedy, J.N. "Prediction of Consumer Innovations: Applications of Multiple Discriminate Analysis." JOURNAL OF MAR-
KETING RESEARCH 5 (February 1968): 64-69.

> Uses multiple discriminant analysis techniques to measure the rela-
> tive importance of the socioeconomic characteristics of consumers
> and the predictive value of the set of characteristics such as:
> venturesomeness, interest range, social mobility, cosmopolitarian-
> ism, integration, and status range.

Root, H. Paul. "The Use of Subjective Probability Estimates in the Analysis
of New Products." In PROCEEDINGS: AMERICAN MARKETING ASSOCIA-
TION FALL CONFERENCE, edited by Philip R. McDonald, pp. 200-207.
Chicago: American Marketing Association, 1969.

> Explains how subjective probability estimates are used for creating
> organizational change in the new product analysis process.

Root, H. Paul, and Klompmaker, Jay. "A Microanalytic Sales Forecasting
Model for New Industrial Products." In PROCEEDINGS: AMERICAN MARKET-
ING ASSOCIATION SPRING CONFERENCE, edited by Fred C. Allvine, pp.
474-77. Chicago: American Marketing Association, 1971.

> Presents a model which incorporates information on industrial adop-
> tion process into sales forecasts of new industrial products.

Schoderbek, Peter P., and Digman, Lester A. "Third Generation PERT/LOB."
HARVARD BUSINESS REVIEW 45 (September-October 1967): 100-10.

> New technique, PERT/LOB, is significant to management because
> it can extend the potential of PERT (Program Evaluation and Review
> Technique) and LOB (Line Of Balance) to encompass the entire
> product development-production life cycle by using a single tech-
> nique. Authors describe the basic principles of LOB and PERT/LOB
> and show how the new technique would be used in a specific case
> to help executives plan and control work on a project.

Schultz, F. "Practical Marketing Model for Short and Long Range Planning." MANAGEMENT ADVISER 10 (March 1973): 17–26.

Seshagiri, N., and Chandrasekhar, P. "Organization of New Product Research in the Electronics Industry in Competitive Environment." IEEE PROCEEDINGS 58 (January 1970): 160–61.

> Nonlinear programming model is developed for describing the organization of new product research in a competitive environment. As an illustration, an optimal strategy is realized for the new product research in electronics instruments industry. Modifications for applying the model to developing countries are suggested.

Shoemaker, R., and Staelin, R. "Effects of Sampling Variation on Sales Forecasts for New Consumer Products." JOURNAL OF MARKET RESEARCH 13 (May 1976): 138–43.

> Outlines a general procedure for estimating the sampling error in sales forecasts of new nondurable consumer products, using the Parfitt and Collins model with actual data from four new product introductions.

Shocker, Allan D., et al. "Toward the Improvement of New Product Search and Screening." In PROCEEDINGS: AMERICAN MARKETING ASSOCIATION FALL CONFERENCE, edited by Philip R. McDonald, pp. 168–75. Chicago: American Marketing Association, 1969.

> Discusses multivariate statistical models available for decisions on new product search and screening.

Silk, Alvin J. "Preference and Perception Measures in New Product Development: An Exposition and Review." SLOAN MANAGEMENT REVIEW 11 (Spring 1969): 21–37.

> Critically evaluates multidimensional techniques for measuring consumer preferences and perceptions. Examines how they can be applied to identify new product opportunities.

Sullivan, H.B. "Using PERT/CPM to Manage the Introduction of New Products." MARKETING FORUM 3 (July–August 1967): 31–34.

Tauber, Edward Maury. "H.I.T. Heuristic Ideation Technique: A Systematic Procedure for New Product Search, With an Experimental Application in the Food Processing Industry." Ph.D. dissertation, Cornell University, Ithaca, 1969. 152 p.

> Surveys and evaluates existing techniques for new product search. Explains and examines specifically a new technique called HIT (Heuristic Ideation Technique). Data from major food processing firms are used in the analysis.

_____. "H.I.T.: Heuristic Ideation Technique – A Systematic Procedure for New Product Search." JOURNAL OF MARKETING 36 (January 1972): 58-70.

> Article presents an idea–generating tool called the heuristic ideation technique (HIT) with illustrations from an application in the food processing industry.

Thomas, Joseph, and Chabria, Prem. "Bayesian Models for New Product Pricing." DECISION SCIENCES 6 (January 1975): 51-64.

> Bayesian technique is used to update prior estimates of demand and distribution parameter values. Interaction of simultaneous production and pricing decision is emphasized. Numerical example of approximate techniques is provided.

Toll, Ray. "Analytical Techniques for New Product Planning." LONG RANGE PLANNING 1 (March 1969): 52-59.

> Article describes a major European consultant's approach to new product planning. Particular attention is drawn to the number of analytical techniques which have been developed for screening new products: PROPLAN, for simple visual and arithmetical comparisons, MARSAN, a more analytical system, ELECTRE, a computer program for making a final selection, and CAPRI, a computer program which enables the planner to select the set of products which provides the best coordinated program of investment.

Urban, Glen L. "Market Response Models for the Analysis of New Products." In PROCEEDINGS: AMERICAN MARKETING ASSOCIATION FALL CONFERENCE, edited by Robert L. King, pp. 105-11. Chicago: American Marketing Association, 1968.

> Proposes the macro behavioral process model which uses mathematical and behavioral ideas in the analysis of new products.

_____. "Mathematical Modelling Approach to Product Line Decision." JOURNAL OF MARKETING RESEARCH 6 (February 1969): 40-47.

> Develops a mathematical model of the interaction among products for normative marketing strategy recommendations, since interdependencies among brands in a firms product line should be considered. Presents an a priori product line model for finding the best marketing mix for each product in a line.

_____. "New Product Analysis and Decision Model." MANAGEMENT SCIENCE 14 (April 1968): B490-B517.

> Presents a model and its practical applications to demonstrate the usefulness and problems of a quantitative approach to new product decisions.

_____. "Perceptor: A Model for Product Positioning." MANAGEMENT SCIENCE 21 (April 1975): 858-71.

Proposes a model and measurement methodology for designing new frequently purchased consumer products, structured as a trial and repeat process that produces an estimate of long run share for a new brand. Physical and psychological product attributes are linked to the trial and repeat probabilities through multidimensional scaling procedures.

_____. "A Quantitative Model of Product Planning with Special Emphasis on Product Interdependency." Ph.D. dissertation, Northwestern University, 1966. 200 p. Ann Arbor, Mich.: University Microfilms. Order no. 66-14083.

By analyzing factors relating to demand, cost, allocation, and uncertainty, this study proposes a new product decision model. Product interdependencies are taken into account by the model which gives a go, no-go on decisions for marketing, rejecting, or undertaking additional studies.

_____. "SPRINTER: A Tool for New Product Decision Makers." INDUSTRIAL MANAGEMENT REVIEW (IMR) 8 (Spring 1967): 43-54.

Provides a new product evaluation model based on the probability of getting back a desired rate of return. It takes into account demand, cost, price, and promotion expenditures.

_____. "SPRINTER: Mod I: A Basic New Product Analysis." In PROCEEDINGS: AMERICAN MARKETING ASSOCIATION SUMMER CONFERENCE, edited by Bernard Morin; pp. 139-50. Chicago: American Marketing Association, 1969.

Describes a new computerized model useful in evaluating alternate product strategies for profit maximization.

_____. "SPRINTER Mod III- A Model for the Analysis of New Frequently Purchased Consumer Products." OPERATIONS RESEARCH 18 (September-October 1970): 805-54.

Presents a model-based information system designed to analyze test-market results, to assist decision making for a new frequently purchased consumer product, and to serve as an adaptive control mechanism during national introduction. The model, SPRINTER, is based on the behavioral process of the diffusion of innovation and can be used normatively in an interactive search mode to find the best marketing strategy for a new product.

Wachsler, Robert A., et al. "News: A Systematic Methodology for Diagnosing New Product Marketing Plans and Developing Actionable Recommendations." Unpublished paper. Batten, Barton, Durstine and Osborn, Inc., New York, Research Department, February 1972.

Wentz, W.B., and Eyrith, G.I. "New Product Forecasting Without Historical or Experimental Data." In PROCEEDINGS: AMERICAN MARKETING ASSOCIATION CONFERENCE, edited by Philip R. McDonald, pp. 215-21. Chicago: American Marketing Association, 1969.

Discusses diffusion theory and applies mathematics to predict new product success in terms of potential market and market penetration rate.

Whiteman, Irvin R. "Improved Forecasting Through Feedback." JOURNAL OF MARKETING 30 (April 1966): 45-51.

Article develops the basis for feedback forecasting, as well as the establishment of control limits for determining which forecasts depart significantly from plan.

Zif, Jay Jehiel. "A System of Models for Quantitative Analysis of Marketing New Products." Ph.D. dissertation, New York University, 1966. 220 p. Ann Arbor, Mich.: University Microfilms. Order no. 66-10584.

Provides an information model to ensure continuous flow of management information for arriving at new product decisions, with maximum cooperation between research, marketing, and management personnel.

Chapter 4

ADOPTION AND DIFFUSION OF INNOVATION

Abernathy, William J., and Utterback, J.M. "Patterns of Industrial Innovation." TECHNOLOGY REVIEW 80 (June-July 1978): 40-47.

Abernathy, William J., and Wayne, Kenneth. "Limits of the Learning Curve." HARVARD BUSINESS REVIEW 52 (September-October 1974): 109-10.

Examines the view that the learning curve concept may lead to a specialized work force with a limited potential for innovation.

Achilladelis, B., et al. A STUDY OF SUCCESS AND FAILURE IN INDUSTRIAL INNOVATION. REPORT ON PROJECT SAPPHO TO SRC. London: Science Research Council and University of Sussex, August 1971.

Ahmad, Imtiaz Uddin. "Time Rate of Diffusion of a Product Innovation in the Manufacturing Sector." Ph.D. dissertation, State University of New York, 1968. 202 p. Ann Arbor, Mich.: University Microfilms. Order no. 68-17335.

Examines the significant economic factors which determine long run rate of entry in an industry following a product innovation. Also analyses the rate of new product turnover.

Ahrens, R.H. "Brainstorming Your Way to New Ideas." MACHINE DESIGN 48 (8 April 1976): 66-68.

Brainstorming is the best known group approach to idea generation. Article illustrates benefits and problems involved.

Alba, Manuel S. "Microanalysis of Socio-Dynamics of Diffusion of Innovation: A Simulation Study." In PROCEEDINGS: AMERICAN MARKETING ASSOCIATION FALL CONFERENCE, edited by Robert L. King, p. 596. Chicago: American Marketing Association, 1969.

Demonstrates the feasibility of simulating the process of diffusion of an innovation.

_____. "Macroanalysis of the Social Dynamics of Diffusion of Innovation." Ph.D. dissertation, Northwestern University, 1967. 317 p.

Formulates a conceptual model of the process of diffusion of innovation in an attempt to demonstrate the feasibility of simulating the process. The basic premise is that the adoption of innovation is stochastic in character.

Albrecht, J.J. "A Corporate View of New Product Development." FOOD TECHNOLOGY 27 (May 1973): 38.

Suggests that innovators must remember that new products are not needed by consumers, but new improvements in existing products are desired by consumer. Provides a list of sources of new product ideas.

Alford, Charles L., and Mason, Joseph Barry. "Generating New Product Ideas." JOURNAL OF ADVERTISING RESEARCH 15 (December 1975): 27-32.

Illustrates the merits and results of a formalized approach to the new product idea generation process.

Allison, David. "The Management Style of Patrick Haggerty." In MANAGING ADVANCING TECHNOLOGY, edited by the staff of INNOVATION magazine, vol. 1, pp. 69-87. New York: American Management Association, 1972.

Describes a technique called "Objectives, Strategy and Tactics" in Texas Instruments Company for promoting innovation.

Allvine, Fred C. "Diffusion of a Competitive Innovation." In PROCEEDINGS: AMERICAN MARKETING ASSOCIATION FALL CONFERENCE, edited by Robert L. King, pp. 341-51. Chicago: American Marketing Association, 1968.

Analyzes the adoption of games by food stores in individual markets, the spread of games within organizations, and the variability of the use of games between markets.

Arthur D. Little, Inc. BARRIERS TO INNOVATION IN INDUSTRY. Prepared for National Science Foundation. Washington, D.C.: 1973. 34 p.

Senior management survey by the firm revealed that the marketing function is a major barrier to innovation.

Ashton, David, et al. "Conditions Favorable to Product Innovation." SCIENTIFIC BUSINESS, May 1965, p. 24.

New product evolution within a company is examined. Management problems of organization and control at each stage from basic research to marketing are discussed as are also the details of research on organizational environments which can be expected to produce new ideas.

Baker, Michael J. "The Diffusion of Industrial Innovations: An Exploration of Factors Associated with the Process, Their Measurement and Predictive Utility." Ph.D. dissertation, Harvard University, 1971. 42 p.

Baldridge, Victor S., and Burnham, R.A. "Organizational Innovation: Individual, Organizational and Environmental Impacts." ADMINISTRATIVE SCIENCE QUARTERLY 20 (June 1975): 165-75.

Deals with the ingredients of successful innovation in organizations and distinguishes them from factors which motivate individual innovators.

Baumgarten, S.A. "The Diffusion of Fashion Innovations among U.S. College Students." In PROCEEDINGS: 31ST EUROPEAN SOCIETY FOR OPINION SURVEYS AND MARKET RESEARCH SEMINAR ON FASHION RESEARCH AND MARKETING, AMSTERDAM, DECEMBER, 1974. Amsterdam: The Society, 1974.

Baumgarten, S.A., and King, C.W. "A Study of Fashion Adoption Among College Students." In PROCEEDINGS: AMERICAN MARKETING ASSOCIATION FALL CONFERENCE, edited by David L. Sparks, p. 124. Chicago: American Marketing Association, 1970.

Highlights the role of the change agent in the process of a fashion product adoption on a college campus.

Beckman, Dale M. "The Process of New Product Adoption." UNIVERSITY OF WASHINGTON BUSINESS REVIEW 30 (Spring 1971): 33-42.

Discusses the results of studies of new drugs used by doctors which illustrate the role of certain factors such as the message channels, amount of information available, characteristics of those who adopt the products and the degree of risk or importance in using the products. Results indicate that salesmen and journals are important in the knowledge stage, and colleagues and other professional sources are increasingly important in the decision stage.

Bradbury, R.F. "Constraints to Innovation." CHEMICAL TECHNOLOGY 7 (January 1977): 23-27.

_____. "Innovation in the Chemical and Allied Industries." CHEMISTRY AND INDUSTRY, 18 October 1975, pp. 852-56.

Describes the process and contributing factors for new product innovation in the chemical and allied industries. Discusses the barriers, such as a diminishing "free space" for innovation, energy costs, capital costs, pollution and environment, and shortage of new ideas.

Bujake, John E. "Programmed Innovation in New Product Development." RESEARCH MANAGEMENT 12 (July 1969): 279-87.

Introduces a programmed approach to new product development creativeness. Discusses the four steps to the procedure: (1) opportunity search, (2) form evaluation, (3) concept expansion, and (4) concept development.

Burns, Robert Obed. INNOVATION: THE MANAGEMENT CONNECTION. Lexington, Mass. D.C. Heath, 1975. 157 p.

Buzzell, Robert D., and Nourse, Robert E.M. PRODUCT INNOVATION IN FOOD PROCESSING. Boston: Harvard Business School, Division of Research, 1967. 220 p.

Deals with product innovation and with some of the problems created by it in the food processing industries. Examines the extent of innovation in twenty-one product categories and the source of new food products. Appraises the effects of new products on retail food costs, corporate growth, and profits.

Cancian, Frank. "Stratification and Risk Taking: A Theory Tested on Agricultural Innovation." AMERICAN SOCIOLOGICAL REVIEW 32 (December 1967): 912-27.

Carmon, James C. "The Fate-of-Fashion Cycles in Our Modern Society." In PROCEEDINGS: AMERICAN MARKETING ASSOCIATION FALL CONFERENCE, edited by Raymond M. Haas, pp. 722-37. Chicago: American Marketing Association, 1966.

Analyzes regular cyclical pattern of women's fashion and a correlation of deviation with changes in our social institutions.

"The Casual Inventor." CONFERENCE BOARD RECORD 8 (October 1971): 54-57.

Discusses the importance of the part-time "casual" inventor and the relationship between the inventor and the manufacturing and marketing company.

Chakrabarti, Alok K. "Industrial Product Innovation: An International Comparison." INDUSTRIAL MARKETING MANAGEMENT 7 (August 1978): 231-37.

Discusses the data obtained from a study of five hundred industrial innovations introduced in major industrialized countries from 1953 to 1973.

_____. "The Role of Champion in Product Innovation." CALIFORNIA MANAGEMENT REVIEW 17 (Winter 1974): 58-62.

Contains case studies of product development based on NASA innovations. Champion is defined as a person intensely interested and involved with the product, and who plays a dominant role.

It was found that in most cases the product's success depended on the presence of such champions.

Christianson, John Alden. "The Determinants of the Rate of Diffusion of New Consumer Products." Ph.D. dissertation, University of Wisconsin, Madison, 1974. 224 p. Ann Arbor, Mich.: University Microfilms. Order no. 74-18924.

There are three stages in a product's life cycle: the youth, maturity, and decline stages. Study analyzes the first of these stages in terms of the growth of the gross national product.

Clutterback, D. "Tapping Employee Creativity for New Product Ideas." IN-TERNATIONAL MANAGEMENT 31 (July 1976): 41.

Employees often spend their own time looking for new product ideas. Article relates how firms can profit by this.

Coleman, James S., et al. MEDICAL INNOVATION: A DIFFUSION STUDY. Indianapolis: Bobbs-Merrill, 1966. 246 p.

Collins, Gwyn. "Management of New Product Development." In PROCEED-INGS: AMERICAN MARKETING ASSOCIATION SUMMER CONFERENCE, edited by John S. Wright and Jack L. Goldstucker, pp. 260-71. Chicago: American Marketing Association, 1966.

Deals with the way corporations stimulate creativity among their personnel and how to channel this creativity for new product development.

"Company Must Recognize the Value of An Idea." INSTRUMENTS AND CON-TROL SYSTEMS 45 (May 1972): 15.

Cooper, Robert G. "Strategic Planning for Successful Technological Innovation." BUSINESS QUARTERLY 43 (Spring 1978): 46-54.

Cooper, Robert G. WINNING THE NEW PRODUCT GAME: AN EMPIRICAL STUDY OF SUCCESSFUL PRODUCT INNOVATION IN CANADA. Montreal: McGill University, Faculty of Management, 1976. 113 p.

Formulates a game plan which most effectively reduces the risks of product innovation. Uses three case histories and flow charts showing the actual processes used by three Canadian companies.

Cooper, Robert G., and Little Blair. "Reducing the Risk of Industrial New Product Development." CANADIAN MARKETER 9 (Fall 1974).

Crookell, Harold. "The Role of Product Innovation in the Trade Flows of Household Appliances Between Canada and the U.S.A." Ph.D. dissertation, University of Western Ontario, Canada, 1971. 45 p.

Danzig, F. "New Products: Stress Renovation Not Innovation." ADVERTIS-
ING AGE 37 (3 January 1966): 2-3.

> Calls for renovating existing products as opposed to innovating
> new products. A number of case studies are presented where a
> successful product was actually a renovated existing product.

Darden, William R., and Reynolds, Fred D. "Generalized Innovation Factors
in Men's Apparel Fashion." In PROCEEDINGS: AMERICAN MARKETING AS-
SOCIATION SPRING - FALL CONFERENCE, edited by Fred C. Allvine, pp.
434-38. Chicago: American Marketing Association, 1971.

> Examines the two new basic alternatives to explain the diffusion
> of men's fashion apparel.

Davis, D.S., and Banfield, T.L. "Maturity and Innovation." CHEMICAL
TECHNOLOGY 3 (October 1973): 584-87.

"Day to Day Work Pressure Makes Companies Dull Innovators." ADVERTISING
AGE 40 (10 March 1969): 3.

Diehl, Rick W. "Achieving Successful Innovation." MICHIGAN BUSINESS
REVIEW 24 (March 1972): 6-10.

> Discusses three key areas in innovation, namely, the internal en-
> vironment of the company, the errors made due to emotional re-
> sponses, and the execution of the innovation. Stresses that if
> these areas are properly approached and handled, successful inno-
> vations can result.

Engel, J.F. "How Information is Used to Adopt an Innovation." JOURNAL
OF ADVERTISING RESEARCH 9 (December 1969): 5-8.

> Finds insufficient knowledge on the part of marketers about the
> process of adoption and the diffusion of an innovation, resulting
> in new product problems.

Exton, William. "The Levels of Innovation." ADVANCED MANAGEMENT
JOURNAL 39 (April 1974): 60-62.

> Examines the cultural, economic, technological, and methodologi-
> cal bases of product or service innovation.

Fabris, Richard Harris. "A Study of the Product Innovation in the Automobile
Industry During the Period 1919-1962." Ph.D. dissertation, University of Illinois, Urbana-Champaign, 1966. 264 p. Ann Arbor, Mich.: University Microfilms. Order no. 66-12321.

> Contains a historical analysis of the nature and rate of product
> innovation in the automobile industry during selected years, spe-
> cifically studies where clusters of innovation occurred and whether
> certain manufacturers were leaders or followers.

Feldman, Laurence P., and Armstrong, Gary M. "Identifying Buyers of a Major Automotive Innovation." JOURNAL OF MARKETING 39 (January 1975): 47-53.

Study of consumer innovations during the process of introduction of the rotary engined Mazda. Study concentrates on the following questions: whether innovators are more influential in innovative behavior, especially in the case of high risk products, whether a high level of interest in the product tend to encourage innovativeness with respect to that product, and whether venturesomeness is associated with innovative behavior.

Fliegel, Frederick C., and Kivlin, J.E. "Attributes of Innovation as Factors in Diffusion." AMERICAN JOURNAL OF SOCIOLOGY 127 (November 1966): 235-48.

Fox, Harold W. "New Products, New Problems." PITTSBURGH BUSINESS REVIEW 43 (January-February 1974): 1-5, 8.

Innovation spurs advances but along with the advance in physical amenities and product innovation, are rising disamenities and civil disutilities. Article reviews social costs of innovation.

Fusfeld, A.R. "How to Put Technology into Corporate Planning." TECHNOLOGY REVIEW 80 (May 1978): 51-55.

Gee, E.A., and Tyler, C. MANAGING INNOVATION. New York: Wiley Interscience, 1977. 267 p.

Discusses aspects of the innovation process--its dynamics, managerial practices, and people problems. Specific topics covered include: relation of innovation to health of an enterprise, budgeting or funding research and development, planning, the managing of a project from conception through marketing, project termination, and controlling risk in new ventures and costs.

Gee, Sherman. "The Role of Technology Transfer in Innovation." RESEARCH MANAGEMENT 17 (November 1974): 31-36.

Distinguishes technological innovation from technology transfer. Analyzes how both are interdependent.

Gerstenfeld, Arthur, and Wortzel, L.H. "Strategies for Innovation in Developing Countries." SLOAN MANAGEMENT REVIEW 19 (Fall 1977): 57-68.

Describes innovations in thirty-three Taiwanese firms from the point of view of product life cycle, impetus for innovations, and information sources used.

"Giving Lone Wolf Inventors a Chance." INTERNATIONAL MANAGEMENT 23 (June 1968): 55.

Globe, Samuel, et al. "Key Factors and Events in the Innovation Process."
RESEARCH MANAGEMENT 16 (July 1973): 8-15.

Contains the results of a comprehensive study of ten outstanding
cases of innovation which revealed that certain events and factors
played key roles in the complex series of activities that led to
success.

Goldberg, Marvin Earl. "Product Innovation: A Study of Personality Factors
in Product Perception." Ph.D. dissertation, University of Illinois, Urbana-
Champaign, 1972. 253 p. Ann Arbor, Mich." University Microfilms. Order
no. 73-9942.

By use of an interactive paradigm consisting of product novelty,
appearance, performance, and social conspicousness, as well as
buyer venturesomeness, practicality, and aestheticism, this study
analyzes the role of personality traits in the evaluation and adoption of new products.

Green, Paul E., and Sieber, Harry F. "Discriminant Techniques in Adoption
Patterns for a New Product." In PROMOTIONAL DECISIONS USING MATHE-
MATICAL MODELS, edited by Patrick J. Robinson, pp. 228-37. Boston:
Allyn and Bacon, 1967.

Green, Robert T., et al. "Innovation in the Service Sector: Some Empirical
Findings." JOURNAL OF MARKETING RESEARCH 11 (August 1974): 323-26.

Contains the results of a study to determine the characteristics of
innovators in one area of the service industry--retailing--and to
examine any overlap existing between retail service innovators and
grocery product innovators. Findings suggest that retail service
innovators are a reasonably distinct group when compared with
the rest of the population.

Greenhaigh, C. "Generating New Product Ideas." In EUROPEAN SOCIETY
FOR OPINION SURVEYS AND MARKET RESEARCH (ESOMAR) CONGRESS,
Helsinki, 22-26 August 1971, pp. 1-26.

Same article also published in ADMAP 7 (September 1971): 300-
301; (October 1971): 342-48; (November 1971): 383-92.

Grimley, S.S. "Canadian Factors in the Generation and Evaluation of New
Ideas." BUSINESS QUARTERLY 39 (Summer 1974): 32-39.

Explains the constraints on the successful development of new products in the Canadian scene and suggests ways and means to over-
ride them.

Gronhaugh, Kjell. "Profiling the Adopters in an Organizational Context."
EUROPEAN RESEARCH 5 (March 1977): 51-55.

Distinguishes between variables related to organizational resources which influence both the rate and speed of adoption and variables related to organization structure, using as a case in point, an internal communication system purchased by a variety of business organizations. Article finds that compared with nonadopters, adopters had more formalized relationships with other organizations.

Gross, Edwin J. "Bureaucracy, the "Gatekeeper" concept, and Consumer Innovation." JOURNAL OF RETAILING 43 (Spring 1967): 9-16, 64.

In order for product innovations to be made available to consumers, acceptance by and distribution through large scale retail organizations with bureaucratic characteristics must be achieved by the innovating manufacturer. The acceptance sequence within critically important bureaucratic retail structures is initially controlled by the buyer who functions as "gatekeeper." This article examines the problem and its ramifications for manufacturers.

Gross, W.A. "Innovation Process." IEEE SPECTRUM 9 (March 1972): 53-57.

Stresses that although many factors determine the success of new products, the important factor is the matching of the user's needs to performance and price.

Hackett, J.T. "Corporate Growth Revisited." BUSINESS HORIZONS 17 (February 1974): 25-31.

Explains the barriers to individual innovativeness in a corporate setup.

Hake, Bruno. NEW PRODUCT STRATEGY: INNOVATION AND DIVERSIFICATION TECHNIQUES. London: Pitman, 1971. 116 p.

Hanieski, John Francis. "An Explanatory Model of Technologically New Products." Ph.D. dissertation, Purdue University, 1970. 206 p. Ann Arbor, Mich.: University Microfilms. Order no. 71-02616.

Examines the processes and motivations necessary for the generation of technological innovations. Surveys a number of theories of economics regarding technological change and substitution.

Hardung-Hardung, Heimo. "A Newcomer: The Innovation Manager." EUROPEAN BUSINESS 34 (Summer 1972): 37-45.

Examines the role of the innovation manager in the launching of new products in different countries at the same time.

Hayward, G. "Diffusion of Innovation in Flour Milling Industry." EUROPEAN JOURNAL OF MARKETING 6 (August 1972): 195-202.

_____. "Market Adoption of New Industrial Products." INDUSTRIAL MARKET-ING MANAGEMENT 7 (June 1978): 193-98.

Hlavacek, James Daniel. "A Comparative Empirical Analysis of Managing Product Innovations in Complex Chemical Organizations." Ph.D. dissertation, University of Illinois, Urbana-Champaign, 1972. 269 p.

> Examines the organization of innovative process in complex institutions, taking the U.S. chemical industry as a case in point. Finds that venture team managers have a comparative advantage in many respects over product managers.

Hlavacek, James Daniel, and Thompson, V.A. "Bureaucracy and New Product Innovation." JOURNAL OF THE ACADEMY OF MANAGEMENT 16 (September 1973): 361-72.

Holmes, John H. "A Note on the Product-Adoption Process." OHIO STATE UNIVERSITY BULLETIN OF THE BUSINESS RESEARCH 44 (July 1969): 1-3.

Holt, Knut. "Information and Needs Analysis in Idea Generation." RESEARCH MANAGEMENT 18 (May 1975): 24-27.

> States that successful innovation requires not only a solid base of technical information but also assessments of user and market needs to spark creative ideas.

_____. "Need Assessment in Product Innovation." RESEARCH MANAGEMENT 19 (July 1976): 24-28.

> Stresses that mere technical competence in product innovation is not enough. Study of user and market need is an equally important part of the innovation process.

_____. PRODUCT INNOVATION: A WORKBOOK FOR MANAGEMENT IN INDUSTRY. London: Butterworth, 1978. 192 p.

> Focuses on the process of innovation, its control, and management. With increasing competition in national and international industry, the ability of a company to survive depends largely on its powers of innovation, on its capacity to anticipate changing needs, and on its development of new market products. Written primarily for those involved in the process of product innovation and management studies.

"How Ideas are Made into Products at 3M." BUSINESS WEEK, 15 September 1973, pp. 224-27.

> Describes the 3M company's approach to supporting innovations for mutual advantage.

Ingledew, William Albert. "The Influence of Major Departmental Chains on Adoption Rates and Developing Patterns of Trade Inflows of New Consumer Products to the Canadian Market." Ph.D. dissertation, University of Western Ontario, Canada, 1975.

"Innovations: The Blind Man's Elephant." TECHNOLOGY REVIEW 79 (June 1977): 72.

"Innovator is Key to New Item Success." AMERICAN DRUGGIST 158 (1 July 1968): 58.

Jacoby, Jacob. "Innovation Proneness as a Function of Personality." In PRO-CEEDINGS: AMERICAN MARKETING ASSOCIATION FALL CONFERENCE, edited by David L. Sparks. Chicago: American Marketing Association, 1970.

> Examines the relationship between personality and consumer behavior in relation to innovation proneness.

Jewkes, John, et al. THE SOURCES OF INVENTION. 2d ed. New York: Norton, 1969. 372 p.

> Surveys the organization, motivation, and the mechanism for trans-forming inventions into innovations.

Johnston, R., and Gibbons, M. "Characteristics of Information Usage in Tech-nological Innovation." IEEE TRANSACTIONS ON ENGINEERING MANAGE-MENT EM-22 (February 1975): 27-34.

Kamien, Norton I., and Schwartz, Nancy L. "Market Structure and Innova-tion: A Survey." JOURNAL OF ECONOMIC LITERATURE 13 (March 1975): 1-37.

> Examines how research and development expenditure relates to tech-nological advances.

Kegerreis, Robert J. "Marketing Management and the Diffusion of Innovations." OHIO STATE UNIVERSITY BULLETIN OF BUSINESS RESEARCH 44 (April 1965): 2-5.

Kegerreis, Robert J., and Engel, James F. "The Innovative Consumer: Char-acteristics of the Earliest Adopters of a New Automotive Service." In PRO-CEEDINGS: AMERICAN MARKETING ASSOCIATION FALL CONFERENCE, edited by Bernard Morin, pp. 357-66. Chicago: American Marketing Associa-tion, 1969.

> Characteristics studied include economic status, social status, and personal correlates of innovativeness.

Kemm, Thomas R. "Scientific Experimentation in Product Innovation." In PROCEEDINGS: AMERICAN MARKETING ASSOCIATION SUMMER CONFERENCE, edited by Raymond M. Haas, pp. 241-46. Chicago: American Marketing Association, 1966.

Describes technique of factorial experimentation and how it can be used to provide market research guidance throughout all stages of product development.

Kieser, M. "Management of Product Innovation: Strategy, Planning and Organization." MANAGEMENT INTERNATIONAL REVIEW 14, no. 1 (1974): 3-19.

Discusses production-innovation strategy (PIS) for the choice of planning procedures for use in the specific phases of the innovation process and also for the design of an innovation-inducing organizational structure.

King, Charles W. "Adoption and Diffusion Research in Marketing: An Overview." In PROCEEDINGS: AMERICAN MARKETING ASSOCIATION FALL CONFERENCE, edited by Raymond M. Haas, pp. 665-84. Chicago: American Marketing Association, 1966.

Surveys research regarding the development of diffusion theory and research.

_____. COMMUNICATING WITH THE INNOVATOR IN THE FASHION ADOPTION PROCESS. Purdue University, Krannert Graduate School of Industrial Administration Institute, Paper no. 121. Lafayette, Ind.: September 1965.

_____. "Communicating with the Innovator in the Fashion Adoption Process." In MARKETING AND ECONOMIC DEVELOPMENT, edited by P.D. Bennett, pp. 425-39. Chicago: American Marketing Association, 1965.

_____. "Communicating with the Innovator in the Fashion Adoption Process." In PROCEEDINGS: AMERICAN MARKETING ASSOCIATION CONFERENCE, edited by Peter Bennett, pp. 324-39. Chicago: American Marketing Association, 1965.

King, Charles W., and Summers, J.O. "Technology, Innovation and Consumer Decision Making." In PROCEEDINGS: AMERICAN MARKETING ASSOCIATION WINTER CONFERENCE, edited by Reed Mayor, pp. 63-68. Chicago: American Marketing Association, 1967.

Examines critical empirical data on consumer predispositions and perceptions in the new product adoption process.

Kleiman, Herbert S. "The Integrated Circuit: A Case Study of Product Innovation in the Electronics Industry." Ph.D. dissertation, George Washington University, 1966. 260 p. Ann Arbor, Mich.: University Microfilms. Order no. 66-09803.

Examines the importance of government-industry relationship in the development of a major innovation. Case study used is that of the development of integrated circuit for which there was a great deal of financial support from government.

Klein, R.W. "Dynamic Theory of Comparative Advantage." AMERICAN ECONOMIC REVIEW 63 (March 1973): 173-84.

Attempts to explain the establishment of U.S. multinational firms as a process of U.S. parent firms developing innovative new products and eventually shifting the new product to a foreign country through a subsidiary.

Kleyngeld, H.P. ADOPTION OF NEW FOOD PRODUCTS. Tilburg Studies on Economics, vol. 12. Netherlands: Tilburg University Press, 1977. 133 p.

Reports a large-scale study concerning the diffusion of food innovations in the Netherlands. Concentrates on questions such as: Are there food innovators?, and if so, What are their characteristics?

Knight, K.E. "A Descriptive Model of the Intrafirm Innovative Process." JOURNAL OF BUSINESS 40 (October 1967): 478-96.

Lancini, Richard A. "The Traditional View of Innovativeness in Relation to Attitude Change and Purchase Behavior: An exception." In PROCEEDINGS: AMERICAN MARKETING ASSOCIATION COMBINED CONFERENCE, edited by Boris W. Becker and Helmut Becker, pp. 439-44. Chicago: American Marketing Association, 1972.

Analyzes traditional theoretical assumption regarding behavior of innovators in the field of fashion, their attitudes and purchase behavior towards new clothing styles. Concludes that the assumptions may not apply to all situations.

Lazer, W., and Bell, W.E. "The Communication Process and Innovation." JOURNAL OF ADVERTISING RESEARCH 6 (September 1966): 2-7.

Leroy, Georges Paul." Multinational Corporate Strategy: A Framework of Analysis of World Wide Diffusion of Products." Ph.D. dissertation, University of California, Berkeley, 1974. 326 p. Ann Arbor, Mich.: University Microfilms. Order no. 75-11486.

Examines the product strategies of multinational companies and their consistency with accepted theories of private direct investment.

_____. MULTINATIONAL PRODUCT STRATEGY: A TYPOLOGY FOR ANALYSIS OF WORLDWIDE PRODUCT INNOVATION AND DIFFUSION. New York: Praeger, 1976. 250 p.

Levit, Theodore. "Innovative Imitation." HARVARD BUSINESS REVIEW 44 (September 1966): 63–70.

> Outlines a strategy for planning and creating innovative imitation, which is just as important as innovation, because surveys reveal that great flow of newness is not innovation but imitation.

_____. MARKETING FOR BUSINESS GROWTH. 2d ed. New York: Mc-Graw-Hill, 1974. 266 p.

> Deals with new product planning and marketing from the point of view of organization of innovation and imitation.

Liles, Patrick R. "Who are the Entrepreneurs?" MSU BUSINESS TOPICS 22 (Winter 1974): 5–14.

> Examines the determinants of entrepreneurial makeup, such as ambition, ability, experience, and situations.

Little, William Blair. "New Product Information Processing: A Descriptive Study of Product Innovation in the Machine Tool Industry." Ph.D. dissertation, Harvard University, 1968. 33 p.

Locke, H.B., et al. "Planning for Innovation." LONG RANGE PLANNING 7 (April 1974): 19–25.

> Explains corporate planning in the National Research Development Corporation. Illustrates the philosophy and approach adopted in planning for innovation.

Lorsch, Jay William. PRODUCT INNOVATION AND ORGANIZATION. Studies of the Modern Corporation. New York: Macmillan, 1965. 184 p.

Lorsch, J[ay].W[illiam]., and Lawrence, P.R. "Organizing for Product Innovation." HARVARD BUSINESS REVIEW 43 (January 1965): 109–18.

> Discusses problems involved in obtaining collaboration and coordination between different departments in a firm, such as research, sales, and production in developing new products and processes.

McGuire, Edward Patrick. "Casual Inventor." CONFERENCE BOARD RECORD 8 (October 1971): 54–57.

> Deals with the independent inventor as a source of new product ideas.

McKay, K.G. "Innovation in Communications Technology." BELL LABORATORIES RECORD 53 (September 1975): 324–32.

> Looks at the innovative process in telecommunications, the various types of innovation, the significance of technical integration, and

the Bell system's record of innovation. The reason that enables an integrated laboratory to excel is its information flow coupled with focused purpose.

Mansfield, Edwin. RESEARCH AND INNOVATION IN THE MODERN COR-PORATION. New York: Norton, 1971. 239 p.

Contains an empirical analysis of the cost and time of development of an innovation, the time lag between invention and commercial use, and effect of the size of the firm on general innovative behavior.

Marks, Norton E. VENDING MACHINES: INTRODUCTION AND INNOVA-TION. Studies in Marketing, no. 11. Austin: University of Texas, 1969. 152 p.

Marquis, Donald G. THE ANATOMY OF SUCCESSFUL INNOVATIONS. Managing Advancing Technology, vol. 1, pp. 35-48. New York: American Management Association, 1972.

Examines the factors leading to the success of nuts and bolts type product innovations.

Massy, William F. A DYNAMIC MODEL FOR MONITORING NEW PRODUCT ADOPTION. Working Paper, no. 95. Stanford, Calif.: Stanford University, Graduate School of Business Administration, 1966. 94 p.

Describes a stochastic model of the new product adoption process and applications.

Mendez, A. "Social Structure and Diffusion of Innovation." HUMAN OR-GANIZATION 27 (Fall 1968): 241-49.

Metcalfe, J.S. "Rewards and Problems of Successful Technological Innovations." METALS AND MATERIALS 4 (February 1970): 63-67.

Midgley, David F. INNOVATION AND NEW PRODUCT MARKETING. New York: Halsted, 1977. 266 p.

Deals with diffusion of innovation within the context of new product introductions. Presents an improved methodology for evaluating and developing new products and new product strategies.

_____. "Innovation in the Male Fashion Market: The Parallel Diffusion Hypothesis." In PROCEEDINGS: 31ST EUROPEAN SOCIETY FOR OPINION SURVEYS AND MARKET RESEARCH SEMINAR ON FASHION RESEARCH AND MARKETING, AMSTERDAM, DECEMBER 1974. Amsterdam: The Society, 1974.

_____. MANAGING NEW PRODUCTS. Cranfield Research Papers in Marketing and Logistics, 1974-75. Cranfield, Bedfordshire, Engl.: Institute Press for School of Management, 1975.

Describes a quantitative theory of new product adoption based on the effectiveness of interpersonal and media communications.

_____. "A Quantitative Theory of Innovative Behavior." Ph.D. dissertation, University of Bradford Management Center, 1974.

_____. "A Simple Mathematical Theory of Innovative Behavior." JOURNAL OF CONSUMER RESEARCH 3 (June 1976): 31-41.

Mittelstaedt, R.A. "Optimal Simulation Level and the Adoption Decision Process." JOURNAL OF CONSUMER RESEARCH 3 (September 1976): 84-94.

Examines the hypothesis that high sensation seekers as consumers would be more aware of new product alterations than other categories.

Morton, Jack Andrew. ORGANIZING FOR INNOVATION - A SYSTEMS APPROACH TO TECHNOLOGY MANAGEMENT. New York: McGraw-Hill, 1971. 171 p.

_____. "A Systems Approach to the Innovation Process." BUSINESS HORIZONS 10 (Summer 1967): 27-36.

Likens the human aspects for managing and innovation to the job of systems engineer for a complex information processing machine.

Myers, Sumner, and Marquis, Donald G. SUCCESSFUL INDUSTRIAL INNOVATIONS: A STUDY OF FACTORS UNDERLYING INNOVATION IN SELECTED FIRMS. Study by the National Planning Association for the National Science Foundation, NSF 69-17. Washington, D.C.: May 1969. 117 p.

Myers, S[umner]., and Sweezy, E.E. WHY INNOVATIONS FALTER AND FAIL: A STUDY OF 200 CASES. Springfield, Va.: National Technical Information Service, 1977, 77 p. Order no. PB 259-208.

Examines the obstacles to innovative success as identified by management officials involved in decisions to scrap innovations and relates these obstacles to other aspects of the innovation process, such as the stages of development at which decisions are made to scrap innovations and the attitudes of management toward these decisions.

Nelson, Richard R., and Winter, Sidney G. "In Search of Useful Theory of Innovation." RESEARCH POLICY 7 (January 1977): 36-37.

Presents an overview of the prevailing theoretical literature on innovation, probes the adequacy of existing theory to guide policy

regarding innovation, and sketches some directions for more fruit-
ful theorizing.

Ness, Eugene Thomas. "Change Agents in Architectural Diffusion Process."
In PROCEEDINGS: AMERICAN MARKETING ASSOCIATION FALL CONFER-
ENCE, edited by Philip R. McDonald, pp. 414-15. Chicago: American Mar-
keting Association, 1969.

Examines how innovations are accepted in the building industry.

_____. "Innovations in the Building Industry: The Architectural Innovator."
In PROCEEDINGS: AMERICAN MARKETING ASSOCIATION FALL CONFER-
ENCE, edited by Philip R. McDonald, pp. 352-56. Chicago: American Mar-
keting Association, 1969.

Compares innovators with noninnovators on a number of dimensions
using multiple discriminant analysis.

Norman, Richard. ORGANIZATIONAL INNOVATIVENESS: PRODUCT VARI-
ATIONS AND REORIENTATION (SIAR, 15). Stockholm: Stiftelsen, foretags-
administrativ forskning, 1969. 31 p.

_____. "Organizational Innovativeness: Product Variations and Reorientation."
ADMINISTRATIVE SCIENCE QUARTERLY 16 (June 1971): 203-15.

Analysis of case studies in product development. Innovation patterns are identified, and explanations of the differences are of-
fered.

North, Jeremy. "Reducing the Risk of Innovation: A Consultant in Diversification and Marketing, Outlines a Strategy for Launching New Products." BUSI-
NESS ADMINISTRATION 3 (March 1970): 33-35.

Oates, D. "How Gould Manages Innovation." INTERNATIONAL MANAGE-
MENT 30 (December 1975): 29-30.

O'Neil, Donald Arthur. "Uncertainty and New Product Innovation Planning."
Ph.D. dissertation, University of California, Los Angeles, 1972. 342 p. Ann
Arbor, Mich.: University Microfilms. Order no. 72-33968.

Develops a simulation model for new product innovation process.
Evaluates whether the model could be used as a procedural guide
in new product planning.

Ostlund, Lyman E. "Identifying Early Buyers." JOURNAL OF ADVERTISING
RESEARCH 12 (April 1972): 25-30.

Study which field tests a model for predicting new product adoption. The following product perception variables were used to
predict new buyers: relative advantage, compatibility, divisibility,
complexity, communicability, and perceived risk.

Ozanne, Urban, and Churchill, G. "Five Dimensions of the Industrial Adoption Process." JOURNAL OF MARKETING RESEARCH 8 (August 1971): 322-28.

> Explains the stages involved in the process of introduction of a new industrial product and its ultimate adoption by the entire industry.

Palda, Kristian S., and Blair, L.M. "An Experimental Approach to the Pricing of Distinctively New Durable Products." In PROCEEDINGS: AMERICAN MARKETING ASSOCIATION FALL CONFERENCE, edited by David L. Sparks, p. 12. Chicago: American Marketing Association, 1970.

> Discusses the questions: What will be the customer behavior in the case of a distinctively new product? How do you gather information in this case which will help set the appropriate price?

Peters, Bruce. "Overcoming Organizational Constraints on Creativity and Innovation." RESEARCH MANAGEMENT 17 (May 1974): 29-33.

> Describes a cell-structured management conducive to research in an organization.

Peters, M.P., and Venkatesan, M. "Exploration of Variables Inherent in Adopting an Industrial Product." JOURNAL OF MARKETING RESEARCH 10 (August 1973): 312-15.

> Finds that personal characteristics, as well as environmental or firm variables play an important role in the new product adoption decision-making process.

Pizam, A. "Psychological Characteristics of Innovators." EUROPEAN JOURNAL OF MARKETING 6 (Autumn 1972): 203-10.

Prince, George M. THE PRACTICE OF CREATIVITY. New York: Collier, 1970. 197 p.

> Discusses a technique called "synectics" for generating new ideas.

Rapoport, John. "Product Innovation Time Cost and Time-Cost Trade-Offs." Ph.D. dissertation, University of Pennsylvania, 1970. 198 p. Ann Arbor, Mich.: University Microfilms. Order no. 71-19273.

> Examines the cost and time of the activities undertaken by a firm when introducing a new product in terms of applied research, preparation of specifications, construction and testing of prototype, and manufacturing start-ups.

Reynolds, Fred D., and Darden, William R. "Analysis of Selected Factors Associated With the Adoption of New Products." MISSISSIPPI VALLEY JOURNAL 8 (Winter 1972-73): 31-42.

_____. "Fashion Theory and Pragmatics: The Case of the Midi." JOURNAL OF RETAILING 49 (Spring 1973): 51-62.

Explores the possibility of obtaining a measure of consumer innovativeness prior to the introduction of a fashion and, thereby,
developing better forecasts of fashion acceptance or rejection.
The above is achieved using an ex-ante measure, intensity of
purchase intentions within the adoption, and diffusion framework
for a recent clothing style, the midi.

Reynolds, William H. "Cars and Clothing: Understanding Fashion Trends."
JOURNAL OF MARKETING 32 (July 1968): 44-49.

Explains that fashion trends can be detected fairly easily if the
marketer is aware of certain factors which help to determine
whether a particular innovation will go on to become an accepted
fashion. These trends may be of two types which facilitate the
prediction of peaks in fashion popularity and the point in time
when the trend is likely to die out.

Riley, D. "Financing Transportation Innovation in Perspective." AERONAUTI-
CAL JOURNAL 77 (April 1973): 181-89.

Examines the methods in which capital is infused to support innovations in the transportation sector.

Robert, Edward. "Entrepreneurs and How to Keep Them." In MANAGING
ADVANCING TECHNOLOGY, vol. 2, pp. 45-57. New York: American
Management Association, 1972.

Explains how to keep individualistic creative entrepreneurs within
a corporate environment.

Roberts, E.B. "Generating Effective Cooperation Innovation." TECHNOLOGY
REVIEW 80 (October-November 1977): 26-33.

Robertson, A. "The Marketing Factor in Successful Industrial Innovations."
INDUSTRIAL MARKETING MANAGEMENT 2, no. 2 (1973): 369-74.

Robertson, Dan Hugh. "An Analysis of New Product Information, Acquisition
and Utilization by Austin, Texas Housewives." Ph.D. dissertation, University
of Texas, Austin, 1971. 158 p. Ann Arbor, Mich.: University Microfilms.
Order no. 72-19657.

Examines the sources of information on new products favorable to
a group of housewives, like newspapers, magazines, television,
and word of mouth. Studies how the information is used by the
group.

Robertson, Thomas S. "Determinants of Innovative Behavior." In PROCEED-

INGS: AMERICAN MARKETING ASSOCIATION WINTER CONFERENCE, edited by Reed Moyer, pp. 328-32. Chicago: American Marketing Association, 1967.

Presents a theoretical model of new product adoption process and examines its predictive validity.

_____. "The New Product Diffusion Process." In PROCEEDINGS: AMERICAN MARKETING ASSOCIATION SUMMER CONFERENCE, edited by Bernard Morin, pp. 80-86. Chicago: American Marketing Association, 1969.

Analyzes how diffusion theory concepts can be used to improve the probability of new product success.

_____. "The Process of Innovation and the Diffusion of Innovation." JOURNAL OF MARKETING 31 (January 1967): 14-19.

Robertson, Thomas S., and Rossiter, John R. FASHION DIFFUSION: THE INTERPLAY OF INNOVATOR AND OPINION LEADER ROLES IN COLLEGE SOCIAL SYSTEMS. Los Angeles: University of California, Graduate School of Business Administration, 1967.

Robertson, Thomas S., et al. "Cultural Compatibility in the New Product Adoption Process." In PROCEEDINGS: AMERICAN MARKETING ASSOCIATION FALL CONFERENCE, edited by Philip R. McDonald, pp. 70-75. Chicago: American Marketing Association, 1969.

Examines whether the new product adoption is dependent upon the compatibility of the new product with the life-styles of a given subculture.

Rockwood, Persis Emmett. "The Diffusion of Innovation Viewed as an Information System." In PROCEEDINGS: AMERICAN MARKETING ASSOCIATION WINTER CONFERENCE, edited by Reed Moyer, pp. 395-96. Chicago: American Marketing Association, 1967.

Examines management of innovative ideas, diffusion of innovation, and innovation process.

Rogers, Everett M. "New Product Adoption and Diffusion." JOURNAL OF CONSUMER RESEARCH 2, no. 4 (1976): 290-301.

Rogers, Everett M., and Shoemaker, F.F. COMMUNICATION OF INNOVATIONS: A CROSS CULTURAL APPROACH. Rev. ed. New York: Free Press, 1971. 476 p.

Discusses the role of communication in individual and organizational adoption of innovations.

Rogers, Everett M., and Stanfield, J. David. "Adoption and Diffusion of New Products: Emerging Generalizations and Hypothesis." In APPLICATIONS OF THE SCIENCES IN MARKETING MANAGEMENT, edited by Frank M. Bass, et al, pp. 227-50. New York: Wiley, 1968.

Romeo, A.A. "Interindustry and Interfirm Differences in the Rate of Diffusion of an Innovation." REVIEW OF ECONOMICS AND STATISTICS 57 (August 1975): 311-19.

Examines the relationship between market structure and technological change taking the British machine tools industry as a case in point.

Root, Paul H. "Implementation of Risk Analysis Models for the Management of Product Innovations." In COMPUTER SIMULATIONS FOR BUSINESS AND ECONOMIC MODELS, edited by W. Goldberg, pp. 93-138. Gothenberg, Sweden: University of Gothenberg, 1972.

Rosenbloom, Richard S. "Product Innovation In a Scientific Age." In PROCEEDINGS: AMERICAN MARKETING ASSOCIATION SUMMER CONFERENCE, edited by John S. Wright and Jack L. Goldstucker, pp. 247-59. Chicago: American Marketing Association, 1966.

Discusses strategic and organizational aspects of research, development, and marketing in product innovation, and requisites for necessary information flow.

Rotandi, Thomas. "The Innovator and the Ritualist: A Study in Conflict." PERSONNEL JOURNAL 53 (June 1974): 439-44.

Deals with a method of encouraging individual creativity without losing organizational control.

Roy, William Randall. "Institutional Constraints in the Marketing of New Plumbing Products." Ph.D. dissertation, University of Michigan, 1967. 334 p. Ann Arbor, Mich.: University Microfilms. Order no. 68-07712.

By using the example of the plumbing industry, this thesis examines the effect of institutional restraints on innovation of new plumbing products and how such constraints can be met.

Rubenstein, A., et al. FINAL TECHNICAL REPORT ON FIELD STUDIES OF THE TECHNOLOGICAL INNOVATION PROCESS. Chicago: Northwestern University, September 1974.

Ryan, J.F., and Murray, J.A. "The Diffusion of a Pharmaceutical Innovation in Ireland." EUROPEAN JOURNAL OF MARKETING 11, no. 1 (1977): 3-12.

Case study of diffusion of an "ethical-drug" available on doctor's prescription only. Data was collected five months after the launch of the new product. Summary of these findings is illustrated.

Sandkull, Bengt. INNOVATIVE BEHAVIOR OF ORGANIZATIONS: THE CASE OF NEW PRODUCTS. Utg.av: Swedish Institute for Administrative Research, Lund, Studentlitteratur, 1970. 165 p.

Sands, Saul. "Successful Business Innovation: A Survey of Current Professional Views." CALIFORNIA MANAGEMENT REVIEW 20 (Winter 1977): 5-16.

Scanlon, Sally. "It Still Pays to Innovate." SALES MANAGEMENT 115 (7 July 1975): 43-44.

Schnee, J.E. "International Shifts in Innovative Activity: The Case of Pharmaceuticals." COLUMBIA JOURNAL OF WORLD BUSINESS 13 (Spring 1978): 112-22.

Schwartz, Jules J. "How an Organization Decides to Innovate?" WHARTON QUARTERLY 7 (Spring 1974): 10-13.

Discusses the formal organization of technological innovation in terms of resource allocation, system for control, and rewards and parts played by various levels of management.

Severiens, J.T. "Product Innovation, Organizational Change and Risk: A New Perspective." ADVANCED MANAGEMENT JOURNAL 42 (Fall 1977): 24-31.

Shankleman, E. "Barrier to Innovation." INDUSTRY AND TECHNOLOGY 5 (June 1967): 110.

Shaw, Steven J. "Behavioral Science Offers Fresh Insights on New Product Acceptance." JOURNAL OF MARKETING 29 (January 1965): 9.

In spite of large sums of money spent on research and development, an estimated ninety percent of all new products fail within four years of their introduction. This does not mean that consumer behavior is fickle and unpredictable, rather marketing managers do not fully understand the processes by which consumers accept or reject an innovation. Article focuses on behavioral science concepts to find out who are the small group of leaders influencing the spread and adoption of innovations, what is the nature of the innovation process, and which attributes of the innovation itself influence its rate of adoption.

Sheth, Jagdish N. "Perceived Risk and Diffusion of Innovations." In INSIGHTS INTO CONSUMER BEHAVIOR, edited by Johan Arndt, pp. 173-88. Boston: Allyn and Bacon, 1968.

Soltanoff, L. "Are You Ready to Become an Inventor?" TECHNOLOGY REVIEW 80 (May 1978): 46-50.

_____. "Innovation Myth." INDUSTRIAL RESEARCH 13 (August 1971): 44-46.

The author says there is a severe innovation crisis in the United States. He calls for measures to redress the situation by promoting creativity.

Sorenson, Ralph Z. "U.S. Marketers Can Learn from European Innovators." HARVARD BUSINESS REVIEW 50 (September 1972): 89-99.

Examines some successes in Europe in translating research discoveries and inventions into commercially viable new products and draws the lessons for American industry.

Steiner, Gary Albert. THE CREATIVE ORGANIZATION. Chicago: University of Chicago Press, 1965. 267 p.

Examines the nature of individual creativity in the context of a large organization.

"Stimulating New Product Ideas." DRUG AND COSMETICS INDUSTRY 113 (October 1973): 36-38.

STRATEGIES AND TACTICS OF PRODUCT INNOVATION. Edited by the Staff of Innovation. Managing Advancing Technology Series. New York: American Management Association, 1972. 245 p.

Summers, John O., and King, C.W. "Interpersonal Communication and New Product Attitudes." In PROCEEDINGS: AMERICAN MARKETING ASSOCIATION FALL CONFERENCE, edited by Philip R. McDonald, pp. 292-99. Chicago: American Marketing Association, 1969.

Examines how critical opinion leadership is in the adoption of four new product categories.

_____. OPINION LEADERSHIP AND NEW PRODUCT ADOPTION. Institute for Research in the Behavioral, Economic and Management Sciences, Paper no. 243. Lafayette, Ind.: Purdue University, Krannert Graduate School of Industrial Administration, 1969. 32 p.

Sutton, C.J. "Effect of Uncertainty on the Diffusion of 3d Generation Computers." JOURNAL OF INDUSTRIAL ECONOMICS 23 (June 1975): 273-80.

Tamura, Masanori. "Structural Model of Personal Influence in the Diffusion Process of a New Product." In ANNALS, pp. 77-95. Japan: Kobe University, School of Business Administration, 1968.

Twiss, Brian. MANAGING TECHNOLOGICAL INNOVATION. London: Longman, 1974. 237 p.

Discusses the function of research and development manager in the area of organization, planning, and control of new products.

Ullman, John. PRODUCT INNOVATION IN SELECTED INDUSTRIES. Hofstra University Yearbook of Business, series 3, vol. 3. New York: Hofstra University Bookstore, 1967. 285 p.

Examines the physical nature of innovations by questioning the kinds of products that constitute innovations and how they differ from their predecessors. It is a study of the physical characteristics of new products in selected industries with an examination of their origins by state. Pinpoints factors determining the volume and results of innovation.

U.S. Department of Commerce. Panel on Invention and Innovation. TECHNOLOGICAL INNOVATION: ITS ENVIRONMENT AND MANAGEMENT. Washington, D.C.: U.S. Government Printing Office, 1967. 83 p.

Utterback, James M. "Innovations in Industry and Diffusion of Technology." SCIENCE 183 (February 1974): 620-26.

Analyzes the departments of a firm's effectiveness in the innovation process.

_____. "The Process of Innovation." IEEE TRANSACTIONS ON ENGINEER-ING MANAGEMENT EM-18 (November 1971): 124-31.

_____. "The Process of Technical Innovation in Instrument Firms." Ph.D. dissertation, Massachusetts Institute of Technology, 1969. 134 p.

Utterback, J.M., et al. "The Process of Innovation in Five Industries in Europe and Japan." IEEE TRANSACTIONS ON ENGINEERING MANAGE-MENT EM-23 (February 1976): 3-9.

Vicas, Alexander George. "The Lag of Unrestricted Imitation Behind Product Innovation." Ph.D. dissertation, Princeton University, 1966. 235 p. Ann Arbor, Mich.: University Microfilms. Order no. 66-13362.

Presents case studies relating to product infusion lag following the introduction of new products. Examines how marketing approaches this problem.

Von Hippel, E.A. "The Dominant Role of Users in the Scientific Instrument Innovation Process." RESEARCH POLICY 5 (July 1976): 212-39.

_____. "THE DOMINANT ROLE OF THE USER IN SEMICONDUCTOR AND ELECTRONIC SUBASSEMBLY PROCESS INNOVATION. M.I.T. Sloan School of Management Working paper, no. 853-76. Cambridge, Mass.: M.I.T., April 1976. 36 p.

_____. "An Exploratory Study of Corporate Venturing - A New Product Innovation Strategy Used by some Major Corporations." Ph.D. dissertation, Carnegie Mellon University, 1973. 161 p. Ann Arbor, Mich.: University Microfilms. Order no. 74-04738.

> Analyzes the need for and capabilities of corporate venture groups. Examines the factors which go to make for successful corporate venturing.

_____. "Has a Customer Already Developed Your Next Product." SLOAN MANAGEMENT REVIEW 18 (Winter 1977): 63-74.

> Examines the view that successful designs which later becomes successful products are typically available from customers or others before the first-to-market manufacturer begins his design work.

_____. "Users As Innovators." TECHNOLOGY REVIEW 80 (January 1978): 30-39.

Webster, Frederick E. "Communication and Diffusion Processes in Industrial Markets." EUROPEAN JOURNAL OF MARKETING 5 (Winter 1971-72): 178-88.

> Reports on the factors which influence the rate of adoption and diffusion of new products. Presents results on identification of the characteristics of early adopters, and on whether the concept of opinion leadership applies in industrial markets.

_____. "New Product Adoption in Industrial Markets: A Framework for Analysis." JOURNAL OF MARKETING 33 (July 1969): 35-39.

> Lack of understanding of the industrial buyer behavior results into new product failures. Article proposes a behavior model in terms of their perception and motivation.

Weiss, E.B. "Do Giant Corporations Need More Dreamers?" ADVERTISING AGE 38 (18 September 1967): 130.

_____. "Product Innovation Comes Out of Its Shell and Goes International." ADVERTISING AGE 41 (9 February 1970): 61.

Wells, Louis Truitt, Jr. PRODUCT INNOVATION AND DIRECTIONS OF INTERNATIONAL TRADE. Cambridge, Mass.: Harvard University, 1966. 23 p.

"Why Industrial Innovations Fail." CHEMISTRY AND INDUSTRY, 4 March 1972, p. 194.

"Why Smaller Firms often Lead the Pace of Change." ENGINEER 228 (12 June 1969): 32-35.

Wilson, Ira G., and Wilson, Marthann E. MANAGEMENT, INNOVATION, AND SYSTEM DESIGN. New York: Auerbach Publishers, 1971. 175 p.

Identifies the process of innovation which requires two quite different kinds of talents and abilities: those of the innovators themselves, and those of the managers who direct and control the innovative process.

Yaney, Joseph P. "The Management of Innovation." MANAGEMENT REVIEW 16 (June 1971): 6-7.

Examines the kinds of people and organizational structure required for innovation management.

Chapter 5

PROMOTIONAL STRATEGY AND BUYER BEHAVIOR

"Admen Can Improve New Product Odds." INDUSTRIAL MARKETING 58 (May 1973): 32.

Discusses how admen can successfully participate in the new product planning and marketing activities from early stages by joining in the firm's new product committees.

Anderson, Beverlee Byler. "The Influence of Seals of Certification on Consumer Attitudes for Selected Products." Ph.D. dissertation, Ohio State University, 1972. 121 p. Ann Arbor, Mich.: University Microfilms. Order no. 72-26968.

Investigates how consumer behavior is affected by seals of certification of products such as Good Housekeeping seals.

Andrus, Roman Raphael. "Measures of Consumer Innovative Behavior." Ph.D. dissertation, Columbia University, 1965. 141 p.

Analyzes the applicability of certain sociological and behavioral theories in the analyses of data on consumer buying habits, in an effort to understand consumer innovative behavior would help reduce new product risks.

Arndt, Johan. "Perceived Risk, Sociometric Integration and Word of Mouth in the Adoption of a New Food Product." In PROCEEDINGS: AMERICAN MARKETING ASSOCIATION FALL CONFERENCE, edited by Raymond M. Haas, pp. 644-48. Chicago: American Marketing Association, 1966.

Measures the factors involved in word-of-mouth process and how they are related to the acceptance of a new consumer food product.

_____. "Perceived Risk, Sociometric Integration and Word of Mouth in the Adoption of a New Food Product." In RISK TAKING IN INFORMATION HANDLING IN CONSUMER BEHAVIOR, edited by Donald F. Cox, pp. 289-316. Cambridge, Mass.: Harvard University, Division of Research, Graduate School of Business Administration, 1967.

_____. "Perceived Risk and Word of Mouth Advertising." In PERSPECTIVES IN CONSUMER BEHAVIOR, edited by Harold H. Kassarjian and Thomas S. Robertson, pp. 330-37. Glenview, Ill.: Scott Foresman, 1968.

_____. "Profiling Consumer Innovators." In INSIGHTS INTO CONSUMER BEHAVIOR, edited by Johan Arndt, pp. 71-83. Boston: Allyn and Bacon, 1968.

_____. "Role of Product-Related Conversations in the Diffusion of New Product." JOURNAL OF MARKETING RESEARCH 4 (August 1967): 291.

Comments on an experiment designed to investigate the short-term sales effects of product-related conversations. Finds that exposure to favorable comments aid acceptance of a new product, while unfavorable comments hinder it.

_____. "Word of Mouth Advertising: The Role of Product Related Conversations in the Diffusion of a New Food Product." Ph.D. dissertation, Harvard University, 1966. 30 p.

_____. WORD OF MOUTH ADVERTISING. New York: Advertising Research Foundation, 1967. 88 p.

_____. "Word of Mouth Advertising and Informal Communication." In RISK TAKING AND INFORMATION HANDLING IN CONSUMER BEHAVIOR, edited by Donald F. Cox, pp. 188-239. Boston: Harvard University, Graduate School of Business, 1967.

Association of National Advertisers. Advertising Management Policy Committee. CURRENT ADVERTISING MANAGEMENT PRACTICES: OPINIONS AS TO FUTURE TRENDS. New York: Association of National Advertisers, 1974. 105 p.

Barker, Stephen M., and Trost, John F. "Cultivate the High Volume Consumer." HARVARD BUSINESS REVIEW 51 (March-April 1973): 118-22.

Deals with the concept that a minority of the consumers of a product are responsible for a large amount of the volume sold, i.e., the high volume consumers. Marketing manager must discover the reason for these high volume sales and then make adjustments so other consumers might increase their consumption.

Barnes, J., and Ayars, W.B. "Reducing New Product Risk Through Understanding Buyer Behavior." INDUSTRIAL MARKETING MANAGEMENT 6, no. 3 (1977): 189-92.

Discusses the importance of perceived risk on the part of industrial buyers and need for marketers to empathize with this.

Barnett, Norman L. "Developing Effective Advertising for New Products." JOURNAL OF ADVERTISING RESEARCH 8 (December 1968): 13-18.

Advises that firms should find out what characteristics consumers desire in a new product which fits its marketing objectives, and then make sure the advertising communicates these characteristics.

Baumgarten, S.A. "Innovative Communicator in the Diffusion Process." JOURNAL OF MARKETING RESEARCH 12 (February 1975): 12-18.

Profiles the characteristics of "innovative communicators"--consumers who are both innovators and opinion leaders, in terms of opinion leadership, early adoption, and innovative communicativeness. This will enable media advertisers to make their advertisements more applicable to that group that is more likely to become consumers.

Beliveau, Donald. "A Cross Cultural Comparison of Foreign Product Images by the Semantic Differential Technique." Ph.D. dissertation, University of California, Los Angeles, 1971. 220 p. Ann Arbor, Mich.: University Microfilms. Order no. 71-16297.

Examines the need for knowing the target markets for successful new product introduction, especially in cases where the new product is being introduced in a different country, where consumer product perceptions may be different than observed in the host country.

Bernado, Nicoletti. "First Time Buyers of a Repurchasable New Product." EUROPEAN JOURNAL OF MARKETING 9, no. 2 (1975): 109-16.

Discusses the estimation of the ratio of "first time buyers" to "repeat buyers" of a new product over a given period of time and at a known rate of consumption. Results are summarized in formulae and tables presented at the end of the article. Three examples of application are illustrated.

Blake, Brian, et al. "Dogmatism and Acceptance of New Products." JOURNAL OF MARKETING RESEARCH 7 (November 1970): 483-86.

Describes a two-category typology of new consumer products to investigate the relationship between consumer personality characteristics and acceptance of new products. Finds that the influence of a consumer's dogmatism upon his acceptance of new products was mediated by the type of new product presented.

_____. "The Effect of Intolerance of Ambiguity Upon Product Perceptions." JOURNAL OF APPLIED PSYCHOLOGY 58 (October 1973): 239-43.

Examines whether the perception of unusual products as new could be a formation of a specified personality characteristic intolerances of ambiguity, and also be related to acceptance of those products.

Boone, Louis E. "The Search for the Consumer Innovator." JOURNAL OF BUSINESS 43 (April 1970): 135-40.

> Examines the traits of consumer innovators, how their leadership is crucial to the success of new products, and their implication for marketing managers.

Bordon, Neil H. "Acceptance of New Food Products by Supermarkets." FOOD TECHNOLOGY 23 (March 1969): 311.

_____. ACCEPTANCE OF NEW FOOD PRODUCTS BY SUPERMARKETS. Boston, Mass.: Harvard University, Division of Research, Business School, 1968. 227 p.

> By using case histories, the author examines three critical elements in the introduction and distribution of new food products by super-markets. These are: the effectiveness of various marketing ele-ments of new product propositions, the effectiveness of various strategies of communicating these propositions, and the importance of supermarket-buying practices and attitudes.

_____. "The Introduction of New Products by Supermarkets." In PROCEED-INGS: AMERICAN MARKETING ASSOCIATION FALL CONFERENCE, edited by Peter Bennett, pp. 674-75. Chicago: American Marketing Association, 1965.

Braun, Michael A., and Srinivasan, V. "Amount of Information as a Deter-minant of Consumer Behavior Towards New Products." In PROCEEDINGS: AMERICAN MARKETING ASSOCIATION COMBINED CONFERENCE, edited by Edward M. Mazze, p. 373. Chicago: American Marketing Association, 1975.

> Paper analyzes consumer purchase behavior intentions and trial pur-chases as based on consumer perception formed from available infor-mation.

Bryk, Terry. "Consumer Buying, Habits and Trends." EUROPEAN RESEARCH 2 (May 1974): 105-7, 122.

> Discusses the grocery market in Canada with particular emphasis on new product development. Two sets of consumers are distin-guised: the end consumer who buys and uses the product, and the retailer distributor who has a major voice in whether the end con-sumer even sees the product.

Burger, Phillipe. "Developing Forecasting Models for New Product Introduc-tions." In PROCEEDINGS: AMERICAN MARKETING ASSOCIATION FALL CONFERENCE, edited by Robert L. King, pp. 112-18. Chicago: American Marketing Association, 1968.

> Analyzes models of buyer behavior using the results of a panel study of new products introduction.

Burgman, Roland. WHEN IS A NEW PRODUCT A NEW PRODUCT. Business paper, no. 5. St. Lucia, Australia: University of Queensland, Department of Management, May 1976. 13 p.

Examines the view that since there is a wide range of consumer behavior which may be exhibited towards any new product introduction, newness to consumers is the most meaningful concept in managerial terms.

Caffyn, J.M., and Loyd, A. "Predicting Effects of Brand Name and Consumer Proposition on Consumer Purchase Decisions." EUROPEAN SOCIETY FOR OPINION SURVEYS AND MARKET RESEARCH (ESOMAR) CONGRESS, pp. 589-604. September 1968. Amsterdam: The Society, 1968.

Chin, G.N. "New Product Success and Failures: How to Detect Them in Advance." ADVERTISING AGE 44 (24 September 1973): 61-66.

Lists and narrates the most common errors in new product promotion strategies.

Coney, K.A. "Dogmatism and Innovation a Replication." JOURNAL OF MARKETING RESEARCH 9 (November 1972): 453-55.

Reports an experiment relating the level of dogmatism of a consumer and his level of innovation. Results confirmed earlier studies that low dogmatic persons are more willing than high dogmatic persons to try new products.

Cooke, J. "How a Food Retailer Looks at New Products." In NEW PRODUCT DEVELOPMENT, edited by J.O. Eastlack. Chicago: American Marketing Association, 1968.

Crespi, Irving. "What Kind of Attitude Measures are Predictive Behavior?" PUBLIC OPINION QUARTERLY 35 (Fall 1971): 327-34.

Cunningham, Scott M. "Perceived Risk as a Factor in the Diffusion of New Product Information." In SCIENCE TECHNOLOGY AND MARKETING, edited by Raymond M. Haas, pp. 698-721. Chicago: American Marketing Association, Fall Conference Proceedings, 1966.

_____. "The Role of Perceived Risk in Brand Commitment and Product among Housewives." Ph.D. dissertation, Harvard University, 1965. 26 p.

Czepiel, John A. "Word of Mouth Processes in the Diffusion of a Major Technological Innovation." JOURNAL OF MARKETING RESEARCH 11 (May 1974): 172.

Attempts a microanalytic study of the use of word of mouth among decision makers in competitive firms in the diffusion of a major technological innovation. Indicates that an active, functioning, informal communications network linked the firms and was in active use in the diffusion process.

Day, George S. "Changes in Attitudes and Intentions as Predictors of New Product Acceptance." Presented at the third Annual Attitude Research Conference of the American Marketing Association, Mexico, March 1970.

Dean, Michael Lewis. "The Influence of Promotional Copy Claims on Consumers Attitudes Towards Selected Products as an Empirical Study." Ph.D. dissertation, Ohio State University, 1971. 185 p. Ann Arbor, Mich.: University Microfilms. Order no. 72-04464.

By using consumer panels under controlled laboratory conditions, this study assesses the impact of standard promotional copy claims, such as new, improved, and so forth, on consumer attitudes towards different products.

Dean, Michael Lewis, et al. "Influence of Package Copy Claims on Consumer Product Evaluations." JOURNAL OF MARKETING 36 (April 1972): 34-39.

Assesses the impact of new and improved package copy claims on consumer evaluations of selected products. Type of product was also considered in the analysis. Article concludes that such claims have little effect on product evaluations.

DeNisco, S. "How the Science Department of an Advertising Agency Help in New Product Development." FOOD TECHNOLOGY 24 (April 1970): 342.

Donnelly, James H., Jr. "Social Character and Acceptance of New Products." JOURNAL OF MARKETING RESEARCH 7 (February 1970): 111.

Examines the relationship between the behavioral attribute "social character" and the acceptance of product innovations. Social character is defined as falling along a continuum from inner- to other-directed.

Donnelly, James H., Jr., and Etzel, Michael J. "Degrees of Product Newness and Early Trial." JOURNAL OF MARKETING RESEARCH 10 (August 1973): 295.

Although numerous demographic and behavioral characteristics have been associated with early triers, little research has been done examining the relationship between early trial and product attributes. Study suggests that the degree of newness of a product is a major factor in determining who tries it.

_____. "The Relationship Between Consumers' Category Width and Trial of New Products." JOURNAL OF APPLIED PSYCHOLOGY 57 (June 1973): 335-38.

Examines the relationship between a housewife's purchase of new
food products and her acceptance of qualitatively different forms
of risk. Explores the relationship between a consumer's tolerance
for errors of exclusion and inclusion and the purchasing of new
products. Results indicate that an individual's breadth of categorization is related to the purchase of new products.

Donnelly, James H., Jr., and Ivancevich, John M. "Methodology for Identifying Innovator Characteristics of New Brand Purchases." JOURNAL OF MAR-
KETING RESEARCH 11 (August 1974): 331.

Demonstrates a method for identifying innovator characteristics of
new branch purchasers. Examines one behavioral characteristic of
the purchasers of a new model automobile during four different
time periods and then compares these purchasers with purchasers
of new versions of similar established models during the same four
time periods.

Engel, James F. "Word of Mouth Communication by the Innovator." JOUR-
NAL OF MARKETING 33 (July 1969): 15-19.

Discusses the results of a study on the post-trial behavior of the
first users of a new automotive diagnostic center. It investigated,
among other things, whether innovators are prone to diffuse innovation through word of mouth, and whether their positive responses
are diffused more rapidly than their negative responses.

Engel, James F., et al. "Sources of Influence in the Acceptance of New
Products for Self-Medication: Preliminary Findings." In PROCEEDINGS:
AMERICAN MARKETING ASSOCIATION FALL CONFERENCE, edited by Ray-
mond M. Haas, pp. 776-82. Chicago: American Marketing Association, 1966.

Explores the consumer decision-making process in the purchase of
a new over-the-counter drug.

Evans, Richard H. "A Behavioral Model for Market Segmentation." UNIVER-
SITY OF WASHINGTON BUSINESS REVIEW 27 (Autumn 1968): 55-72.

"Fewer New Products, More Government Activity Slows Research Spending."
ADVERTISING AGE 43 (24 April 1972): 32.

Examines the view that government restrictions on advertising have
restricted many new product introductions and reduced the corporate
expenditure on market research.

Fiedler, J.A. "Choose a Remedy for Sick Sales: Product Change or Advertising Change." JOURNAL OF MARKETING 39 (April 1975): 67-68.

Describes a two-step procedure for identifying causes of the problem of a product suffering from poor sales. The first step is to
investigate the product itself to determine if consumers were op-

posed to it, and consider an alternative product that might have
a unique appeal for a limited segment of the population. The
second step is, if a superiority claim for the product could be
justified, build an advertising and marketing strategy around it.

Fisk, George. "Impact of Social Sanctions on Product Policy." JOURNAL
OF CONTEMPORARY BUSINESS 4 (Winter 1975): 1-20.

Explains how life-styles and social values affect product planning
and strategy.

Fliegel, Frederick C., and Sekhon, G.S. "A Cross National Comparison of
Farmers' Perceptions of Innovations as Related to Adoption Behavior." Paper
presented at the Meeting of the Rural Sociological Society, Boston, August
1968.

"Food Industry Survey Ties New Product Success to Specific Ad Promotion
Plans." ADVERTISING AGE 38 (25 December 1967): 2.

Reports on a survey which found that companies which had specific promotional plans had a better chance for acceptance from
supermarket distributors. Retailers also demonstrated an interest
in test market performances.

Fox, Harold W. "How to Sell a New Product to Industry." ADVANCED
MANAGEMENT JOURNAL 41 (Summer 1976): 23-33.

Analyzes the critical marketing factors in motivating industrial
users to adopt a new product.

Frevert, Fred. "Consumer Purchasing is the Best Measure of New Product Acceptance." EUROPEAN RESEARCH 5 (May 1977): 127-30.

Examines whether the behavioral evidence of sales potential is a
more significant point of focus of new grocery product marketing
research than attitudinal measures. While two products may have
similar acceptance on an attitudinal "intention to buy" scale,
when evaluated in terms of the customer's willingness to spend
money to purchase the product, one product often greatly outper-
forms the other.

Ginter, James L. "An Experimental Investigation of Attitude Change and
Choice of a New Brand." JOURNAL OF MARKETING RESEARCH 6 (February
1974): 30-40.

Describes research on the relationships between change in attitude
towards a new brand and exposure to advertising for that brand
and the relationship between attitude and choice and the use of
the brand. Attitude dynamics are combined with choice and behavior and advertising exposure at the individual level.

_____. "A Study of Attitude Change and Choice Behavior During New Product Introduction in a Laboratory Setting." Ph.D. dissertation. Purdue University, Lafayette, Ind., 1972. 323 p. Ann Arbor, Mich.: University Microfilms. Order no. 72-21195.

>   Examines the relationship between attitude change and brand choice over time, by using data collected in a laboratory experiment with a group of housewives who were selectively exposed to commercials and also participated in a simulated shopping trip.

Ginter, James L., and Bass, Frank M. AN EXPERIMENTAL STUDY OF ATTITUDE CHANGE, ADVERTISING, AND USAGE IN NEW PRODUCT INTRODUCTION. Lafayette, Ind.: Purdue University, Herman C. Krannert Graduate School of Industrial Administration, 1972. 20 p.

Goldberg, Marvin E. "Identifying Relevant Psychographic Segments: How Specifying Product Functions Can Help." JOURNAL OF CONSUMER RESEARCH 3 (December 1976): 163-69.

>   Characterizes new products according to the degree of novelty and the type of product novelty (appearance or performance) with a view to identify product functions as a basis for predicting consumer preferences.

Gorman, Walter P. III. "Market Acceptance of a Consumer Durable Goods Innovation." Ph.D. dissertation, University of Alabama, 1966. 231 p.

>   Examines the applicability of the sociological analyses to the demographic and behavioral characteristics of early acceptors-- adopters or innovators--in a segmented market. Product chosen here is a color television receiver.

Green, Irwin. "Advertising Creativity: Controlling the Uncontrollable Through Research. In PROCEEDINGS: ANA WORKSHOP, Association of National Advertisers, New York, February 1968.

>   Analyzes how some new advertising research concepts could be applied to new product research.

Green, R.T., and Langeard, E. "Cross National Comparison of Consumer Habits and Innovator Characteristics." JOURNAL OF MARKETING 39 (July 1975): 34-41.

>   Reports the results of a cross-national study conducted to compare the characteristic of samples of consumers in France and the United States. Focuses on the consumption of both grocery products and retail services. Provides a comparative profile of samples of French and United States consumers along several dimensions relating to consumption behavior, and to compare the profiles of the innovators identified in the two samples.

Grese, Thomas David. "Product Usage Patterns As a Basis for the Determination and Analysis of Market Segments for New Products." Ph.D. dissertation, University of Missouri, 1976.

> Investigates the segmentation of markets for new products by the use of consumption patterns.

Gross, E.J. "Selected Benchmarks for Consumer Evaluation of New Products." SOUTHERN JOURNAL OF BUSINESS 2 (October 1967): 57-62.

Grubb, Edward Lee. "Consumer Perception of Self-Concept and Its Relation to Brand Choice of Selected Product Types." Ph.D. dissertation, University of Washington, 1965. 201 p. Ann Arbor, Mich.: University Microfilms. Order no. 65-15382.

> Examines the applicability of two conceptual areas of behavioral science--self-theory and symbolism--to consumption of individual brands.

"Guidelines for Marketing New Brands in the Toilet Goods Field." NIELSEN RESEARCHER, no. 2, 1965, pp. 3-13.

> Discusses some of the most important factors involved in a product's introduction, specifically, toiletry products. To establish some general guidelines for successful brand introductions, factual case histories, recording both failures and successes, are analyzed. These guidelines are related to the total advertising and promotional expenditures on competing products, and the relationship between these expenditures and the share-of-sales are derived.

Haines, George H. "A Study of Why People Purchase New Products." In PROCEEDINGS: AMERICAN MARKETING ASSOCIATION CONFERENCE, edited by Raymond M. Haas, pp. 685-95. Chicago: American Marketing Association, 1966.

> Analysis of why consumers buy new products and the role of marketing strategy in the light of such analysis in promoting the product's adoption and diffusion.

Haines, George H., and Silk, A.J. "Does Consumer Advertising Increase Retail Availability of a New Product.: JOURNAL OF ADVERTISING RESEARCH 7 (September 1967): 9-15.

> Reports on a study which found that there is no simple pattern of relationship between consumer advertising and products availability.

_____. THE EFFECT OF CONSUMER ADVERTISING ON THE RETAIL AVAILABILITY OF A NEW PRODUCT. Research paper, no. 10. Los Angeles: University of California, Division of Research, 1966. 17 p.

Hallaq, John Hana. "An Analysis of the Development of Original Brand Loyalty for Nondurable Consumer Products." Ph.D. dissertation, University of Washington, 1972. 258 p. Ann Arbor, Mich.: University Microfilm. Order no. 73-13829.

> Investigates how original brand loyalty develops and what factors cause it, in view of the fact that consumers go through a period of search before settling on the product.

Hanan, Mack. LIFE-STYLED MARKETING. Chicago: American Marketing Association, 1972. 146 p.

_____. "Marketing Management: Growth Products From Real Life." SALES MANAGEMENT 109 (16 October 1972): 25-28.

> Suggests that initial knowledge of the customer's daily activities not only reduces risk of new product failure but awakens the marketing executive to a whole new world of product possibilities.

Hargreaves, George, et al. "New Product Evaluation: Electric Vehicles for Commercial Applications." JOURNAL OF MARKETING 40, no. 1 (1976): 74-77.

> Investigates product characteristics which are more important to potential buyers, and the weight given to them by buyers in selecting as alternative to existing technology. Suggests the use of conjoint measurement to assess attribute trade-offs.

Haugh, L.J. "Sales Promo Plans Can Mean Success for Your New Product." ADVERTISING AGE 49 (20 February 1978): 40-41.

Hauser, J.R., and Urban, G.L. "Normative Methodology for Modelling Consumer Response to Innovation." OPERATIONS RESEARCH 25 (July 1977): 579-619.

Hempel, Donald Jay. "An Experimental Study of the Effects of Information on Consumer Product Evaluation." Ph.D. dissertation, University of Minnesota, 1966. 243 p. Ann Arbor, Mich.: University Microfilms. Order no. 66-12208.

> Studies application of communications theory to consumer product selection and brand choice. Information received in this case by the consumer came from two different sources: a consumer magazine, and a salesperson.

Hendrickson, A.E. CHOICE BEHAVIOR AND ADVERTISING: A THEORY AND TWO MODELS. THE ST. JAMES MODEL. London: Admap World Advertising Workshop, 1967.

Herniter, Jerome D., et al. "Macrosimulation of Purchase Behavior for New and Established Products." Paper presented at the University of Chicago Conference on Behavioral and Management Science in Marketing, June 1969.

Hirsch, Paul M. "Processing Fads and Fashions: An Organisation - Set Analysis of Cultural Industry Systems." AMERICAN JOURNAL OF SOCIOLOGY 77 (January 1972): 639-59.

> Suggests that in order for new products or ideas to reach consumers, they first must be processed favorably through a system of organizations whose units filter out large numbers of candidates before they arrive at the consumption stage. Proposes the concept of an industry system as a useful frame of reference which can trace the flow of new products and ideas as they are filtered at each level or organization and examine relations among organizations.

Hise, Richard T. "New Product Acceptance Overlap: A Measure of General Innovativeness." AKRON BUSINESS AND ECONOMICS REVIEW 2 (Summer 1971): 34-37.

Hise, Richard T., and Donnelly, James H. "A Sociological Framework for a New Product Acceptance and Its Implications for Marketing Management." UNIVERSITY OF WASHINGTON BUSINESS REVIEW 27 (Summer 1968): 34-44.

> Describes the relationship of sociology to new product acceptance within a theoretical system-oriented context and indicates the significant role that sociology plays in the new product acceptance.

Hix, John Lloyd. "An Inquiry into the Decision Criteria Used by Men's Wear Buyers in Department and Specialty Stores in Determining Whether to Include a New Product in Their Offering." Ph.D. dissertation, University of Arkansas, 1972. 132 p. Ann Arbor, Mich.: University Microfilms. Order no. 72-10210.

> Change is introduced with such rapidity in some industries that retail buyers will have to be careful when dealing with new retail products. This study examines decision criteria used by men's wear buyers in the selection of a new product.

Honomichl, J.J. "Test Marketing Practices are Documented in Private Survey." ADVERTISING AGE 43 (10 April 1972): 30.

> Surveys promotional plans, which include consumer promotional plans, store level promotional plans, store-shelf location, trade promotion, trade channel emphasis, and brand names.

"Hoopla Works... In Industry Too." SALES MANAGEMENT 89 (19 October 1962): 55.

> Discusses new product introduction and promotional efforts by Western Mineral Products Company.

Hopper, L.C. "How Advertising and Sales Promotion Can Make or Break Your New Product." INDUSTRIAL MARKETING 61 (September 1976): 132-34.

> Illustrates how it takes a strong introductory promotional program to successfully launch a new product in today's market-place where competitive pressures and hard-nosed buyers are the rule.

Howard, John A., and Sheth, Jagdish N. THE THEORY OF BUYER BEHAVIOR. New York: Wiley, 1969. 458 p.

"How to Put a New Product on Top in One Year." INDUSTRIAL MARKETING 47 (April 1962): 90.

> Discusses ways and means to push a new product to the top of the market quickly. Existing product promotion techniques could be used in order to achieve the above if properly focused.

"How to Sell New Products to Supermarkets." SALES MANAGEMENT 100 (15 February 1968): 64.

> Deals with the importance of written communications about new products and effective sales presentations.

Hutt, Michael David. "The New Product Selection Process of Retail Buying Committees: An Analysis of Group Decision-Making." Ph.D. dissertation, Michigan State University, 1975. 148 p. Ann Arbor, Mich.: University Microfilms. Order no. 76-5576.

> Examines the impact of group decision making in the form of a buying committee in firms on the new product introduction. The sample studies includes chains, voluntary group wholesalers and co-operative group wholesalers in metro areas.

Hutt, Michael David, et al. "A New Versus an Established Product: A Comparison of Consumer Profiles." In PROCEEDINGS: AMERICAN MARKETING ASSOCIATION FALL CONFERENCE, edited by David L. Sparks, pp. 122-23. Chicago: American Marketing Association, 1970.

> Study to estimate optimum product positioning. Uses data gathered from the introduction of a new product in an established competitive market.

"Industrial Marketing: All Eyes Are on the Buyers." SALES MANAGEMENT 99 (15 October 1967): 71-78.

> Examines the BUYGRID model of the Marketing Science Institute. Explains how the industrial buyers' perception is important for the acceptance of a new industrial product.

Ironmonger, D.S. NEW COMMODITIES AND CONSUMER BEHAVIOR. University of Cambridge, Dept. of Applied Economics. Monograph 20. Cambridge, Engl.: University Press, 1972. 200 p.

Jacoby, Jacob. "Personality and Innovation Proneness." JOURNAL OF MAR-
KETING RESEARCH 8 (May 1971): 244-47.

Personality variable of dogmatism has been shown to be a criterion
for predicting new product acceptance. Based upon both theoretical rationale and the weight of related empirical evidence, article
predicts that low dogmatics will be more likely to make innovative
selections than will high dogmatics.

Jenssen, Ward J. "Pretesting the Effectiveness of Advertising and Other Marketing Influences Via In-Store Tests." In PROCEEDINGS: AMERICAN MAR-
KETING ASSOCIATION SUMMER CONFERENCE, edited by John S. Wright
and Jack L. Goldstucker, pp. 440-49. Chicago: American Marketing Association, 1966.

How to measure the extent to which exposure to TV or radio ads
motivate consumers to buy advertised product.

Johnson, Barbara. "New Products: Put More Ad Dollars on Potential Winners:
Forget Mediocre Ones." INDUSTRIAL MARKETING 56 (December 1971):
16-17.

Illustrates how a meager advertising budget hinders new product
potential.

Johnson, Richard M. "Market Segmentation: A Strategic Management Tool."
JOURNAL OF MARKETING RESEARCH 8 (February 1971): 13-18.

Uses a market structure analysis to decide product space based on
consumer perceptions of brands within product category.

Jolibert, Alain J.P. "Perception of Product Failure: An Application of Attribution Theory." Ph.D. dissertation, University of Texas, Austin, 1975.
230 p. Ann Arbor, Mich.: University Microfilms. Order no. 75-16688.

Using attribution theory, this is an attempt to analyze consumer
perceptions of new product failures into categories, such as product
defect, consumer ignorance, and misuse. This may help marketing
managers in their decisions on marketing mix.

Kerby, Joe K. "Semantic Generalization in the Formation of Consumer Attitudes." JOURNAL OF MARKETING RESEARCH 4 (August 1967): 314-17.

Evaluates the tendency of purchasers who transfer attitudes developed
about one product to another product via the brand name.

Kernan, Jerome B. "The Product Or the Brand: The Advertisers Dilemma."
UNIVERSITY OF WASHINGTON BUSINESS REVIEW 25 (February 1966): 61-
65.

King, C.W., and Summer, J.O. "Overlap of Opinion Leadership Across Consumer Product Categories." JOURNAL OF MARKETING RESEARCH 7 (February 1970): 43-50.

King, Stephen. "Advertising Research for New Brands." JOURNAL OF MARKET RESEARCH SOCIETY 10 (July 1968): 145-56.

Klein, Frederick C. "How a New Product Was Brought to Market Only to Flop Miserably." WALL STREET JOURNAL, 5 January 1973, 1.

> Explains the process of predicting consumer response to a new product, using the case of a new whiskey.

Kondos, A., and Clunies-Ross, C. "Sources of Bias in Sensory Evaluation as Applied to Food and Beverages." EUROPEAN SOCIETY FOR OPINION SURVEYS AND MARKET RESEARCH (ESOMAR) CONGRESS, Brussels, September 1966.

Kotler, Philip, and Zaltman, Gerald. "Targeting Prospects for a New Product." JOURNAL OF ADVERTISING RESEARCH 16 (February 1976): 7-18.

> Reviews the literature on early adopters for choosing prospects early in the campaign: the prospect's heavy-volume propensity, the prospect's early-adoption propensity, the prospect's influence propensity, and the cost of effectively reaching the particular prospect group.

Lambert, Z.V. "Perceptual Patterns, Information Handling and Innovativeness." JOURNAL OF MARKETING RESEARCH 9 (November 1972): 427-31.

> Investigates innovative purchasing of inexpensive, mass-marketed products in relation to five general factors: consumers product perceptions, patterns of acquiring new product information, interpersonal communication behavior, consumer's self-perceptions, and perceived risk.

Lampert, Shlomo Izhak. "Word of Mouth Activity During the Introduction of a New Food Product." Ph.D. dissertation, Columbia University, 1971. 237 p. Ann Arbor, Mich.: University Microfilms. Order no. 74-8192.

> Examines the correlation between consumer-buyer product perceptions and word-of-mouth activity in terms of the level, type, and timing of conversations, and the kind of people who engage in it.

Lawless, P.A., and Katzenstein, A.K. "Advertising Agency and Product Development." FOOD TECHNOLOGY 23 (March 1969): 294-95.

Lehmann, Donald R. "Product Attitude Learning for Consumer Durable." In PROCEEDINGS: AMERICAN MARKETING ASSOCIATION COMBINED CON-

FERENCE, edited by Ronald C. Curhan, pp. 71-74. Chicago: American Marketing Association, 1974.

> Presents an example which follows attitudes toward a new consumer durable product over time. Describes how these attitudes relate to sales.

Lessig, V.P., and Tollefson, J.O. "Market Segmentation Through Numerical Taxonomy." JOURNAL OF MARKETING RESEARCH 8 (November 1971): 480-87.

> Discusses methods for identifying customers likely to respond similarly to marketing stimuli. Examines evidence of relationship between consumer characteristics and buying behavior.

Lester, William Bernard. "Measurements, Effects and Implications of an Educational Promotion for a Dairy Food Product." Ph.D. dissertation, Texas A & M University, 1965. 184 p. Ann Arbor, Mich.: University Microfilms. Order no. 66-02430.

> Examines the promotional strategies needed and used to boost sales of new agricultural products. Looks into the use of a recipe pamphlet and in-store display.

"Lifestyle Is Key Word." ADVERTISING AGE 44 (19 February 1973): 28.

> Stresses that anticipating and capitalizing on changing life-styles is the key to success in new products whether they be appliances, automobiles, or cigars.

Linehan, Thomas A. "Communications Boosts Chance of New Product Acceptance." INDUSTRIAL MARKETING 62 (September 1977): 46-52.

> Describes the role of corporate advertising manager in helping boost the acceptance of new products.

Lovell, M.R.C., et al. "The Pretesting of Press Advertisements." ADMAP 4, no. 3 (1968): 90-104.

McConnell, John Douglas. "A Behavioral Study of the Development and Persistence of Brand Loyalty for a Consumer Product." Ph.D. dissertation, Stanford University, California, 1967. 196 p. Ann Arbor, Mich.: University Microfilms. Order no. 67-17459.

> Examines the impact of product perception and time on brand loyalty, using a controlled field experiment.

McNeal, James U. "Packaging for the Young Consumer: A Descriptive Study." AKRON BUSINESS AND ECONOMIC REVIEW 7 (Winter 1976): 5-11.

> Explains that an important ingredient of success of a new children's

product is the attractiveness of the packaging. Also deals with the various attractive methods of packaging a product.

Mancuso, Joseph R. "Why Not Create Opinion Leaders of New Product Introduction?" JOURNAL OF MARKETING 33 (July 1969): 20-25.

Discusses how to improve the understanding of the process of introducing new products or services. Suggests a technique and conceptual framework designed to increase the likelihood of new product success. Technique described deals with the "creation" of opinion leaders.

Martin, Warren S. PERSONALITY AND PRODUCT. Austin: University of Texas, Bureau of Business Research, 1973. 74 p.

Studies the relationships that exist between personality and groups of people that are classified by application of the theory of product symbolism. A wide range of products were tested by use of a convenience sample. Results contribute toward an understanding of human behavior.

Massey, Morris Edgar. "An Exploratory Study on the Role of Professional Occupational Status as an Influence on Product Perceptions." Ph.D. dissertation, Louisiana State University and A. & M. College, 1969. 186 p. Ann Arbor, Mich.: University Microfilms. Order no. 70-09078.

Examines the relationships, if any, between occupations on consumer behavior, i.e., whether or not product perceptions are influenced by the occupational situations of the perceivers.

Merims, Arthur M. "Marketing's Stepchild: Product Publicity." HARVARD BUSINESS REVIEW 50 (November-December 1972): 107-113.

Many new product launchings often are carried through with inadequate promotional efforts. Article deals with the need for and objectives of such promotional efforts and also tells how to do it effectively.

Mertes, John E. "The Elegant and the Novel: Consumer Behavior and Product Innovation." MISSISSIPPI VALLEY JOURNAL OF BUSINESS & ECONOMICS 2 (Fall 1966): 19-27.

Michaels, P.W. "Consumer Research in New Product Planning." DRUG & COSMETIC INDUSTRY 96 (February 1965): 161-62.

Mintz, H.K. "How to Prepare Good New Product Releases." INDUSTRIAL MARKETING 55 (February 1970): 69.

Describes how properly prepared publicity releases can let you make full use of the new products pages of business publications read by firms, customers, and prospects.

Mizerski, Richard William. "Attribution Theory and Consumer Processing of Unfavorable Information About Products." Ph.D. dissertation, University of Florida, 1974. 163 p. Ann Arbor, Mich.: University Microfilms. Order no. 75-16423.

Examines whether the attribution theories relating to prediction of trait attribution in personal perception can be generalized to the casual attribution of information about products.

Montgomery, David B. "New Product Distribution: An Analysis of Supermarket Buyer Decisions." JOURNAL OF MARKETING RESEARCH 12 (August 1975): 255-64.

To reduce new product failures and to understand the buyers' criteria for evaluating proposed new products, multiple discriminant analysis is used to determine the extent to which variables are associated with obtaining distribution in supermarkets.

"More Idea Sources Would Help Cut Product Failures." ADVERTISING AGE 40 (26 May 1969): 3.

Describes new product marketing and promotion strategies. Gives four reasons for lack of success in the new product field.

Morris, John T. "Diving and Tapping the Consumers Psyche." MARKETING/ COMMUNICATIONS 299 (January 1971): 24-27.

Describes four simple basic steps which provide a surefire formula to prevent new product failure: know who the consumer for the product really is, find out what problems or feelings this consumer has regarding the product category, and use the knowledge to fashion a selling message which will punch through the consumers' boredom barrier.

Muse, William V., and Kegerreis, Robert J. "New Product Awareness and Purchasing Behavior." MARQUETTE BUSINESS REVIEW 16 (September 1972): 19-27.

Myers, John G. "Patterns of Interpersonal Influence in the Adoption of New Products." In PROCEEDINGS: AMERICAN MARKETING ASSOCIATION FALL CONFERENCE, edited by Raymond M. Haas, pp. 750-57. Chicago: American Marketing Association, 1966.

Examines the role of interpersonal influences on forming product attitudes and changes.

Myers, Robert H. "Marketing Opportunities." BUSINESS HORIZONS 15 (February 1972): 5-6.

Analyzes the implications for new product development, of changes in life-styles, technology, and government services.

Nevers, John V. "Extensions of a New Product Growth Model." SLOAN MANAGEMENT REVIEW 13 (Winter 1971): 77-90.

Reveals by an analysis of survey data that imitiative and innovative behavioral forces explain adoptive human behavior across many market sectors.

Nicoletti, Bernado. "First Time Buyers of a Repurchasable New Product." EUROPEAN JOURNAL OF MARKETING 9, no. 2 (1975): 109-116.

O'Reilly, A.J.F. "The Conservative Consumer." MANAGEMENT DECISION 10 (Summer 1972): 168-86.

Examines how in marketing advanced technology and new products the food manufacturing industry has to face the very substantial hurdles of a rapidly changing distribution system and an essentially conservative consuming population. Also discusses in detail distributor power and its consequence, increasing media cost and high economic risk and basic technological and packaging difficulties.

Ostlund, Lyman E. "Factor Analysis Applied to Predictors of Innovative Behavior." DECISION SCIENCES 4 (January 1973): 92-108.

_____. "The Interaction of Self Confidence Variables in the Context of Innovative Behavior." In PROCEEDINGS: AMERICAN MARKETING ASSOCIATION SPRING-FALL CONFERENCE, edited by Fred C. Allvine, pp. 351-57. Chicago: American Marketing Association, 1971.

Examines whether or not self confidence is related to innovative behavior in judging given new products.

_____. "Perceived Innovation Attributes as Predictors of Innovativeness." JOURNAL OF CONSUMER RESEARCH 1 (September 1974): 23-29.

Examines whether a new test product perceived innovation attributes are strong predictors of new product purchase and whether personal characteristics of the potential buyer have little to offer as predictors of new product purchase.

_____. "The Role of Product Perceptions in Innovative Behavior." In PROCEEDINGS: AMERICAN MARKETING ASSOCIATION FALL CONFERENCE, edited by Philip R. McDonald, pp. 259-66. Chicago: American Marketing Conference, 1969.

Examines whether or not product perception should be incorporated in new product diffusion studies.

_____. "A Study of Innovativeness Overlap." JOURNAL OF MARKETING RESEARCH 9 (August 1972): 341-43.

Assesses the extent of innovativeness overlap among six new products from different product categories. Innovativeness towards each product was assessed by a purchase intentions measure of how likely each person said she was to buy the given product within the first few weeks after it would be on sale in the Boston area.

Ostlund, Lyman E., and Tellefsen, Brynulf. "Relationship Between Consumers' Category Width and Trial of New Products: A Reappraisal." JOURNAL OF APPLIED PSYCHOLOGY 59 (December 1974): 759-60.

Attempts a critique of an early study conducted in 1973 by Donnelly, Etzel, and Roeth which concluded that an individual's breadth of categorization is related to his purchase of new products. Raises questions about how the products studied were selected, choice of subjects, and the measure of association used.

Parsons, Leonard J. "Econometric Analysis of Advertising Retail Availability and Sales of a New Brand." MANAGEMENT SCIENCE 20 (February 1974): 938-47.

Develops a dynamic model to examine whether consumer advertising increases the retail availability of a new product.

Pessemier, Edgar A. "Can New Product Buyers be Identified?" JOURNAL OF MARKETING RESEARCH 4 (November 1967): 349-54.

Provides an insight into the characteristics of buyers and nonbuyers of a new branded product. It was found that if the consumer made at least one purchase of the new product, differences between early and late trial tended to relate to socioeconomic factors.

Peters, Michael Paul. "Characteristics of Adopters and Non-Adopters of an Industrial Product." Ph.D. dissertation, University of Massachusetts, 1972. 159 p. Ann Arbor, Mich.: University Microfilms. Order no. 72-18027.

Examines how variables like individual behavior, demographic variables, and environmental factors influence the adoption and non-adoption of new industrial products. Also looks into sources of information in the adoption process.

Peterson, Robert A., and Ross, Ivan. "How to Name New Brands." JOURNAL OF ADVERTISING RESEARCH 12 (December 1972): 29-34.

Examines whether or not consumers are more likely to associate a certain word or sound with certain categories than with others, and what personal characteristics moderated this hypothesized relationship between phonetic word sounds and product categories.

Popielarz, D.T. "Exploration of Perceived Risk and Willingness to Try New Product." JOURNAL OF MARKETING RESEARCH 4 (November 1967): 368.

Consumer decisions involving new products are generally recognized

as potentially high-risk situations. Article explores the relationship between willingness to try new products and willingness to
accept different forms of risk expressed as a dimension of cognitive
style relates to trying new products.

Quinlan, J.C. "Sixteen Ways to Stretch the Product Press Release Budget."
PUBLIC RELATIONS JOURNAL 33 (November 1977): 48.

"Rapid Lifestyle Changes Causes Some New Product Failures." ADVERTISING
AGE 41 (28 September 1970): 26.

Suggests that one reason for new product failure is that companies
do not perceive in time the change in consumer life-styles.

Rawlings, T.C., and Sparks, D.N. "The Use of Repeat Buying Measures in
Evaluating New Product Launches." In MARKET RESEARCH SOCIETY CON-
FERENCE, pp. 95-118. March 1975. London.

Presents models that require only purchasing data as an input. Different measures of repeat purchase used are: period-to-period repeat, cumulative repeat buying, and depth of repeat. Four methods
of prediction relating to new brand launches are considered. Traditional methods of evaluating new brand launches are reviewed
and their practical usefulness assessed.

Richard, Lawrence Milton. "An Analysis of the Relationship Between Personality
Structure, New Product Awareness, and Purchase-Behavior in Convenience Goods
Buying." Ph.D. dissertation, Louisiana State University and A. & M. College,
1973. 218 p. Ann Arbor, Mich.: University Microfilms. Order no. 74-7255.

Examines the relationships between personality and consumer behavior, specifically purchase behavior. It was found that there was
no significant relationship between a selected demographic variable
and new product awareness and purchase behavior in the market
place.

Roberts, Mary Low, and Taylor, James R. "Analyzing Proximity Judgements in
an Experimental Design." JOURNAL OF MARKETING RESEARCH 12 (February 1975): 68-72.

Reports the results of a study designed to determine the effect of
the experimental manipulation on the respondent's perception of a
hypothetical new coffee product relative to seven types currently
available.

Robertson, Thomas S. "Consumer Innovators: The Key to New Product Success." CALIFORNIA MANAGEMENT REVIEW 10 (Winter 1967): 23-30.

Suggests that the probability of new product success can be in-
creased by understanding the consumer innovator. Tests an empirical model of innovator characteristics and advises that a desirable

new product marketing program should take into account such knowledge of innovator characteristics at the initial levels of penetration.

_____. "The Effect of Informal Group Upon Member Innovative Behavior."
In PROCEEDINGS: AMERICAN MARKETING ASSOCIATION FALL CONFER-
ENCE, edited by Robert L. King, pp. 334–40. Chicago: American Marketing
Association, 1968.

Studies the effect of aggregate group response to innovation on
individual innovative behavior.

_____. INNOVATIVE BEHAVIOR AND COMMUNICATION. New York:
Holt, Rinehart and Winston, 1971. 331 p.

Examines the role of personal influence and opinion leadership in
the process of adoption and diffusion of innovation.

_____. "Purchase Sequence Responses: Innovators Vs. Noninnovators." JOUR-
NAL OF ADVERTISING RESEARCH 8 (March 1968): 47–52.

Reports results of a survey of touchtone telephone owners. Contains an analysis of the hierarchy of effects model which consists
of the following steps of purchase: cognitive awareness and knowledge, affective - liking and preference, and cognitive - conviction and purchase. Suggests that the conviction step is the most
critical stage in the purchase sequence and that marketing efforts
should be directed to assist in this conviction process.

Roshwalb, Irving. "How Much is an Ad Test Worth?" JOURNAL OF ADVER-
TISING RESEARCH 15 (February 1975): 17–23.

Russ, Frederick Ansley. "Consumer Evaluation of Alternative Product Models."
Ph.D. dissertation, Carnegie-Mellon University, 1971. 210 p. Ann Arbor,
Mich.: University Microfilms. Order no. 75-9086.

Studies the methods used by decision makers in evaluating multiple
attribute alternatives like alternative models of the same product.

Ryans, Adrian Bernard. "Estimating Consumer Preferences for a New Durable
Brand at a Given Price in an Established Product Class - The Development of
a Model and an Experimental Test." Ph.D. dissertation, Stanford University,
California, 1973. 287 p. Ann Arbor, Mich.: University Microfilms. Order
no. 74-6540.

Using perceived product characteristics data, this study examines
the possibility of estimating the level of preferences consumers
would exhibit towards a brand at a given price.

_____. "Estimating Consumer Preferences for a New Durable Brand in an Established Product Class." JOURNAL OF MARKETING RESEARCH 11 (November 1974): 434.

> Theoretical model is developed to aid in the estimation of demand for a durable brand at a given price in an established product class. The operationalization and an experimental test of the model in the new product context are described and the results discussed.

Sampson, P. "Can Consumer Create New Products?" JOURNAL OF THE MARKET RESEARCH SOCIETY 12 (January 1970): 145-66.

Schiffman, Leon Gene. "Communication and Experience: The Acceptance of a New Food Product by Elderly Consumers Living in Geriatric Housing." Ph.D. dissertation, City University of New York, 1971. 285 p. Ann Arbor, Mich.: University Microfilms. Order no. 71-16542.

> Examines the importance of certain variables in the new product trial behavior of some elderly consumers. Variables include flow of communication, need, experience, perceived risk, shopping behavior, and demographic attributes.

_____. "Perceived Risk in New Product Trial by Elderly Consumers." JOURNAL OF MARKETING RESEARCH 9 (February 1972): 106.

> Examines the relationship between risk handling and new product trial behavior of the elderly consumer. Focuses on perceived error tolerance, a new complementary variable to perceived risk. Indicates that elderly consumers may demonstrate consistent risk strategies for new products within a broad product category.

Sheth, Jagdish N. IMPORTANCE OF WORD OF MOUTH IN THE DIFFUSION OF LOW RISK AND HIGHLY ADVANTAGEOUS INNOVATIONS. Graduate School of Business, Working Paper, no. 16. New York: Columbia University, 1969.

Sheth, Jagdish N., and Venkatesan, M. "Risk-Reduction Processes in Repititive Consumer Behavior." JOURNAL OF MARKETING RESEARCH 5 (August 1968): 307-10.

> Studies consumer decision making over time. Explores risk reduction processes of information seeking, prepurchase deliberation, and brand loyalty. Perceived risk was manipulated by creating low-risk and high-risk groups.

Shoemaker, Robert W., and Shoaf, F. Robert. "Behavioral Changes in the Trial of New Products." JOURNAL OF CONSUMER RESEARCH 2 (September 1975): 104-9.

> Discusses a consumer diary panel study which indicates the follow-

ing: individual household purchases a smaller quantity of a new brand on a trial purchase than an established brand, but on second purchase, the quantity is larger. However, there is only inconclusive evidence to judge the effects on free sample receivers on their purchases of new brands after receipt of the samples.

Singh, P. "New Product Releases Don't Belong in the Round File." INDUSTRIAL MARKETING 52 (February 1967): 70-72.

Srinivasan, V., and Braun, Michael A. AMOUNT OF INFORMATION AS A DETERMINANT OF CONSUMER BEHAVIOR TOWARD NEW PRODUCTS. University of Rochester, working paper series, Studies in Applied Economics, no. 3. New York: University of Rochester, February 1973.

Summers, John O. "Media Exposure Patterns of Consumer Innovators." JOURNAL OF MARKETING 36 (January 1972): 43-49.

Knowledge of the innovator or early buyer's media exposure characteristics is essential to the new product advertiser. An analysis is presented which will provide the new product manager with an operational guide for the media selection process. Investigation considers the relationship between six broad categories and twelve types of media vehicles.

Szybillo, George J. "Situational Influence on the Relationship of a Consumer Attitude to New Product Attractiveness." JOURNAL OF APPLIED PSYCHOLOGY 60 (October 1975): 652-55.

Examines both the effects of a situational influence and a personal tribute on new product attractiveness. Effects of perceived fashion scarcity on the relationship of fashion-opinion leadership to new fashion attractiveness is considered.

Talarzyk, William Wayne. "An Empirical Study of an Attitude Model for the Prediction of Individual Brand Preference for Consumer Products." Ph.D. dissertation, Purdue University, 1969. 276 p. Ann Arbor, Mich.: University Microfilms. Order no. 70-08980.

Studies consumer characteristics with emphasis on attitudes as they relate to individual brand preference. Examines whether or not measurements, which are specific to the preference alternatives, will lead to better predictions than general measurements such as socioeconomic variables.

Tauber, E.M. "Predictive Validity in Consumer Research." JOURNAL OF ADVERTISING RESEARCH 15 (October 1975): 59-64.

Report of a study made to determine whether any of the attitude and intention questions typically asked in concept and product tests relates to and can pretest the subsequent states of behavior awareness, trial, and repeat.

_____. "Reduce New Product Failures: Measure Needs As Well As Purchase Interest." JOURNAL OF MARKETING 37 (July 1973): 61-70.

Article contends that research may deceive marketers to introduce products with limited potential, because consumers may be favorably disposed to a new brand yet have no need for it. Presents an approach for measuring perceived needs and discusses this measure in relation to the traditional purchase intention scale.

Taylor, James R. "Unfolding Theory of Applied to Market Segmentation." JOURNAL OF ADVERTISING RESEARCH 9 (December 1969): 39-46.

Since substantial numbers of new products fail each year, there is a growing realization that at least part of this failure is the result of insufficient knowledge about innovation. Study has used an automobile diagnostic center as an example of innovation. Personal interviews have been held as people waited for their vehicles to be diagnosed. Methodology used and the results are presented.

Taylor, James W. "A Striking Characteristic of Innovators." JOURNAL OF MARKETING RESEARCH 14 (February 1977): 104-07.

Examines the effects of perception of product class on innovative behavior. Indicates that innovative behavior is very dependent on product class use. This relationship holds for products that very few households try, as well as for products that many households try. Also suggests that new product development should be conducted among heavy users of the product class rather than simply among general users of the product class.

Taylor, James W., et al. "The Purchase Intention Question in New Product Development: A Field Test." JOURNAL OF MARKETING 39 (January 1975): 90-92.

Investigates the real meaning of respondents reply of "definitely interested" in the course of test marketing a product. Analyzes the results of the "intention - to-buy" question. Could it be really used in predicting purchase behavior? Authors find from their field study the purchase intention questions are likely to be useful in identifying the "losers" and that it is still a potent tool for use in new product development.

Tillman, Rollie, and Kirkpatrick, C.A. PROMOTION: Rev. ed. Homewood, Ill.: R.D. Irwin, 1972. 536 p.

Watts, Reginald. REACHING THE CONSUMER: THE ELEMENTS OF PRODUCT PUBLIC RELATIONS. London: Business Books, 1970. 168 p.

White, Irving S. "New Product Differentiation: Physio and Symbolic Dimension." In PROCEEDINGS: AMERICAN MARKETING ASSOCIATION SUMMER CONFERENCE, edited by Bernard Morin, pp. 99-103. Chicago: American Marketing Association, 1969.

Discusses the need for an effective marketing campaign which will highlight the perceived product differences on the part of consumers for new product success.

Wolf, L. "How to Make Your New Product Advertising Work Harder." ADVERTISING AGE 45 (21 October 1974): 57-58.

Presents a case study of successful examples of new product advertising to explain some basic tenets of promotional strategy.

Wood, D. "Consumer Durables Differentiation Strategy and Consumer Response in Relation to Real and Apparent Risk." EUROPEAN JOURNAL OF MARKETING 6 (Winter 1972-73): 249-56.

Examines the desirability of measuring consumer response in a prepurchase position rather than measuring the objective qualities of the article. Stresses the importance of identifying the special attributes where variation produces significant response from consumers. Also discusses whether new product introduction should be followed by an effort to identify variables which are taken by consumers as indicators of quality.

Woodside, Arch G. "Social Character, Purchasing New Products and Word of Mouth Advertising." MARQUETTE BUSINESS REVIEW 16 (Winter 1972): 184-91.

Wortuba, Thomas R., and Duncan, P.L. "Are Consumers Really Satisfied?" BUSINESS HORIZONS 18 (February 1975): 85-90.

Chapter 6

MARKETING RESEARCH

Abrams, Jack. "Reducing the Risk of New Product Marketing Strategies Testing." JOURNAL OF MARKETING RESEARCH 6 (May 1969): 216-20.

> Describes a design for evaluation of new product ideas. Gives the results of a study to determine the differences between reactions from: 1) controlled mail panel members, 2) respondents interviewed face to face, and 3) alternative rating devices.

Ahl, David H. "New Product Forecasting Using Consumer Panels." JOURNAL OF MARKETING RESEARCH 7 (May 1970): 160.

> Increased importance of bringing successful products to the marketplace makes it critical that research techniques provide a timely indication of progress developed. Such a technique using data from a consumer diary panel is discussed.

Albrecht, J.J. "Determining Consumer Needs and Preferences." RESEARCH MANAGEMENT 13 (March 1970): 149-62.

> Determining consumer needs is essential for the success of a company. Market research can determine what to make before spending money on production. Stresses that survey techniques must be scrutinized very carefully to insure validity and reliability.

Applied Marketing, Inc. A CONCEPTUAL FRAMEWORK FOR MORE SUCCESSFUL NEW PRODUCT INTRODUCTIONS. New York: 1968. 27 p.

> Deals with opinion leadership and the possibility of creating specific opinion leaders for specific products. Presents a universal framework by which a marketer can increase the likelihood of success of a new product.

Aucamp, J., ed. THE EFFECTIVE USE OF MARKET RESEARCH. London: Staples Press, 1971. 320 p.

Bell, J.B. "Market Research Can Help in New Product Development." STEEL 156 (1 February 1956): 26.

Claims that market research can be used to search for new product ideas and it can also help define probable success of a new product.

Bieda, John C., and Kassarjian, H.H. "An Overview of Market Segmentation." In PROCEEDINGS: AMERICAN MARKETING ASSOCIATION SUMMER CONFERENCE, edited by Bernard Morin, pp. 249-53. Chicago: American Marketing Association, 1969.

Calls for the application of multidimensional techniques to marketing research in preference to previously employed univariate techniques.

Bruce, Robert D. "Marketing and the Management of Technological Change." In SCIENCE, TECHNOLOGY AND MARKETING, edited by Raymond Haas, pp.33-34. Chicago: American Marketing Association, 1966.

Examines the marketing function in innovation management in terms of market evaluation, product concepts, and competitive atmosphere.

Canning, G., Jr. ."Increasing the Odds of Product Success." INDUSTRY WEEK 181 (13 May 1974): 31.

Clunies-Ross, C. "Different Uses of Market Segmentation." In THE EFFECTIVE USE OF MARKET RESEARCH, edited by J. Aucamp, London: Staples Press, 1971.

Colby, S. "Lonely Field Interviewer: Why and How Your Research With Her is Going Wrong." ADVERTISING AGE 46 (30 June 1975): 33-36.

Reports on the problems associated with field interviewing in the areas of scheduling, wages, quotas, and lengthy questionnaires. Calls for prompt payment for field labor, uniform hourly rates, allowing supervisors a living wage, improving the questionnaires, and alleviating quotas.

Connell, D.F. "Watch Out for Shortcuts in Measuring New Products." PRINTERS INK 291 (27 August 1965): 74.

Warns against shortcut marketing research techniques that have been developed to test the success of a new product. These shortcuts usually involve very few interviews which are interpreted to speak for the entire market. New computerized system of new-product measurement and evaluation is discussed.

Cooper, Robert G., and Little, Blair. "Determinants of Market Research Expenditures for New Industrial Products." INDUSTRIAL MARKETING MANAGEMENT 6 (1977): 103-12.

Presents a model outlining the situational factors to be considered in deciding the actual amount of marketing research expenditures. Also deals with the cost of gathering information.

Crawford, C. Merle. "Marketing Research and the New Product Failure Rate." JOURNAL OF MARKETING 41 (April 1977): 51-61.

Examines why the rate of new product success has not climbed as a result of many advances in marketing research technology over the past twenty-five years.

Day, R.L. "New Products and Market Research." EUROPEAN MARKETING RESEARCH REVIEW 2 (Winter 1967): 13-23.

Dillon, T.F. "How Purchasing Handles New Product Evaluation." PURCHAS-ING 63 (13 July 1967): 77-79.

Deals with the importance to a company of knowing what new prod-ucts are on the market and having someone who can determine the products' potential success or failure.

Drake, Nick J., and Winton, David S. "The Contribution Made by a Market-ing Research Programme Towards the Development of a New Industrial Product." EUROPEAN RESEARCH 12 (January 1977): 34-44.

Describes all the stages a market research program has to go through before giving the go-ahead to the development of a new product. A new insurance plan is used as a case in point. Same article also in PROCEEDINGS: MARKET RESEARCH SOCIETY CONFERENCE, London, March 1975, pp. 187-97.

Ehrenberg, A.S.C. "The Neglected Use of Data." JOURNAL OF ADVERTIS-ING RESEARCH 7 (June 1967): 2-7.

Demonstrates the immediate usefulness of basic marketing research in terms of a practical marketing problem, namely that of assess-ing the likely success or failure of a new product. Two practical examples are outlined, followed by a summary of the relevant basic research findings and their application to the practical prob-lems.

England, L., and Grosse, W. "Why the Perfect Product Stays on the Shelf." DIRECTOR 25 (July 1972): 64-66.

Discusses the importance of market research. Often products that are technically "perfect" will not sell for reasons that could have been determined with a more efficient market research program. Stresses the need for communication between the marketer and consumer.

Erdos, Paul L. "Modern Mail Surveys." Paper presented at the 15th Annual Conference of the Advertising Research Foundation, New York, 1969.

Field, J.G. "Gamesmanship in New Product Research." Paper presented at the Market Research Society Annual Conference, London, March 1972.

Three new product research strategies that can encourage product failure and sabotage success are given. To avoid this, firms must insure that a consumer would play a larger part in market research as a person rather than as an object.

_____. "The Study of Preference in Market Research." EUROPEAN SOCIETY FOR OPINION SURVEYS AND MARKET RESEARCH (ESOMAR) CONGRESS, Vienna, 21-24 August 1967, pp. 455-68.

"Field Service Data - A Must." STORES 51 (August 1969): 42.

Foster, W.K. "Marketing Can Help New Product Development." FOOD TECHNOLOGY 21 (November 1967): 1454-57.

Gittos, D.G. "Marketing and Product Development." MANAGEMENT ACCOUNTING (ENGLAND) 45 (August 1967): 312-22.

Goodyear, J.R. "Qualitative Research Studies." In THE EFFECTIVE USE OF MARKET RESEARCH, edited by J. Aucamp. London: Staples Press, 1971

"Group Analyses the Market then Plans the Product." PRODUCT ENGINEERING 40 (24 February 1969): 34-36.

Describes how Stanford Research Institute in California has launched a program designed to give clients a thorough grounding in economic information before they embark on new product development efforts or in major expansion.

Heaton, Eugene E. "Increasing Mail Questionnaire Returns with a Preliminary Letter." JOURNAL OF ADVERTISING RESEARCH 5 (December 1965): 36-39.

Survey reveals that significant higher return was obtained by first writing a personalized letter informing the respondent of the questionnaire's impending arrival. This idea can be used in concept testing.

Hilton, Peter. "Product Development: Market Research: Unexpected Sources of New Product Opportunities." FOOD TECHNOLOGY 24 (May 1970): 557-59.

Holmes, John H. "Profitable Product Positioning." MSU BUSINESS TOPICS 21 (Spring 1973): 27-32.

Relationship of the new product and proper positioning in the marketplace is examined. Survey was conducted for the favorite brand of detergent and rating along selected scale dimensions of each of the low phosphate brands, as well as the ideal. Analysis of the rating scales is accompanied with a figure plotting the responses. Positioning for profit is examined and guidelines to be followed are set forth.

Homayounfar, Firooz. "Evaluation of Market Potential for New Industrial Products: An Application of Multidimensional Scaling Techniques." Ph.D. dissertation, Stanford University, 1970. 272 p. Ann Arbor, Mich.: University Microfilms. Order no. 71-12922.

Examines whether useful, and if so, how useful are the techniques of nonmetric multidimensional scaling in estimating market potential of new industrial products.

Johnson, Bruce W. "New Products: Serendipity or Plan." BUSINESS QUARTERLY 30 (Spring 1965): 46-50.

Article is concerned with the use of market research in new product work. Analyzes how greater value can be attained from market research.

Jones, P.M.S. "Market Research in the Novel Product Field." IMRA JOURNAL 7 (February 1971): 32-47.

Forecasting aspects in the new product field by reference to real case studies is illustrated.

Kraushar, Peter M. "The Cost Effectiveness of Market Research With Particular Application to the Search for New Product Ideas in Fast Moving Consumer Goods." EUROPEAN SOCIETY FOR OPINION SURVEYS AND MARKET RESEARCH (ESOMAR) CONGRESS, Hamburg, 1974, pp. 285-99.

Discusses the need for cost effectiveness in market research, and examines whether research is capable or cost effective in identifying consumer needs leading to new product opportunities in fast-moving markets. Also touches upon the role of research in the context of concept testing and suggests procedures from concept hypothesis to validation.

Lantos, Peter R. "What R&D Can Expect From Marketing Research." CHEMICAL TECHNOLOGY (October 1973): 588-91.

Modern marketing research function involves more than what was done traditionally. Includes data collection, analysis, as well as product-market planning. Article examines what is expected of today's market research department.

Lavidge, Robert J. "The Role of Marketing Research in New Product Development." OREGON BUSINESS REVIEW 27 (June 1968): 1-3.

Marketing research is discussed from four phases: concept generation, preliminary evaluation, product refinement, and sales success prediction. Typical steps for each phase are identified.

Little, Blair, and Copper, Robert G. "Role of Marketing Research in New Technology Ventures." RESEARCH MANAGEMENT 20 (May 1977): 20-25.

Describes guidelines which answers troublesome questions like: what kind of studies should be done for marketing research, and how much should be spent on research.

Little, Blair, et al. "Putting the Market into Technology to Get Technology into the Market." BUSINESS QUARTERLY 37 (Summer 1972): 62-67.

Describes the role of marketing research in Canadian firms.

Long, Durwood. "Selectivity: Key to Effective Sampling Techniques." ADVERTISING AND SALES PROMOTION 19 (November 1971): 38-41.

Examines how several companies use sampling, how selective sampling became important, what the marketing objectives are, and what the problems are.

"Market Probing Expands to Avert Product Flops." INDUSTRIAL MARKETING 52 (September 1967): 81-83.

Stresses the importance of market research before new product introduction.

Martinez, Arthur. "Communications, Research Gaps and Their Roles in New Product Mishaps." INDUSTRIAL MARKETING 25 (10 March 1970): 10-11.

Analyzes the common causes of new product failures such as lack of proper market research of consumer needs and faulty analysis.

Mayeur, J.P. "Marketing Research and Innovation." EUROPEAN SOCIETY FOR OPINION SURVEYS AND MARKET RESEARCH (ESOMAR) CONGRESS. Budapest, 9-13 September 1973, pp. 339-51.

Corporate planners need to base their decisions on a detailed know-how of the future marketplace in heavy industrial goods. Article explains how market research can help in this area.

Miles, V. "Avoid Those Errors in New Product Research." ADVERTISING AGE 45 (15 July 1974): 26.

Failure to research the market adequately during the new product prenatal period is the cause of the majority of new product failures.

Mooney, P.B., and Wicks, Anne. "The Use of Market Research in the Launching of a New Evening Newspaper." MARKET RESEARCH SOCIETY CONFERENCE, London, 1967, 20.

Morse, R.E. "Product Development, Market Research, Developing New Food Products For Foreign Markets." FOOD TECHNOLOGY 24 (May 1970): 560.

Muije, Cornelius S. "How Decisions are Made to Stop Developing or Testing New Products." In PROCEEDINGS: AMERICAN MARKETING ASSOCIATION COMBINED CONFERENCE, edited by Thomas V. Green, pp. 160–62. Chicago: American Marketing Association, 1973.

> Discusses the involvement of marketing research in the new product decision process. Describes a case of product failure and a case of product part-failure.

"New Items in Action: The Payoff at Point-of-Purchase." PROGRESSIVE GROCER 47 (June 1968): 46–57.

> Based on research and an in-store study in the Boston area. Article reveals how retailers and customers feel about new items in supermarkets and how effective specialized merchandising methods are in presenting these new items. Data on customer opinions and on sales are presented, and promotional ideas, such as "new idea centers" and shelving and sign techniques are suggested.

Nichols, J.B. "Developing New Products: The Role of Research." MECHANICAL ENGINEERING 98 (November 1976): 33–35.

> Explains the importance of searching out and definition of markets and the timely development on new product and product lines.

Pannenborg, A.E. "Technology Push Versus Market Pull: The Designer's Dilemma." ELECTRONICS AND POWER 21 (15 May 1975): 563–66.

> While fulfilling customer's needs is the obvious objective, finding out what the customer wants is not always easy. Article discusses how to deal with this problem.

Pessemier, Edgar A. "Analyzing Research Strategies for Selecting Alternative New Product Opportunities." In PROCEEDINGS: AMERICAN MARKETING ASSOCIATION CONFERENCE, edited by Fred C. Allvine, pp. 143–46. Chicago: American Marketing Association, 1971.

> Analyzes the objective and subjective data needed for a rational decision on most promising new product venture from among a group of equally competing ideas.

Plummer, Joseph T. "Psychographics: What Can Go Right?" In PROCEEDINGS: AMERICAN MARKETING ASSOCIATION COMBINED CONFERENCE, edited by Ronald C. Curham, pp. 41-50. Chicago: American Marketing Association, 1974.

> Examines how psychographic research has been useful to marketers and advertisers in the area of new products.

Pratt, Robert W. "Using Research to Reduce Risks Associated With Marketing New Products." In PROCEEDINGS: AMERICAN MARKETING ASSOCIATION WINTER CONFERENCE, edited by Reed Moyer, pp. 98-104. Chicago: American Marketing Association, 1967.

Discusses the need to establish marketing information systems which will insure flow of all information needed to make appropriate marketing decisions.

"Product Development Market Research: Symposium." FOOD TECHNOLOGY 24 (April-May 1970): 332-34, 557-60.

"Research Can Help Marketer Gain Lead Time for New Product." ADVERTISING AGE 36 (8 March 1965): 3.

Since companies feel the need to quickly enter the market, lead time is often cut down sharply. Market research can help solve some of this problem.

Roberts, P. "Market Research and the Development of New Products." In PROCEEDINGS: MARKET RESEARCH SOCIETY ANNUAL CONFERENCE, London, March 1972, pp. 149-57.

Expresses concern about the ability of existing research techniques which measure static market situations and predict the effects of the changes within that market situation resulting from the introduction of a new product. Questions the wisdom of trying to establish consumer needs, of relying on gap analysis as a source of ideas, and the use of some screening techniques. Also doubts traditional methods of market segmentation and suggests that until the planning for the production of a new product had reached the media planning stage, normal segmentation classifications are of little use to the product developer.

Robinson, Richard Kent. "An Organizational Study of Marketing Research Acquisition in Product Management." Ph.D. dissertation, Northwestern University, 1975. 288 p. Ann Arbor, Mich.: University Microfilms. Order no. 75-29734.

Examines the results of a survey of product managers' perception and use of market research function and how it relates to individual, organizational, and situational variables.

Shocker, Allan D., and Srinivasan, V. "An Analytic Methodology for Generation of New Product Ideas." In PROCEEDINGS: AMERICAN MARKETING ASSOCIATION COMBINED CONFERENCE, edited by Fred C. Allvine, pp. 158-62. Chicago: American Marketing Association, 1971.

Suggests an approach which involves product-market research, discovering user perceptions and preferences.

Smith, S.A. "Research and Pseudo Research in Marketing." HARVARD BUSI-
NESS REVIEW 52 (March 1974): 73-76.

Argues that a great deal of market research has no influence at
all on marketing decisions. Executives just use it to play organizational politics, giving the company a better image.

Thomas, Michael J. "Making R & D Pay: The Role of Market Research."
CHEMISTRY AND INDUSTRY 16 (18 August 1973): 766-68.

Presents organizational models which will help prevent nontechnical mistakes of research and development department resulting from
a communications gap between itself and marketing department.

Tomlin, Edward R. "New Product Research--A Different Approach." EURO-
PEAN SOCIETY FOR OPINION SURVEYS AND MARKET RESEARCH (ESOMAR)
CONGRESS, pp. 263-83. Hamburg, 1974.

Examines some of the causes of high new product failure rate at-
tributed partly to political pressures within marketing teams and
partly to the inadequacy of market research techniques currently
available to provide a quantitative estimate of likely offtake.
Also presents a hypothetical case to establish whether a new sham-
poo, successfully marketed by the U.S. parent company and Canadian and French subsidiaries, will sell in Australia.

Twedt, D.W. "What about Other Sources of Sampling Error." JOURNAL OF
MARKETING 30 (October 1966): 62-63.

States that the real concern of the researchers attempting to measure consumer acceptance of a product should be the existence of
still another source of sampling error and that source of error is
variance in the product itself. Product testing for uniformity is
stated as an essential precaution.

Vaughan, Richard L. "Pet Peeves in New Products Marketing Research." In
PROCEEDINGS: AMERICAN MARKETING ASSOCIATION COMBINED CON-
FERENCE, edited by Ronald C. Curhan, pp. 521-24. Chicago: American
Marketing Association, 1974.

New products have a high failure rate which can be reduced or
minimized by sound management and planning. Paper discusses a
few suggestions.

Wei, James. "Planning and Marketing of Research." CHEMICAL ENGINEER-
ING PROGRESS 67 (March 1971): 22-29.

Explains how marketing research can reveal consumer needs. Suggests that if research and development pays better attention to this
they can come up with winners.

Yoell, William A. "The Abuse of Psychology by Marketing Men." MARKET-ING/COMMUNICATIONS 298 (August 1970): 42-44.

Zarecor, William D. "High-Technology Product Planning." HARVARD BUSI-NESS REVIEW 53 (January-February 1975): 108-15.

Describes what is involved in market analysis which must be done prior to development of high technology products.

Zernisch, P. "Agitative Market Research As a Guide in Developing New Prod-ucts." EUROPEAN SOCIETY FOR OPINION SURVEYS AND MARKET RESEARCH (ESOMAR) CONGRESS, Cannes, 10-14 September, 1972, pp. 481-90.

Discusses a concept called prototypical product development (PPD), which is basically a flow chart analysis of the product develop-ment process. Explains how the market research department can use this concept to their best advantage.

Chapter 7

RESEARCH AND DEVELOPMENT

Albala, A. "Financial Planning for New Products." LONG RANGE PLAN-
NING 10 (August 1977): 61-69.

Describes how to formulate a matching overall long-range budget
planning policy which will answer the questions of how many projects to approve and how much to fund.

_____. "Stage Approach for the Evaluation and Selection of R&D Projects."
IEEE TRANSACTIONS ON ENGINEERING MANAGEMENT EM-22 (November 1975): 153-64.

Allen, D.H. "Optical Selection of a Research Project Portfolio Under Uncertainty " THE CHEMICAL ENGINEER 238 (1970): CE278-28.

Aram, John D. "Innovation Via R & D." RESEARCH MANAGEMENT 13
(November 1973): 24-26.

Stresses the importance of successfully managing the interface between research and development, marketing department, and the
field.

Arthur D. Little, Inc. MANAGEMENT FACTORS AFFECTING RESEARCH AND
EXPLORATORY DEVELOPMENT. Report for the Director of Defense Research
and Engineering, contract SD-235. Cambridge, Mass.: 1965. Available from
NTIS: AD-618321. Microfiche.

Baker, Norman, and Freeland, James. "Recent Advances in R & D Benefit
Measurement and Project Selection Methods." MANAGEMENT SCIENCE 21
(June 1975): 1164-75.

Surveys quantitative methods for selecting research and development
projects and resource allocation between competing projects.

Bass, Lawrence Wade. THE MANAGEMENT OF TECHNICAL PROGRAMS,
WITH SPECIAL REFERENCE TO THE NEEDS OF DEVELOPING COUNTRIES.

Prepared by Arthur D. Little, Inc. Praeger Special Studies in International Economics and Development. New York: Praeger, 1965. 138 p.

Becker, S.W., and Whisler, T.L. "The Innovative Organization: A Selective View of Current Theory and Research." JOURNAL OF BUSINESS 40 (October 1967): 462-69.

Bennett, Keith W. "Put Research Division to Work As a Management Tool." IRON AGE 213 (3 June 1974): 37-38.

Explains what the management can and must get out of its research and development department such as relating new technology to existing product lines and coordinating projects which run across product lines.

Berman, S.I. "Integrating the R & D Department into the Business Team." RESEARCH MANAGEMENT 16 (July 1973): 16-19.

Explains the need for the inventors working closely with the organization for the ultimate success of the new product.

Berton, L. "Introducing New Products: A Longer Look Before the Leap." MANAGEMENT REVIEW 56 (April 1967): 50-52.

As the economy slows down, industries have a smaller margin for research and development error. Several examples are given of companies which lost money before more selective development was undertaken. Suggests ways to cut research and development costs.

Biller, Alan D., and Shanley, Edward S. "Understanding the Conflicts Between R & D and Other Groups." RESEARCH MANAGEMENT 18 (September 1975): 16-21.

Discusses how to avoid conflicting interests and coordinate the activities of departments like research and development, manufacturing, marketing, and management for efficient development process.

Bissell, Herbert D. "Research and Marketing--Rivals or Partners." RESEARCH MANAGEMENT 14 (May 1971): 65-73.

Marketing department is necessary for locating a customer need, while the research department should work on a product which fulfills the need. Article stresses coordination between the departments to achieve a maximum effort.

Blood, Jerome W. UTILIZING R & D BY-PRODUCTS. New York: American Management Association, 1967. 127 p.

Bobbe, Richard A. "What to Do When There are No Corporate Research Goals." RESEARCH MANAGEMENT 13 (1970): 251-63.

Deals with the problem of new product research managers who do not have clear-cut goals given by top management.

Bobis, A.H., et al. "A Funds Allocation Method to Improve the Odds for Research Success." RESEARCH MANAGEMENT 14 (1971): 34-39.

Boliek, Paul E. "Setting Up Corporate R & D As an Independent Company." CHEMICAL ENGINEERING 9 (29 May 1975): 50 .

Suggests creating a research and development group as an independent profit center which would cut down high costs of support for research and development activity.

Bours, W.A. "Imagination Wears Many Hats." JOURNAL OF MARKETING 30 (October 1966): 59-61.

New product ideas can result from any of three types of research programs: Market oriented, in which new product ideas are solicited from consumers to determine what there is a market for, Product oriented, in which particular products are developed that will meet marketing needs. Fundamental or Pure Research, in which new product ideas result from the research itself.

Bradley, H.A. "Selling Your Pet Project to Management." AUTOMATION 21 (July 1974): 63-64.

Explains how to convince management of the commercial feasibility of an idea.

Brown, Alfred E. "Twelve Ways to Improve R & D Corporate Relations." RESEARCH MANAGEMENT 13 (May 1970): 183-88.

Examines the probable areas of conflict between the research and development and the rest of corporate departments. Suggests ways of resolving conflicts.

Brown, G.H. "The Increasing Importance of R & D in New Product Development and Corporate Profitability." In PROCEEDINGS: THIRD ANNUAL NATIONAL CONFERENCE ON INDUSTRIAL RESEARCH, 22 January 1968.

Cathey, P.J. "New Venture Funding: Mad Money for Managers." IRON AGE 214 (29 July 1974): 36-38.

Discusses the advantages of new venture funding for discovering product ideas. By providing funds for researchers who want to pursue special interests, new ideas are likely to result. Various approaches to new venture funding are studied in relation to a particular firm, Teleflex, Inc.

Centron, Marvin J., and Goldhar, J.D. "The Science of Managing Organized Technology." IEEE TRANSACTIONS ON ENGINEERING MANAGEMENT EM-17 (February 1970): 20–43.

Surveys the literature on research and development management aimed at nontechnical manager.

Collier, Donald W. "The Creative Link Between Market and Technology." CHEMICAL TECHNOLOGY 3 (February 1975): 90–93.

Reports a survey which found lack of communication between research and marketing departments. Suggests establishing venture groups consisting of members from all departments.

_____. "Innovation System for the Larger Company." RESEARCH MANAGE-MENT 13 (September 1970): 341–49.

Deals with resource allocation, project planning, research and development goal setting and department coordination required for corporate development projects.

Commander, M. "Ten Ways Not to Make a New Material." ENGINEERING 218 (March 1978): 236–37.

Cordtz, Dan. "Bring the Laboratory Down to Earth." FORTUNE 83 (January 1971): 106.

Stresses the need for bringing the efforts of research department in conformity with what the market wants.

"Creative Staff Pools Ideas Each Week for New Products." PRODUCT EN-GINEERING 37 (21 November 1966): 156.

Daniels, Draper. "How to Keep Research from Getting In the Way." In PRO-CEEDINGS: AMERICAN MARKETING ASSOCIATION SUMMER CONFERENCE, edited by Keith Cox and Ben E. Enis, pp. 177–80. Chicago: American Marketing Association, 1968.

Discusses the barriers to new product development in research and development department, such as the lack of communication and lack of purpose. Stresses the need for coordinated and well-directed research efforts.

Davis, John C. "Brewing New Product Ideas." CHEMICAL ENGINEERING 80 (12 November 1973): 108–10.

Describes the practice followed by leading companies to promote new and successful product ideas.

Dean, Burton Victor. EVALUATING, SELECTING AND CONTROLLING R &

D PROJECTS. Research study, no. 89. New York: American Management Association, 1968. 127 p.

Discusses all phases of project management from idea generation to commercialization or termination.

Dean, Burton Victor, and Nishry, M.J. "Scoring and Profitability Models for Evaluating and Selecting Engineering Projects." OPERATIONS RESEARCH 13 (July 1965): 550–69.

Presents a profitability model for allocating manpower resources in a company and selecting from a set of engineering projects those which are to utilize these resources.

Dessauer, John H. "How a Large Corporation Motivates Its Research and Development People." RESEARCH MANAGEMENT 14 (May 1971): 51–55.

Describes the techniques used by Xerox for motivating its research team.

_____. "Some Thoughts on the Allocation of Resource to Research and Development Opportunities." RESEARCH MANAGEMENT 10 (March 1967): 77–89.

"Developing a Product -- From Idea to Marketing Plan." ADVERTISING AGE 46 (10 November 1975): 55.

Dov, A.G. Beged. "Optimal Assignment of Research and Development Projects in a Large Company Using a Integer Programming Model." IEEE TRANSACTIONS ON ENGINEERING MANAGEMENT EM-12 4 (December 1965): 138–42.

Dutton, R.E. "Creative Use of Creative People." PERSONNEL JOURNAL 51 (November 1972): 818–22.

Explains how to create an organizational climate conducive to research.

Fast, Norman D. "New Venture Departments: Organizing for Innovation." INDUSTRIAL MARKETING MANAGEMENT 7 (April 1978): 77–78.

Reports on a study of new venture departments in eighteen companies and assesses their usefulness in new product development.

Fazia, Harry. "How Marketing and Technical Development Information Can be Utilized." MODERN TEXTILES 172 (March 1972): 65–67.

Case study of how guidance from marketing department can get best ideas out of research and development department.

Fox, Harold W. "Toward Market Acceptance of New Products." ADVANCED MANAGEMENT JOURNAL 39 (April 1974): 51–59.

Explains how marketing department can help research and development solve new product problems regarding risk and other factors which are barriers to product acceptance.

Gancer, Carson L. "Is That New Product Worth Developing?" MACHINE DE-SIGN 46 (18 April 1974): 118-23.

Discusses the use of the risk-analysis approach in evaluating research and development projects. By this method it is possible to get an indication of the dispersion that surrounds the most likely outcome, along with a related degree of confidence. Two basic present value indicators are used: internal rate-of-return, and discounted payback.

Gerstenfeld, A. "A Study of Successful Projects, Unsuccessful Projects and Projects in Process in West Germany." IEEE TRANSACTIONS ON ENGINEER-ING MANAGEMENT EM-23 (August 1976): 116-23.

Gladstone, Edgar J. "How Systems Analysis Can Help R & D." MANAGE-MENT REVIEW 61 (February 1972): 41-43.

Discusses the application of systems analysis techniques in research and development management which will improve project planning, selection and control, and interdepartmental coordination.

Grassi, P.G. "Network Project Development." DATA PROCESSING 13 (November 1971): 441-44.

Hanan, Mack. "Effective Coordination of Marketing with Research and Development." In HANDBOOK OF MODERN MARKETING, edited V.P. Buell, pp. 17-28. New York: McGraw-Hill, 1970.

Discusses the formation, composition, and functions of "marketing action teams" used by top management to coordinate activities between research and development and marketing.

Hart, A. "Chart for Evaluating Product Research and Development Projects." OPERATIONAL RESEARCH QUARTERLY 17 (December 1966): 347-58.

Hatfield, M.R. "Going Down the Rat Hole with New Products Research." BUSINESS MANAGEMENT 40 (June 1971): 18.

Develops the view that the probability of commercial success of a new venture is inversely proportional to the sequence of the distance between the marketing and technical people.

Haussler, Warren M. "What Makes for Successful Product Development." In PROCEEDINGS: AMERICAN MARKETING ASSOCIATION SUMMER CONFER-ENCE, edited by R.E. Vosburgh and M.S. Moyer, pp. 61-63. Chicago: American Marketing Association, 1967.

Analyzes how corporations in the aerospace industry encourage research and development and flow of research ideas into commercially successful ventures.

Hertz, David B. "The Management of Innovation." MANAGEMENT REVIEW 54 (April 1965): 49-52.

Results of a survey into a number of firms as to how they have organized research and development activities and their interface with management and executives for best results.

Herzog, Raymond E. "Marketing: The Link Between Customer and Engineer." MACHINE DESIGN 46 (July 1974): 113-16.

Offers suggestions for developing better coordination between marketing and engineering departments which will always result in product improvement.

Heyke, H.E. "Organization of Product Development in Chemical Industry." MANAGEMENT INTERNATIONAL REVIEW 7, no. 1 (1967): 3-40.

Hitchcock, L.B. "Selection and Evaluation of R & D Projects." RESEARCH MANAGEMENT 6 (May 1963): 231-44; (July 1963): 259-75.

"How to Generate New Product Ideas." BUSINESS MANAGEMENT 33 (October 1967): 82-91.

Describes how two new product firms work, and how large in-company research and development programs are incorporating some of the practices of the small, independent innovators.

Johnston, R.D. "Product Selection and Evaluation." LONG RANGE PLANNING 5 (September 1972): 40-45.

Examines a number of techniques which are available for the selection and evaluation of research and development projects. This would in turn insure a range of new products and processes which will meet the requirements of the company's policy for business growth and strength.

Joselyn, Robert William. "An Exploratory Study of Marketing Considerations Relating to the Sale or License of Research and Development by Product Technology." Ph.D. dissertation, University of Colorado, 1971. 223 p. Ann Arbor, Mich.: University Microfilms. Order no. 71-25842.

Reports the results of a survey of members of Licensing Executive Society regarding the ways in which firms deal with the by-products of their research and development efforts, i.e., whether to further develop them or to sell or license them.

Kebernick, O.C. "Unique Relationship of Engineering and Marketing in a New Product Development." ADVANCED MANAGEMENT JOURNAL 32 (July 1967): 45-49.

Stresses that engineering and marketing can work together in pursuit of new products. They should draw close in order to succeed in fields where technology is advancing rapidly, where product lifetime continues to shorten, and where investments must be recovered quickly.

Kellog, Marion S. "Don't Isolate Your R & D Staff." HYDROCARBON PROCESSING 51 (December 1972): 104.

Some companies do not see the need for letting research and development department deal with other departments in its own right. This leads to poor results. Article gives tips on avoiding this situation.

Kidder, R.C. "Selling the Super Project to Management." CHEMICAL TECHNOLOGY 3 (January 1973): 18-20.

Laffy, R. "A System for the Research Selection and Introduction of New Products." REVUE FRANCAIS DU MARKETING, no. 22, 1967, pp. 45-62.

Lanitis, Tony. "How to Generate New Product Ideas." JOURNAL OF ADVERTISING RESEARCH 10 (June 1970): 31-35.

Most new product development programs place major emphasis on the screening and testing of "given" ideas. These ideas are solicited from throughout the company or come from the "brain storm" or "creative flash" program. This article suggests procedures for developing new product ideas which are not a series of steps but offer meaningful approaches for generating innovative and pertinent concepts.

Leiter, L.I. "Improving the Odds in Product R & D." MACHINE DESIGN 50 (9 February 1978): 80-83.

McCarthy, J.F., and Ginn, A. "Systematic Approach to Setting and Implementing Project Objectives." MANAGEMENT REVIEW 59 (January 1970): 2-11.

Product planning involves developing realistic goals. Authors discuss their experience in planning for aerospace systems products involving setting of clear-cut objectives and development of practical plans. Procedures could be applied to other new product planning.

McGuire, Edward Patrick. GENERATING NEW PRODUCT IDEAS. Conference Board Report, no. 456. New York: Conference Board, 1972. 70 p.

Deals with internal and external stimulation of creativity and utilization of inventors and licensors. Gives examples of corporate waiver forms and policy statements.

Mansfield, Edwin, and Wagner, Samuel. "Organizational and Strategic Factors Associated with Probabilities of Success in Industrial R & D." JOURNAL OF BUSINESS 48 (April 1975): 179-98.

Uses organizational structural data from twenty major industrial firms to estimate probabilities of success of research and development projects.

Marton, Katherine, and Berkman, K.A. "A System Approach for the Generation of New Product Ideas." JOURNAL OF THE ACADEMY OF MARKETING 4 (Spring 1976): 520-26.

Generating new product ideas represents a highly specialized kind of problem solving. Article suggests adoption of a systems approach model which will explore all relevant factors involved in the decision.

Miles, Robert H. "How Job Conflict and Ambiguities Affect Research and Development Professionals." RESEARCH MANAGEMENT 18 (July 1975): 32-37.

Deals with communications difficulties resulting from knowledge specialization in research and development people.

Miller, James R. "Management Mix in Research and Hourglass Concept." AMERICAN ECONOMIC REVIEW 23 (March-April 1973): 8-15.

Discusses how to choose research goals and how personnel can achieve the goals in a corporate context.

Minkes, A.L., and Samuels, J.M. "Allocation of Research and Development Expenditure in the Firm." JOURNAL OF MANAGEMENT STUDIES 3 (1966): 62-72.

Moore, K. "Ingredient Applications in New Product Categories." FOOD PRODUCT DEVELOPMENT 12 (August 1978): 27.

Moore, R.F. "Five Ways to Bridge the Gap Between R & D and Production." RESEARCH MANAGEMENT 67 (September 1970): 367-73.

To coordinate the various processes, article suggests creation of data processing systems for better information, improving communication, use of product-process manager, and upgrading production personnel.

Morgenthaler, G. "How to Make By-Product R&D Pay." MANAGEMENT REVIEW 60 (July 1971): 41-45.

Many firms fail to exploit research and development ideas related to planned product lines, i.e., the by-product spin-off ideas which are potential assets. Article develops a mechanism to take advantage of these.

Mortimer, J. "Factoring of a New Product Can Save those R and D Costs." ENGINEER 239 (July 1974): 31.

"Moving Your Product from Research to Manufacturing." FACTORY 123 (August 1965): 66-69.

Muse, William V., and Kegerreis, Robert J. "Technological Innovation and Marketing Management: Implications for Corporate Policy." JOURNAL OF MARKETING 33 (October 1969): 3-9.

Discusses new directions for research and development management through infusion and involvement of marketing executives, application of the "test of marketing feasibility" in the allocation of research and development effort, and adherence to profit-motivated marketing orientation throughout the stages of new product development.

Nagy, Stephen F., and Herbert, Terry. "R & D As a Closely Managed Activity." INDUSTRIAL RESEARCH 16 (August 1974): 38-41.

Explains how lack of proper documentation in research and development department makes it difficult for the product manager to accurately evaluate its effectiveness.

Naslund, Bertil, and Sellstedt, B. "An Evaluation of Some Methods for Determining the R & D Budget." IEEE TRANSACTION ON ENGINEERING MANAGEMENT EM-21 (February 1974): 24-29.

Nienow, Robert B., and Coltman, Robert A. "Putting R & D on a Profit Making Basis." MANAGEMENT SERVICES 6 (May-June 1969): 21-27.

Examines what should be done in terms of each project to make it profitable. This includes cash-flow projects, project cut-offs, and periodic reviews.

Oates, D. "French Firm Tries Creative Methods." INTERNATIONAL MANAGEMENT 27 (October 1972): 54-55.

O'Mulloy, J.B. "Research and Development of New Products." ADMAP 4 no. 5 (1968).

Owens, Richard N. "Product Research: Product Design." In his MANAGEMENT OF INDUSTRIAL ENTERPRISES. Homewood, Ill.: R.D. Irwin, 1965, pp. 225-58.

Park, Ford. "The Technical Strategy of 3M." In MANAGING ADVANCING TECHNOLOGY, edited by staff of INNOVATION magazine, vol. 1, pp. 51-68. New York: American Management Association, 1972.

> Describes how people at 3M company advance their new product ideas.

"Payoff From New Products." MACHINE DESIGN 42 (2 April 1970): 70-73.

> Outlines how one company solved financial problems of its corporate research division. Rex Chainbelt, Inc. operates its technical center in a way that is designed to insure a profitable return on research dollars.

Peach, Leonard H. "The Responsible Management of Technological Change." PERSONNEL MANAGEMENT 5 (August 1973): 18-21.

> Explains how marketing and technical personnel get on opposing sides and tells how to avoid pitfalls in this area.

Peters, J.I. "Scavenging Successful New Products." INDUSTRIAL RESEARCH 15 (April 1973): 52-55.

> Puts forward the view that the vast array of technical development is lying fallow in company archives or scientists' notebooks. Stresses need for successfully exploiting creativity.

Quinn, J.B. "Budgeting for Research." In HANDBOOK OF INDUSTRIAL RESEARCH MANAGEMENT, edited by Carl Heyel, pp. 281-313. New York: Reinhold, 1968.

RESEARCH DECISION MAKING IN NEW PRODUCT DEVELOPMENT. PROCEEDINGS, edited by Victor J. Danilov, National Conference on Industrial Research 3d Illinois Institute of Technology, 1968. Beverly Shores, Ind.: Industrial Research, 1968. 206 p.

Rhodes, Clifford. "The Centrality of R & D." ENGINEERING 214 (June 1974): 456-59.

> Discusses the research planning diagram technique which would help coordinate research and development's relationship vis-a-vis other units.

Roberts, George A. "The Communication Imperative between the Management and R & D." RESEARCH MANAGEMENT 15 (March 1972): 67-72.

> Explains why communication breaks down and how to bridge the gap.

Rosen, Charles E. "New Product Decisions - Creative Measurements and Realistics Applications." In NEW PRODUCTS, CONCEPTS, DEVELOPMENT AND STRATEGY, edited by Robert Scrace, pp. 11-17. Ann Arbor: University of Michigan, Graduate School of Business Administration, 1967.

Narrates the experiences of the president of a research firm in promoting creativity.

Rosen, E.M., and Souder, W.E. "A Method for Allocation of R & D Expenditure." IEEE TRANSACTION ON ENGINEERING MANAGEMENT EM-12, 3 (September 1965): 87-93.

Ryan, M.F. "Scientist and Marketer, Cultures in Conflict." CHEMICAL TECHNOLOGY 6 (October 1976): 623-25.

Sherman, R.F. "R & D's Role in Product Development." INDUSTRIAL RESEARCH 8 (July 1966): 32-34.

Blames lack of overall coordination for the high rates of product failure. Explains where research and development fits in the process.

Souder, William E. "Effectiveness of Nominal and Interacting Group Decision Processes for Integrating R & D and Marketing." MANAGEMENT SCIENCE 23 (February 1977): 595-605.

Research and development and marketing are dependent on each other for new product development. Both have different viewpoints. There is need for a process that will bridge dissonant viewpoints of both. Author describes three properties involved in the bridging process: nominal, interacting, and combined nominal-interacting. These are applied to actual cases and results are discussed.

Steele, L.W. "Speeding the Transition of R & D to Commercial Use." RESEARCH MANAGEMENT 18 (September 1975): 30-34.

Discusses how effective solutions call for flexible ad hoc arrangements to fit individual circumstances, and actions involving plant locations, reporting relationships, financial support, and people.

Stumpe, Warren R. "Venture Management is Part R & D." RESEARCH/DEVELOPMENT 27 (November 1976): 32-40.

First-hand account of the operations of a corporate research center. Discusses budgeting, organization, communication problems, and how to hire the right people.

Swan, John E. "The Creative Link Between Market and Technology." CHEMICAL TECHNOLOGY 3 (February 1975): 90-93.

Deals with the communications gap between research and development and marketing which acts as a barrier to innovation.

Tatler, M.A. "Turning Ideas Into Gold." MANAGEMENT REVIEW 64 (March 1975): 4-10.

Describes the formation, purpose, procedures, and motivating aspects of idea development system employed by corporations.

Tauber, E.M. "How Market Research Discourages Major Innovation." BUSINESS HORIZONS 17 (June 1974): 22-26.

Author makes a case for reduced utilization of marketing research when major innovations are concerned. He feels that the research techniques are biased to discourage major innovations. Test and survey results favor a "go" decision for minor innovations as they cause the least disturbance in the established consumption patterns, unlike the major innovations.

Thomas, K.L. "Idea Generation and Collection." FOOD TECHNOLOGY 19 (October 1965): 1511-15.

Tietjen, K.H. "New Direction for New Product R & D." PRINTERS INK 290 (12 February 1965): 14-16.

Explains how research and development can help smoke out good new product ideas from bad ones.

Udell, J.G. "Unsolicited Product Ideas: A New Evaluation Program." RESEARCH MANAGEMENT 19 (July 1976): 14-17.

Describes an experimental, noncorporate system, currently underway for selecting and testing new ideas and inventions for industry.

UNCERTAINTY IN RESEARCH MANAGEMENT, AND NEW PRODUCT DEVELOPMENT. Edited by Raymond M. Hainer, et al. New York: Reinhold, 1967. 234 p.

"Unmarketed Moneymakers." PRODUCT ENGINEERING 36 (11 October 1965): 97.

Discusses the study released by Barnes Research Associates which delved into the causes for an apparent decline in research productivity. It surveyed directors of research from 100 of the largest corporations and private research labs and 150 of the country's outstanding inventors. One of their important conclusions was that top management of U.S. industry is reluctant to commercialize new patents. Article goes on to discuss what the reasons are for the above conclusions.

Usury, Milton F., and Hess, John L. "Planning and Control of Research Development Activities." JOURNAL OF ACCOUNTANCY 124 (November 1967): 43-48.

Research and development project planning and control involve project selection and resource allocation. Article discusses how this is done to achieve effective financial control.

Utterback, James M., and Brown, James W. "Monitoring for Technological Opportunities." BUSINESS HORIZONS 15 (October 1972): 5-15.

Calls for a continuous system of watching out for opportunities resulting from technological change. The photographic industry is used as a case in point.

Vinson, Donald E., and Jackson, J.H. "New Product Ideas Need Special Management." MANAGEMENT REVIEW 62 (December 1973): 24-29.

Describes how to create an organizational climate for the encouragement and development of new product ideas.

Watson, Spencer C. "A Vote for R & D Profit Centers." MANAGEMENT ACCOUNTING 56 (April 1975): 50-52.

Discusses traditional and current methods for allocating cost and expenditures of the research and development department.

Watt, S.O. "New Blue Bloggo: A Study of Household Product R & D." RESEARCH MANAGEMENT 13 (1970): 55-62.

Discusses the advantages of new product development through establishment of research and development committee. Also notes other factors to remember in new product development.

White, George R., and Graham, M.B.W. "How to Spot a Technological Winner." HARVARD BUSINESS REVIEW 56 (March-April 1978): 146-52.

How does a manager tell the difference in advance between a winner and a loser in a new product line up? This article presents a framework for evaluation.

Williams, D.J. "Study of a Decision Model for R & D Project Selection." OPERATIONAL RESEARCH QUARTERLY 20 (September 1969): 361-73.

Wrist, P.E. "How R & D Men Can Eliminate Road Blocks to New Product Success." PAPER TRENDS 150 (7 November 1966): 46-48.

Chapter 8

MARKETING TECHNIQUES

Abrams, George J. "Why New Products Fail." ADVERTISING AGE 45 (22 April 1974): 51-52.

Narrates the experience of a foremost new product developer.

Adler, Lee. "Systems Approach to Marketing." HARVARD BUSINESS REVIEW 45 (May-June 1967): 105-18.

Provides a work flow and systems chart for new product management.

Angelus, Theodore L. "Improving the Success Ratio in New Products." FOOD TECHNOLOGY 24 (April 1970): 333-34.

In the past, nearly 80 percent of all new product introductions have resulted in failures because of poor product positioning, poor product differentiation, bad timing, poor performance, or wrong market. Suggests that producers must make a distinction between marketing opportunity and new product opportunity.

_____. "Why Do Most New Products Fail." ADVERTISING AGE 40 (24 March 1969): 85-86.

By an analysis of new products not reaching full expected potential, the author finds the following common denominators: poor product positioning, lack of product differentiation, and failure to use the right timing.

"Avoiding New Product Failure." ACCOUNTANT 176 (19 May 1977): 574.

Offers suggestions which may help limit the risk involved in new product launches.

Baker, Michael J. MARKETING NEW INDUSTRIAL PRODUCTS. New York: Holmes and Maier, 1975. 209 p.

Balassie, Eugene G. "Planning Must Begin With Marketing Opportunities." MANAGERIAL PLANNING 22 (September-October 1973): 21-25.

Barnett, Norman L. "Beyond Market Segmentation." HARVARD BUSINESS REVIEW 46 (January-February 1969): 152-66.

Reviews and evaluates various segmentation techniques used for new product development such as: demographics; social structure, i.e., reference group theory, family life cycle, and usage patterns. A new concept is discussed--product segmentation--whereby people differentiate among the various brands in a market according to their perception of the brands' real or imagined characteristics. Although brands vary widely in their perceived characteristics, they tend to be relatively stable. Consequently, each brand occupies a unique "niche" in the market.

Bennett, K.W. "Reducing New Product Mortalities." IRON AGE 202 (19 December 1968): 48-49.

Too often new product ideas are lost before they are fully developed. By giving the marketing personnel a greater role in new product development and having the marketing and engineering divisions work together, one can determine more rapidly which products are producible and marketable.

Bjorksten, Johan. "New Products Fail--Why." PLASTIC WORLD 24 (February 1966): 48-49.

Explores the reasons why new products fail in the plastics industry and makes recommendations which may help new products succeed.

Boger, C.K., Jr. "New Product Marketing: The Small Operation." TAPPI 49 (August 1966): 137A-38A.

Discusses new product marketing at the small marketing operation level, such as the "family" or "do-it-yourself" businesses. Suggests that the goal of a small operation should be to create and market its own products, rather than improve on some existing product.

Borden, Neil Hopper, Jr. THE INTRODUCTION OF NEW PRODUCTS TO SUPERMARKETS. Cambridge, Mass.: Harvard University, 1965. 26 p.

Boykin, A.L. "Policies for Growth." CANADIAN CHARTERED ACCOUNTANT 89 (October 1966): 287-89.

Deals with the product life cycle as an analytical concept which, in conjunction with other factors, is particularly useful in planning for success. Stages of a product life cycle are defined.

Britt, Steuart Henderson. "Marketing Importance of the Just Noticeable Differences." BUSINESS HORIZONS 19 (August 1976): 38-40.

Discusses how much a product must be improved before consumers notice the difference and choose it over competing brands.

Burger, Phillip Clinton. "Market Segments and Information Flows in a New Product Introduction." Ph.D. dissertation, Purdue University, 1968. 383 p. Ann Arbor, Mich.: University Microfilms. Order no. 68-12528.

Examines the key variables governing the rate and depth of new product diffusion and develops a methodology for monitoring new product introduction.

"The Care and Feeding of a New Product." BROADCASTING 74 (11 November 1968): 73-76.

Consumers have a strong appetite for newness, and there seems to be a growing dependence among manufacturers on new products. According to a poll of fifty consumer goods manufacturers, the average percentage of current sales attributable to new products is twenty-two percent. The costs and risks of new product introduction are discussed.

Carlson, Bjorn, and Kusoffsky, Bertil. DISTRIBUTOR BRANDS VERSUS PRODUCER BRANDS: AN ANALYSIS OF THE BRAND POLICY PROBLEMS OF DISTRIBUTORS IN A FRAMEWORK OF DECISION THEORY. Stockholm: Economic Research Institute, Stockholm School of Economics, 1966. 125 p.

Chilcutt, J. "Proliferation of New Products Curbs Their Acceptance Amidst Problems of Shelf Space, Store Growth." ADVERTISING AGE 35 (6 July 1964): 71-72.

Discusses why only a few of the submitted new product ideas are actually chosen for marketing. To be accepted a product must increase corporate profits, present a new service to the consumer, be better in quality than the competition, and replace rather than duplicate old products.

Clifford, Donald K. "Managing the Product Life Cycle." In THE ARTS OF TOP MANAGEMENT, edited by R. Mann. New York: McGraw-Hill, 1971.

Explains how to locate the life cycles for a firm's product line and arrive at marketing strategies for the same.

Cochran, B., and Thompson, C.G. "Why New Products Fail?" CONFERENCE BOARD RECORD 1 (October 1964): 11-18.

Most common reasons for new product failure are: inadequate market analysis, product defect, higher costs than expected, poor timing, competition, insufficient marketing effort, inadequate sales force, and weakness in distribution. Suggests remedies, including improved screening and evaluation, organization changes, changes in procedures, improved development work, production, and quality control and selective development.

Corey, E. Raymond. "Key Options in Market Selection and Product Planning." HARVARD BUSINESS REVIEW 53 (September-October 1975): 119-23.

Discusses how to decide what end markets to serve and at what stage of manufacture to serve them.

Cox, William E. "Product Life Cycles as Marketing Models." JOURNAL OF BUSINESS 40 (October 1967): 375-84.

Survey of over 700 drug firms to illustrate the advantages of product life cycle concept to a multiproduct firm in allocating resources.

CREATING AND MARKETING NEW PRODUCTS: VIEWPOINTS OF LEADING AUTHORITIES. Collected and edited by Gordon Wills, et al. London: Crosby Lockwood Staples, 1973. 484 p.

Daignault, Phyllis. "Packaging Sell Gets Organized." SALES MANAGEMENT 94 (19 March 1965): 59-62.

Illustrates how a product's package can be used effectively in introducing a new product.

Davidson, J. Hugh. "Why Most New Consumer Brands Fail?" HARVARD BUSINESS REVIEW 54 (March-April 1976): 117-72.

Explains the much ignored criteria for successful products which management and marketers can use as weapons against new consumer brand failure, such as price or performance advantage, product differentiation, and new untried ideas.

Davis, E.J. EXPERIMENTAL MARKETING. Chicago: Nelson Hall, 1970. 186 p.

_____. THE SALES CURVES OF NEW PRODUCTS. London: Market Research Society Conference, J. Walter Thompson, 1965.

Dhalla, Nariman K. "Forget the Product Life Cycle Concept." Harvard Business Review 54 (January-February 1976): 102-12.

Challenges the concept and existence of product life cycle. Suggests alternative systems which will give managers data on deciding how and whether to continue promoting a product.

Dore, J.B. "How to Learn From Product Failures." DIRECTOR 25 (July 1972): 73-76.

By an analysis of some new product failures, article identifies key problem areas related to organization, marketing, and technology.

Doyle, Peter, and Weinberg, Charles B. "Effective New Product Decisions for Supermarkets." OPERATIONAL RESEARCH QUARTERLY 24 (March 1973): 45-54.

Current methods by which supermarkets decide which new products to stock are reviewed. Certain limitations of these subjective and ad hoc procedures are suggested and an alternative approach based on a screening technique is developed.

Dunn, M.J. "Interface of Marketing and R & D Personnel in the Product Innovation Stream." JOURNAL OF THE ACADEMY OF MARKETING SCIENCE 3 (Winter 1975): 20-33.

Reports on the product development component of research in a Canadian context.

Eastlack, J.O., Jr., ed. MARKETING NEW PRODUCTS UNDER TODAY'S COMPETITION. New York: American Marketing Association, 1966. 50 p.

Proceedings of the Fourth Annual New Products Conference sponsored by the New York Chapter of the American Marketing Association, 31 March 1966. Papers cover such topics as creating, marketing, timing, and strategy of new product introduction abroad, and new product development.

Field, G.A. "Do Products Really Have Life Cycles?" CALIFORNIA MANAGEMENT REVIEW 14 (Fall 1971): 92-95.

Discusses whether products do or do not have life cycles. Suggests that products have "acceptance" cycles rather than life cycles since products will be used or not used several times during its marketing life.

Fox, Harold W. "Product Life Cycle: An Aid to Financial Administration." FINANCIAL EXECUTIVE 41 (April 1973): 28-34.

Like the fiscal year concept, business needs an operational and financial system which is more sensitive to critical events than to a fixed date. Article outlines a system based on product life cycles, which could satisfy the above objective.

Foy, G.E. "Marketing a New Chemical." CHEMICAL ENGINEERING 73 (26 September 1966): 130-31.

Frand, Erwin A. "Why New Products Fail." INDUSTRY WEEK 186 (11 August 1975): 58-60.

Reasons new products fail vary, but most failures fall into four categories as follows: management failure to fully comprehend the implications of developing new products, the lack of adequate marketing organization, management's failure to fully recognize corporate limitations, and a lack of demand. Strategies for prevention and/or cure of this malady affecting the success of new products are prescribed.

Frank, L.K. "Don't Over Achieve in Your Market." INDUSTRIAL MARKETING 53 (February 1968): 46-48.

Cautions against frequent tendency to design products in terms of performance instead of markets and capacities.

Frederixon, Martin Shelton. "An Investigation of the Product Life Cycle Concept and its Application to New Product Proposal evaluation Within the Chemical Industry." Ph.D. dissertation, Michigan State University, 1969. 529 p. Ann Arbor: University Microfilms. Order no. 70-09536.

Attempts to formulate a predictive multivariate model for a new industrial chemical product and to identify the structural characteristics of the product which relate to sales performance. Also classifies product life cycles by pattern of sales, profits and other related financial data.

French, Norman, and Brooksher, William R. "Marketing New Products: By Segmenting Product Lines." UNIVERSITY OF MISSOURI BUSINESS AND GOVERNMENT REVIEW 10 (September-October 1969): 5-10.

Fruham, William E., Jr. "Pyrrhic Victories in Fights for Market Share." HARVARD BUSINESS REVIEW (September-October 1972): 100-07.

Cautions against trying for a larger piece of the action in a new product area when success of such efforts will spell disaster in the form of government control and so forth. Cites examples for computer, airlines, and food businesses.

Gisser, Philip. LAUNCHING THE NEW INDUSTRIAL PRODUCT. New York: American Management Association, 1972. 183 p.

_____. "New Products are a Gamble, But the Risk Can be Reduced." INDUSTRIAL MARKETING 58 (May 1973): 28-32.

One reason for new products' failure is as follows: the right decision for one situation can be the wrong decision for another. Three factors to be considered in the decision making process are: 1) new product introduction is a risk decision, 2) getting the necessary information to make key decisions, and 3) maintenance of objectivity - avoidance of product infatuation. The advertising programs should be conducted in such a way that a clear picture of the viability of the product can be obtained as early as possible. Early introduction of the product is also important.

_____. "Taking the Chances Out of Product Introductions (Using PERT)." INDUSTRIAL MARKETING 50 (May 1965): 86-91.

New product introduction programs are often a hodgepodge of last minute plans and unfilled needs. Article outlines a coordination technique which help smooth such a program.

Gubitz, A.C. "Introducing a New Product." INDUSTRIAL MARKETING 60 (May 1975): 53-58.

Offers some new and relatively low cost solutions to product intro-duction problems.

Haley, Russell I. "The Implication of Market Segmentation." CONFERENCE BOARD RECORD 6 (March 1969): 43-47.

Discusses various kinds of market segmentation and its implications for the product-market manager.

Hamilton, Michael, et al. LAUNCHING A NEW PROJECT: A CHECKLIST FOR MARKETING MANAGEMENT. Marketing Management series. London: Institute of Marketing, 1970. 16 p.

Hanan, Mack. THE MARKET ORIENTATION OF R & D: A RECOMMENDA-TION FOR MINIMIZING NEW PRODUCT RISK. New York: American Man-agement Association, 1965. 22 p.

Describes a management method, referred to as the marketing ac-tion committee for minimizing new product risk. It is an expres-sion of management thinking designed to anticipate the market's ultimate judgment by seeking out its needs, installing them into the research and development process from the beginning and then validating the preproduct concepts, all before a product itself is ever manufactured, distributed, or sold.

Harper, Paul C., Jr. "New Product Marketing: The Cutting Edge of Corporate Policy." JOURNAL OF MARKETING 40 (April 1976): 76-85.

New product success depends on aggressive marketing and a strong corporate policy. Shifts in the corporate scene, a changed busi-ness environment and a more cautious consuming public with dimin-ishing real disposable personal income call for a new product stra-tegy.

Harris, J.S. "New Product Marketing: A Case Study in Decision Making Un-der Uncertainty." APPLIED STATISTICS 16, no. 1 (1967): 39-42.

Headen, Robert Speir. THE INTRODUCTORY PHASES OF THE LIFE CYCLE FOR NEW GROCERY PRODUCTS: CONSUMER ACCEPTANCE AND COMPE-TITIVE BEHAVIOR. Cambridge, Mass.: Harvard University, 1966. 22 p.

Marketing Techniques

Heininger, S.A. "From Laboratory to Consumer in One Easy (?) Step." FOOD TECHNOLOGY 23 (March 1969): 298.

Hopkins, David S., and Barley, Earl L. "New Product Pressures." CONFERENCE BOARD RECORD 8 (June 1971): 16-24.

Discusses new product failures and some means to minimize them.

Howard, Fred. "Unorthodox Way in New Product Production." BUSINESS MANAGEMENT 40 (September 1971): 35.

When a company is small and its product is new, big outlets usually wait and see how the market reacts to the product before going ahead with handling it. Article describes how one small company got around this obstacle.

Howard, John A. MARKETING MANAGEMENT: OPERATING STRATEGIC AND ADMINISTRATIVE. 3d ed. Homewood, Ill.: R.D. Irwin, 1973. 560 p.

"How do You Get Salesman to Push New Products." SALES MANAGEMENT 99 (1 December 1967): 34-36.

Survey of the opinions of top selling marketing executives as to how to motivate salesmen and overcome the common inertia on a new product introduction.

"How Many New Products Die." PRINTERS INK 293 (26 August 1966): 19.

Questions the generally accepted norm that four out of five new products fail.

Hussey, Edward O. "Developing and Marketing a Safe Product." RESEARCH MANAGEMENT 18 (March 1975): 20-22.

Describes how one corporation met the new, stiffer safety regulations for fabrics and at the same time strengthened its position in the marketplace.

Hustad, Thomas P., et al. "Advances in Product Research Improve the Marketer's Decision Making." CANADIAN MARKETER 7 (Spring 1974): 7-12.

Describes the new methods used for product design decisions and explains where they fit into the entire product development process.

"The Implication of Market Segmentation." CONFERENCE BOARD RECORD 6 (March 1969): 43-47.

"Improving the New Products Equation." NIELSEN RESEARCHER, no. 1, 1974, pp. 2-13.

Analyzes the share of the market for new grocery products and draws conclusions for corporate growth.

International Labor Office. CREATING A MARKET. ILO Publications in the Field of Management. Geneva, Switzerland: 1968. 180 p.

Kamien, N.I., and Schwartz, N.L. "Market Structure Rivals Response and the Firm's Rate of Product Improvement." JOURNAL OF INDUSTRIAL ECONOMICS 20 (April 1972): 159-72.

Kotler, Philip. MARKETING MANAGEMENT: ANALYSIS, PLANNING AND CONTROL. Englewood Cliffs, N.J.: Prentice-Hall, 1976. 529 p.

Lazo, H. "Finding a Key to Success in a New Product Failure." INDUSTRIAL MARKETING 50 (November 1965): 74-77.

Investigates the reasons for new product failures and establishes means of making products successful. Eight reasons for product failure are identified and seven steps to reduce product failure are discussed.

Leduc, Robert, and Wardle, John. HOW TO LAUNCH A NEW PRODUCT. London: Crosby Lockwood, 1966. 130 p.

Lemont, Fred L. "New Products: How They Differ, Why They Fail, How to Help Them Do Better." ADVERTISING AGE 42 (5 April 1971): 43-48.

Examines two different kinds of new product successes, and also goes into the question why promising new products fail.

Levit, Theodore. "Exploit the Product Life Cycle." HARVARD BUSINESS REVIEW 43 (November-December 1965): 81-94.

Explains how the concept can be used to plan ahead based on anticipated changes in the products sales and profits.

"The Life Cycle of Grocery Brands." NIELSEN RESEARCHER, no. 1, 1968, pp. 4-19.

Explains how to identify the factors affecting primary and secondary share cycles.

Macdonald, Morgan B. "New Product Risk in Industrial Markets." CONFERENCE BOARD RECORD 4 (November 1967): 26-31.

McKay, Samuel F. "The High -Technology Trap: Product Preoccupation - A Case in Point: The Laser Industry." IEEE TRANSACTION ON ENGINEERING MANAGEMENT EM-19 (February 1972): 31-34.

Contends that little attention has been paid to basic marketing
principle. Products have been developed with only foggy ideas
of market potential. As a result the development of an industry
around the laser has failed to match early expectations. Industry
has been giving all of its attention to the miracle product, rather
than to the magic market.

MacKenzie, George E. "Product Life Cycle Make ROI Analysis Relevant:
Can Tell You When to Run the Ads." INDUSTRIAL MARKETING 56 (June
1971): 100-05.

Effective use of product life cycle requires well-documented market and appropriate product conception. Article warns against
companies initiating new products more on the basis of opinion,
interest or challenge than on well-researched markets.

Margulies, W.P. "Positioning Demands Research Design Communication." AD-
VERTISING AGE 39 (13 May 1968): 66.

Describes a four step process which will help create an optimum
product positioning. This involves skills in market research, product design, and communication techniques.

_____. "Should You Treat a New Product Like a Family Member?" ADVER-
TISING AGE 39 (22 January 1968): 63-64.

Examines whether a new product should resemble a well-established
brand, how strong the resemblance should be, and would it hurt or
help sales.

"Marketing: New Products, Packaging, Timing Mark Texize Successes." AERO-
SOL AGE 19 (August 1974): 19-21.

"Marketing a New Product." BANK OF AMERICA. SMALL BUSINESS RE-
PORTER 10 (1971): 12 p.

Discusses the marketing of a new product including assessing the
product, product life cycle, determining the market, selling to a
manufacturer, going it alone, patents, trademarks, and copyrights.

"Market Methods for New Products Interest." ADVERTISING AGE 43 (24 April
1972): 32.

Relates the new product techniques used by Dow Chemical Co. and
General Mills.

Marketing Communications Research Center. PROCEEDING OF AN ANNUAL
CONFERENCE ON DEVELOPING AND MARKETING NEW PRODUCTS FOR
BUSINESS AND INDUSTRY. Princeton, N.J., 20 January 1970. 28 p.

Various aspects of developing and marketing new products are discussed. These include: the birth pains of a new welding process, a major new product line, form concept to simultaneous world-wide introduction, and application of an existing technology for the development of a new product line.

MARKETING NEW PRODUCTS TO BUSINESS AND INDUSTRY. Princeton, N.J.: Marketing Communications Research Center, 1971. 126 p.

Based on a survey of eighty-eight industrial companies, this study presents basic guidelines in developing and marketing new products for business and industry. Three major types of manufacturers are considered separately: materials, components, and finished products, and within these three groups, standard and complex products are treated. The objective of the study is to discover principles of good practice, planning, and organization that will reduce the number of failures, increase the efficiency of the development and introduction process and improve the quality, appropriateness, and profitability of the new products of future years. Detailed descriptions are given for twenty medium size and large companies.

Mazzoni, Dominick J. "New Product Reception: Tactical Use of Competitive Product Life Cycles in Multinational Marketing." MEDICAL MARKETING AND MEDIA 8 (March 1973): 13-21.

Timing of introduction of a new product is usually related to getting the new product to the market as soon as possible. Few marketers related timing of introduction to a far more critical aspect of marketing -- the receptivity of the marketplace. Article examines how this is approached to international marketing.

Meck, L.L. "Marketing Climate is Manmade: Change It to Suit Your Product." INDUSTRIAL MARKETING 55 (October 1970): 52.

Describes how product success depends upon a variety of factors which prove a given product superior to competition. These include design, packaging, appearance, performance, distribution, and communication.

Medcalf, Gordon. MARKETING AND THE BRAND MANAGER. Oxford, N.Y.: Pergamon Press, 1967. 252 p.

Mills, M.J. "New Products: How to Avoid Joining the Failures." DIRECTOR 19 (August 1966): 242-46.

Miracle, Gordon E. "Product Characteristics and Marketing Strategy." JOURNAL OF MARKETING 29 (January 1965): 18-24.

Presents a model which provides a means of predicting, or justifying, a market mix for a product with given characteristics. The prediction is approximate ideal.

Mockler, Robert J. "How to Avoid Costly Mistakes When Introducing a New Product." ADVANCED MANAGEMENT JOURNAL 31 (July 1966): 45-52.

Describes a number of guidlines on how mistakes can be avoided when introducing new products.

Moran, William T. "Why New Products Fail." JOURNAL OF ADVERTISING RESEARCH 13 (April 1973): 5-13.

Morley, John, ed. LAUNCHING A NEW PRODUCT. London: Business Books, 1968. 172 p.

Moss, Arthur. SUCCESSFUL INDUSTRIAL DESIGN: ITS CREATION BY GOOD MANAGEMENT. London: H. Witherby, 1968. 70 p.

"Name Game: Find Your Way Through This Hazardous Maze: Pitfalls for New Products." ADVERTISING AGE 36 (5 April 1965): 134.

Explains how DuPont solves the problem of naming new products, taking into account trademarks and market orientations.

"New Food Products From Concept to Marketing: Symposium." FOOD TECH-NOLOGY 19 (October 1965): 1506-44.

"New Product Introduction." RETAIL BUSINESS 12 (March 1969): 42-47.

Article presents a simple approach to the problems of planning new product introduction with particular emphasis on the role of market research. It is based on the central role of the product manager or any company officer responsible for the development of a new product. New items and new products introduction are considered separately. New items are defined as modifications to lines already being sold; new products are lines never before sold by the company.

"New Product Introduction is Not Faint." INDUSTRY WEEK 170 (6 September 1971): 40-42.

"New Product Introductions." SM/SALES MEETINGS 24 (February 1974): 44.

Views new product introductions as serious, hard working events, rather than the razzle dazzle spectaculars of the past. Case histories show how new product programs make the entire presentation a learning experience for the attendees.

"New Product Risk in Industrial Markets " CONFERENCE BOARD RECORD 4 (November 1967): 26-31.

Deals with problems of marketing new industrial products and the risks therein.

"New Products: The Push is On Marketing." BUSINESS WEEK, 4 March 1972, pp. 72-77.

Reviews new product development process from the point of view of market monitoring, reducing development time, and risk bearing.

NEW PRODUCTS IN THE GROCERY TRADE. London: Kranshar, Andrews and Eassie, 1971.

Derives failure rates from a study of new products' off-shelf disappearance.

"New Product Success Ratio." NIELSEN RESEARCHER, no. 5, 1971, pp. 2-10.

Summary of several Nielsen studies relating to new product launches and profitability.

"Nonwhites Too Often Ignored in New Product Plans." ADVERTISING AGE 38 (17 July 1967): 91-92.

Calls all marketers and researchers to develop a marketing approach to urban blacks before introducing new products.

Norwood, G. Joseph, et al. "New Product Marketing Practices by Pharmaceutical Firms." MEDICAL MARKETING AND MEDIA 5 (1970): 19-28.

Perhaps the most fundamental consideration in marketing new products is the marketing concept which considers the most important characteristic for a product is a need for the product by the market. The pharmaceutical industry has a tendency to neglect this principle beginning with marketing considerations after the product has been developed.

Nourse, Robert Eric Martin. DEMAND FOR NEW PRODUCTS IN PROCESSED FOOD INDUSTRIES. Cambridge, Mass.: Harvard University, 1967. 30 p.

O'Connell, F. "Birth of a New Product Merchandising and Marketing View." FOOD TECHNOLOGY 26 (April 1972): 43-44.

Paschkes, Michael. "How to Guarantee New Product Failure." SALES AND MARKETING MANAGEMENT 117 (12 July 1976): 40-42.

New products will have to prove themselves in a relatively short time. Assuming that the product is basically sound, author points out some common pitfalls which the marketer should avoid.

Pegram, R.M., and Bailey, E.L. "What Marketing Executives Want- New Products." CONFERENCE BOARD RECORD 4 (May 1967): 17-22.

Discusses the result of a Conference Board survey of some 300 top ranking marketing men to determine how they solve major marketing problems, and the importance given to product development. Reports the reasons for impetus for new product innovation which are: to match new product entries marketed by competitors, to cope with changing requirements and preferences of customers, and to keep pace with accelerating gains in technology.

Peterson, Robert Allen. "Identifying Predictors of New Product Acceptability for Selected Grocery Products." Ph.D. dissertation, University of Minnesota, 1971. 131 p. Ann Arbor, Mich.: University Microfilms. Order no. 71-08263.

Examines the characteristics of good and bad predictors of new products and compares the predictions with those estimated from more traditional sources.

"Pitfalls of Introducing a New Product." INDUSTRIAL DISTRIBUTOR NEWS 60 (August 1970): 58-60.

Poisson, W.H. "Creation of Markets for New Products in the Textile Industry." MODERN TEXTILE MAGAZINE 49 (October 1968): 87-92.

Polli, R., and Cook, V. "Validity of the Product Life Cycle." JOURNAL OF BUSINESS 42 (October 1969): 385-400.

Develops an operational model of product life cycle, methods of evaluating the model results of tests which make use of the observed sales in 140 categories of consumer nondurables.

"Prime Weapons in Sales War: New Products." IRON AGE 199 (20 April 1967): 25.

Explains how new products are the best weapons to stay ahead of competition.

Ragnitz, K., and Ungureanu, Marie. "How to Use Market Segmentation for Determining New Product Ideas." EUROPEAN SOCIETY FOR OPINION SURVEYS AND MARKET RESEARCH (ESOMAR) CONGRESS, Barcelona, 1970, pp. 235-47.

Unfilled needs existing in a specific market which a new product could filfill are discussed. Other points described are as follows: what the features of this new product should be, to what segment of this market should this new product be directed, which of the competitors this new product would attack most efficiently, and what the probable market share of the new product would be.

Reynolds, William H. "More Sense About Market Segmentation." HARVARD BUSINESS REVIEW 43 (September-October 1965): 107-14.

Argues that a product strategy based on the policy of offering a variety of products to the general market is better than the policy of attempting to serve a multitude of small markets, i.e., segmentation.

_____. PRODUCTS AND MARKETS. New York: Appleton-Century Crofts, 1969. 244 p.

Ricker, H.S. "Product Development from a Marketing Viewpoint." FOOD TECHNOLOGY 23 (March 1969): 290-92.

Robertson, A.B. THE LESSONS OF FAILURE. London: Macdonald and Janes, 1974. 106 p.

Robertson, Andrew. "Today's High Flier Tomorrow's Flop." BUSINESS ADMINISTRATION (July-August 1975): 27.

Predicting the decline and fall of a product is one of the most important and difficult aspects of marketing.

Rothschild, S.R. "Responding to Consumer Needs in New Product Development." FOOD PRODUCT DEVELOPMENT 12 (February 1978): 17-18.

"Routes Vary for Launching New Products." STEEL 165 (17 November 1969): 64a-64b.

Schwartz, D.A. "Consumer Research: Sometimes It Does Not Pay to Follow the Leader." SALES MANAGEMENT 109 (16 October 1972): 42.

Disproves the view that developing a product with broadest consumer appeal is the fastest route to maximum sales.

Sheeran, J.J. "New Products: Building Winning Momentum." SALES MANAGEMENT 103 (1 October 1969): 52-60.

Marketers run the least risk when they add something new to an existing product. Risk is greatest when both the product and the market are new. Product innovations that go against current sociological trends often go awry.

Shocker, Allan D., and Srinivasan, V. "Consumer Based Methodology for the Identification of New Product Ideas." MANAGEMENT SCIENCE 20 (February 1974): 921-37.

Suggests a procedure which analytically ties a model to predict users' predisposition to purchase different brands in a product market with a search process to identify optimal new product ideas.

"Should Products be Created for the Negro Market." GIBSON REPORT 8 (1968): 4.

"Short Comings Predominante in Market Planning." INDUSTRIAL MARKETING 52 (July 1967): 60-62.

> Results of a survey which explains why industrial companies are putting time and effort into market planning without a corresponding return.

Silvern, David H. "Product Opportunity Analysis." MANAGEMENT ACCOUNTING 50 (February 1969): 44-46.

> Explains how to critically appraise new product opportunities by using concepts of the time value of money and risk factors for technical development.

Simon, Leonard, et al. "Managerial Uses of Price and Product Preference Data." In PROCEEDINGS: AMERICAN MARKETING ASSOCIATION COMBINED CONFERENCE, edited by Thomas V. Greer, pp. 145-50. Chicago: American Marketing Association, 1973.

> Information from consumer surveys regarding price and preferences can be used in designing, developing, and marketing products or services. Taking the case of women's clothing items, this paper discusses methods for using such data.

"Simple Chart Gets New Products to Market." STEEL 161 (31 July 1967): 48.

Skelly, F., and Nelson, E.H. "Market Segmentation and New Product Development." SCIENTIFIC BUSINESS 4 (1966): 13.

Skinner, Richard N. LAUNCHING NEW PRODUCTS IN COMPETITIVE MARKETS. New York: Wiley, 1973. 184 p.

Smallwood, John C. "The Product Life Cycle: A Way to Strategic Market Planning." MSU BUSINESS TOPICS 21 (Winter 1973): 29-35.

> Explains how to use this concept in product planning, forecasting, pricing, and promotion.

Smith, H. "Six Steps in Presenting Your Product at a Sales Meeting." SALES AND MARKETING MANAGEMENT 116 (14 June 1976): 68.

> Describes that the success of acceptance of a new product by a distributing organization is improved if sales representatives present the product in the right way.

Smith, R. Kenneth. "Look First, Then Leap." In NEW DIRECTIONS IN MARKETING, edited by F. Webster, pp. 674-81. Chicago: American Marketing Association, 1966.

Discusses why an industrial goods manufacturer must develop new products and bring them to market as quickly as possible.

Spencer, Edson W. "The Marketing Man as Entrepreneur." INDUSTRIAL MARKETING 61 (June 1976): 112.

Discusses the view that marketing men should develop bold new products that represent an entirely new but real customer need. This requires an investment of capital and creative people and also a willingness to take risks.

Staudt, T.A. "Keeping Products in Tune with Times." SALES MANAGEMENT 107 (15 November 1971): 33-34.

Describes how effective marketing strategies can keep a new product afloat against intense competition and depressed market conditions.

Struse, R.W. "Marketing and Researching Techniques Can Lead to New Product Failures." FOOD PRODUCT DEVELOPMENT 11 (November 1977): 12.

Taylor, William F. "Fast Changing Market Conditions Call for a Flexible Marketing Communications Plan." INDUSTRIAL MARKETING 59 (June 1974): 58-62.

Describes the importance of effective communication on the part of the product manager to solve changing market conditions.

Thornton, C. RANKING NEW PRODUCT OPENINGS IN MULTIDIMENSIONAL SPACE. London: Market Research Society Conference, 1970.

"To Sell Customers, First Sell Salesman." STEEL 165 (10 November 1969): 31.

Twedt, D.W. "How Long Does it Take to Introduce New Products." JOURNAL OF MARKETING 29 (January 1965): 71-72.

States the reasons as to why it takes time to introduce a new product in the market. Presents a graphic tabulation of the replies received from twenty-three companies as to how long it actually takes large grocery product manufacturers to introduce a new item. Two-and-one-half years was the norm for getting new products started.

Udell, Jon G. "The Perceived Importance of the Elements of Strategy." JOURNAL OF MARKETING 32 (January 1968): 34-40.

Summarizes a study of the marketing strategies of 485 successful products. Also presented is a theoretical approach for determining the relative importance of product efforts and sales efforts in the marketing programs of manufacturing companies.

Udell, Jon G., and Anderson, Evan E. "The Product Warranty As an Element of Competitive Strategy." JOURNAL OF MARKETING 32 (October 1968): 1-8.

Discusses when and how to take effective advantage of the new product promotional warranty. These situations include high price, buyer ignorance, and product complexity.

Verma, Dharmendra T. "Marketing New Products: Experiences of Utah Manufacturers." UTAH ECONOMIC BUSINESS REVIEW 28 (August 1968): 1-3.

Wainwright, C.A., and Gerlach, J.T. "Want to Reduce the Risk on New Products." MARKETING/COMMUNICATIONS 297 (February 1969): 43-46.

Warder, Rita, and Strong, Sally. "New Products: Out of the Lab Into the Market." INDUSTRIAL MARKETING 56 (December 1971): 18-20.

Wasson, C.R. DYNAMIC COMPETITIVE STRATEGY AND PRODUCT LIFE CYCLES. Rev. ed. St. Charles, Ill.: Challenge Books, 1974. 311 p.

_____. "How Predictable are Fashion and Other Product Life Cycles." JOURNAL OF MARKETING 32 (July 1968): 36-43.

States that the cyclical nature of fashion rests on a firm foundation of individual and social psychology. Outlines a model of fashion acceptance and oscillation which he believes can lead to a better understanding of both fads and fashions as well as market acceptance of new products.

Weinberg, Charles B. "The Decay of Brand Segments." JOURNAL OF ADVERTISING RESEARCH 13 (February 1973): 44-47.

Discusses how a new product brand which is successful should be able to hold its ground against its competitors. This defense should be part of the introductory marketing plan. The marketing actions of competitors and customers' use of information sources preclude the maintenance of brand segments over time. Successful marketing policies in these cases should then be based on appealing to users of multiple brands.

Weiss, E.B. "Potential Marketing Successes Can be Dug From the New Product Morgue." ADVERTISING AGE 37 (15 August 1966): 37-71.

_____. "Products With Shorter Life Span Will Make it in Anti-Materialistic Society." ADVERTISING AGE 42 (27 September 1971): 73.

Well, Louis T., comp. THE PRODUCT LIFE CYCLE AND INTERNATIONAL TRADE. Boston: Division of Research, Graduate School of Business Administration, Harvard University, 1972. 259 p.

Wesson, W.S. "How Marketing Men Can Eliminate Road Blocks of New Product Success." PAPER TRENDS 150 (7 November 1966): 49-50.

Wilkie, William L. "The Product Stream of Market Segmentation." In PROCEEDINGS: AMERICAN MARKETING ASSOCIATION SPRING-FALL CONFERENCE, edited by Fred C. Allvine, pp. 317-21. Chicago: American Marketing Association, 1971.

> Discusses important characteristics of product stream method of market segmentation and a methodology for segmentation creation and evaluation.

Winston, Arthur H. "Appraising New Products for International Markets." MARKETING FORUM 5 (May-June 1969): 21-22.

Wixon, Theodore M. "New Product Marketing - A Total System." INDUSTRIAL ENGINEERING 5 (July 1973): 10-13.

> Discusses the importance of a total approach to new product marketing. Illustrates a complete marketing system.

Yeck, John D. HOW TO PROMOTE A NEW PRODUCT IN THE U.S.A. New York: Y and Y Publication, 1965. 16 p.

> Outlines a step-by-step procedure for developing the promotion of a new product. Lists the steps normally taken in order to introduce a new product or service to business or industry and the promotion materials usually needed before the product can be sold successfully.

Zif, Jay Jehiel, et al. MARKETING A NEW PRODUCT: PLAYER'S MANUAL. New York: Macmillan, 1971. 96 p.

Chapter 9

COST, PRICE, AND PROFITS

Abernathy, William J., and Baloff, N. "International Planning for New Product Introduction." SLOAN MANAGEMENT REVIEW 14 (Winter 1972-73): 25-43.

Explains how to develop joint production and marketing plans for new product introductions which will reduce investment costs and risks.

American Institute of Certified Public Accountants. COST ANALYSIS FOR PRODUCT LINE DECISIONS. Management Services Technical Study, no. 1. New York: 1965. 132 p.

Angear, T.R. "Product Profile Analysis." DIRECTOR 23 (April-May 1971): 121-26.

Discusses profile analysis stage of new product development. Product profile analysis is a quantified checklist approach to new product development. Basic procedure for product profile analysis is explained and several examples are discussed.

Aurora Electronics Company. "New Product Design and Pricing Factors." In FUNDAMENTALS OF MARKETING, edited by William J. Stanton, pp. 242-43. 2d ed. New York: McGraw-Hill, 1967.

Baloff, Nicholas, and Kennelly, John W. "Accounting Implications of Product and Process Startups." JOURNAL OF ACCOUNTING RESEARCH 5 (Autumn 1967): 131-43.

Argues that explicit recognition and estimation of the entire productivity path of a start-up will result in more effective accounting, whereas the application of a constant cost or productivity standard may result in misleading internal and external reporting. When the effects of a start-up are not explicitly recognized, uncertainty arises in the interpretation of internal and external reports.

Balog, J. "Forecasting Drug Earnings: Impact of New Products." FINANCIAL ANALYSTS JOURNAL 22 (July 1966): 39–40.

Examines the earnings impact of new products, particularly within the pharmaceutical industry, in terms of some general factors influencing earnings such as population growth, economic factors, and the means of financing health care.

Berliner, Joseph S. "Flexible Pricing and New Products in USSR." SOVIET STUDIES 27 (October 1975): 525–44.

Examines the new product market in the USSR and their methods of pricing. A "temporary price" concept is introduced as the Soviet method of price competition. Reasons for the failure of this concept are also discussed.

Blecke, Curtis J. "Profitability Review by Products." In his FINANCIAL ANALYSIS FOR DECISION MAKING, pp. 94–105. Englewood Cliffs, N.J.: Prentice-Hall, 1966.

Brickner, William Homer. "Pricing Strategies for New Industrial Products in Oligopolistic Industries." Ph.D. dissertation, Stanford University, 1966. 299 p. Ann Arbor, Mich.: University Microfilms. Order no. 66-08601.

Examines the factors which are taken into consideration in a new product initial pricing decision, such as life cycle of the product, rate of adoption, demand, competitive reaction, and barriers to entry. Article published as a book by Varian Associates, 1966. 299 p.

Blitch, Charles Parrish. "Product Innovation and Price Discrimination: A Case Study of Cellophane." Ph.D. dissertation, University of North Carolina, Chapel Hill, 1966. 211 p. Ann Arbor, Mich.: University Microfilms. Order no. 67-00964.

Studies the effect of price discrimination on competition in an industrial market by an empirical analysis of the pricing policy of an innovator of a major new industrial material.

"Budget Guidelines are Wanted for Introduction of New Product." INDUSTRIAL MARKETING 52 (February 1967): 25.

Deals with the problems in budgeting new product introductions. Stresses the need for guidelines within the corporation that would simplify the budgeting procedure, since not all products require a large budget.

Buzzell, Robert D. "Market Share: A Key to Profitability." HARVARD BUSINESS REVIEW 53 (January–February 1975): 97–106.

Describes how profitability depends on the share of the market of the product. Explains the implications of the concept for product managers.

Buzzell, Robert D., et al. PRODUCT PROFITABILITY MEASUREMENT AND MERCHANDISING DECISIONS: A PILOT STUDY IN RETAIL FOOD STORES. Boston: Harvard University, Division of Research, Graduate School of Business Administration, 1965. 104 p.

Clifford, Donald K., Jr. "Leverage in the Product Life Cycle." DUNS REVIEW 85 (May 1965): 62-64, 66, 68, 70.

Cooper, Robert Gravein. "Market Assessment Expenditures in Industrial New Product Ventures." Ph.D. dissertation, University of Western Ontario, Canada, 1973. 27 p.

Dean, Joel. "Pricing a New Product." In THE PRICING STRATEGY, edited by B. Taylor, and G. Wills, pp. 534-40. London: Staples Press, 1969.

_____. "Pricing Pioneering Products." JOURNAL OF INDUSTRIAL ECONOMICS 17 (July 1969): 165-79.

Explains the considerations which go into the pricing decision, such as dynamic competition, demand, elasticity, buyer alternatives, cost and rate of return, promotion, and distribution options.

_____. "Pricing Policies for New Products." HARVARD BUSINESS REVIEW 54 (November 1976): 141-53.

Outlines the possible price strategies for each stage of a products' market evolution and the various grounds of making a choice, geared to the dynamic nature of a new products competitive status, not just cost.

Dearden, John. "The Case Against ROI Control." HARVARD BUSINESS REVIEW 47 (May-June 1969): 124-35.

Describes the Return on Investment (ROI) system of decentralized financial control and explains why it creates conflicts between company and division interests, and why it is often of limited use in evaluating division performance.

Desrosier, Norman W., and Desrosier, John N. ECONOMICS OF NEW FOOD PRODUCT DEVELOPMENT. Westport, Conn.: Avi Publications, 1971. 217 p.

Edelman, Franz, and Greenberg, J.S. "Venture Analysis: The Analysis of Uncertainty and Risk." FINANCIAL EXECUTIVE 37 (August 1969): 56-62.

Discusses management techniques, cost, and revenue comparisons for competing corporate investments.

Elnicki, R.A. "ROI Simulations for Investment Decisions." MANAGEMENT ACCOUNTING 51 (February 1970): 37-41.

Deals with the use of return on investment simulations by management for deciding on order rankings for investment alternatives of similar magnitudes.

Enein, Gaber Abou, el-. DEVELOPMENT OF NEW PRODUCTS MARKETING AND PRICING CONSIDERATIONS. Urbana: University of Illinois, 1965. 104 p.

Ferrell, Odies Collins, Jr. "An Empirical Investigation of Attitudes Toward the Life Insurance product, Price and Promotion." Ph.D. dissertation, Louisiana State University and A. & M. College, 1972. 177 p. Ann Arbor, Mich.: University Microfilms. Order no. 72-28340.

Examines consumer perceptions and attitudes following the introduction of a new insurance product in terms of the product, its price, and promotion.

Flanagan, Robert James, Jr. "Stochastic Network Analysis as an Approach to Cost Analysis in Product Research and Development." Ph.D. dissertation, Arizona State University, 1971. 278 p. Ann Arbor, Mich.: University Microfilms. Order no. 71-13242.

By using stochastic network planning, this study attempts to develop a model for help in allocating funds for research and development and establishing a cost control program for the same.

Friedman, I. Paul. COST CONTROLS AND PROFIT IMPROVEMENT THROUGH PRODUCT ANALYSIS. Englewood Cliffs, N.J.: Prentice-Hall, 1966. 238 p.

Gale, Bradley T. "Selected Findings from the PIMS Project; Market Strategy Impact on Profitability." In PROCEEDINGS: AMERICAN MARKETING ASSOCIATION COMBINED CONFERENCE, edited by Ronald C. Curhan, p. 471. Chicago: American Marketing Association, 1974.

Goodman, S.R. "Expanded Uses of the ROI Concept." FINANCIAL EXECUTIVE 36 (March 1968): 28.

Gould, Douglas P. "Opportunity Accounting for Product Line Decisions." MANAGEMENT ACCOUNTING 50 (April 1969): 33-37.

Explains accounting concepts used in new product development. These include: price volume curves, marginal income, break-even points, and discounted cash flow.

Hackborn, Richard. "Discounted Cash Flow of the Return on Engineering Investment." IEEE SPECTRUM 2 (October 1965): 86-95.

Explains the DCF analysis which governs investment in new product programs. Takes into account the effect of the time value of money.

Imbro, Andrew. "New Products and Their Related Costs." MANAGEMENT ACCOUNTING 53 (August 1971): 43-44.

Shows how a manufacturer can process a new product through various stages of development analyzing the cost in each stage and determining whether or not to continue.

James, Barrie. "A Contemporary Approach to New Product Pricing." In THE PRICING STRATEGY, edited by B. Taylor, and G. Wills, pp. 521-33. London: Staples Press, 1969.

_____. "Market Share Strategy and Corporate Profitability." MANAGEMENT DECISION 10 (Winter 1972): 243-52.

Attempts to identify the latent factors in the areas of market vulnerability, innovation and promotion and the opportunity-cost factors which must be evaluated when planning product-marketing strategies, and the individual effect which these hidden factors can have on the brand leader's profitability. Also provides some insight into the problems of correlating brand profitability with market share as a tool for product-market strategy planning on three levels: intrabrand, interbrand, and intercompany.

Jamison, Ward. "Agency's New Rating Scale Sets Products Prices." INDUSTRIAL MARKETING 51 (March 1966): 62-65.

Describes a new, relatively simple system for pricing new products. Illustrates how a performance and price index can be used to evaluate how well a new product will compete at a given price level.

Kallimanis, William S. "Product Contribution Analysis for Multiproduct Pricing." MANAGEMENT ACCOUNTING 49 (July 1968): 3-14.

Develops a price-cost-volume-contribution analysis by the life cycle of each product. Present value of the products contribution is treated as the key information in management planning of product pricing during product introduction period.

Kamien, N.I., and Schwartz, N.L. "Limit Pricing and Uncertain Entry." ECONOMETRICA 39 (May 1971): 441-54.

Pricing policy of the existing unit is a factor affecting the likelihood of entry of competitors. Article examines the question of what should be the sellers' optimal price policy or limit price which will ban potential new entrants.

Kenny, J.M., and Meile, C.H. "How to Design Profit into New Products." MANAGEMENT REVIEW 59 (May 1970): 46–49.

Details the use of value techniques and principles to the design of a new product before it goes into actual production. This procedure to control the parameters involved in a new product development program maximizes profit. Use of value control ensures: predetermined profit margins and lower costs.

King, Edmund B. "A Control System of Profitability of New Products." MANAGEMENT ACCOUNTING 49 (July 1968): 35–42.

Discusses a closed loop system which is designed in order to minimize the profit squeeze. The system presented incorporates key component set points, two feedback circuits, accelerated communication, and sensitivity of response.

Lere, John C. PRICING TECHNIQUES FOR THE FINANCIAL EXECUTIVE. New York: Wiley, 1974. 195 p.

McDonald, Dwight J. "The Mechanics of Profit." MACHINE DESIGN 46 (19 September 1974): 114–18.

Describes the factors which affect the profit making of a new product or design improvement. Discusses the parameters of profit and explains the theory of the equations of profit.

McNeill, Winfield L. "How to Measure Product Profitability." In his EFFECTIVE COST CONTROL SYSTEMS, pp. 143–60. Englewood Cliffs, N.J.: Prentice-Hall, 1965.

Maw, J. Gordon. RETURN ON INVESTMENT: CONCEPT AND APPLICATION. New York: American Management Association, 1968. 32 p.

Miles, John Karl. AN EMPIRICAL APPROACH TO PRODUCT DESIGN. Urbana: University of Illinois, Urbana-Champaign, 1966. 56 p.

Monroe, Kent Bourdon. "A Method for Determining Product Line Prices With End-Price Constraints." Ph.D. dissertation, University of Illinois, Urbana-Champaign, 1968. 135 p. Ann Arbor: University Microfilms. Order no. 69-01394.

Develops a technique for determining product line prices when product prices are limited to a specified range.

Miller, Myron M., and Viosca, Robert R. USING DIRECT COSTING FOR PROFIT AND PRODUCT IMPROVEMENT: A TOOL FOR MANAGEMENT DECISION MAKING. Englewood Cliffs, N.J.: Prentice-Hall, 1967. 239 p.

Moulson, T.J. "How Much Profit Should a New Product Make?" PRINTERS INK 291 (23 July 1965): 13-20.

> Explains how to solve the problem which management frequently faces when planning the introduction of new products, that of determining the optimum margin-to-volume relationship to achieve satisfactory profitability for the operation as a whole. Illustrates the methods of arriving at the needed volume-margin requirements.

Murray, John R. "Sensitivity Analysis in the Return on Investment Computation." MANAGEMENT ACCOUNTING 50 (May 1969): 23-25.

> Described the application of sensitivity analysis and the return on investment concept.

Newman, M.S. "Return on Investment: An Analysis of the Concept." MANAGEMENT SERVICES 3 (July 1966): 15-23.

Oxenfeldt, Alfred Richard. PRICING STRATEGIES. New York: AMACOM, Division of the American Management Association, 1975. 255 p.

> New product pricing differs from old product price in its uncertainty regarding conditions of cost and demand. Initial guess work must be correct by constant monitoring. Article, in one chapter, describes how.

_____. "Product Line Pricing." HARVARD BUSINESS REVIEW 44 (July-August 1966): 137-44.

> Discusses the considerations which operate in selecting price differentials between items within the same product class and also of complimentary items within a product mix.

Pashigian, B. Peter. "Limit Price and the Market Share of the Leading Firm." JOURNAL OF INDUSTRIAL ECONOMICS 16 (1968): 165-77.

Robinson, Bruce, and Lakhani, Chet. "Dynamic Price Models for New-Product Planning." MANAGEMENT SCIENCE 21 (June 1975): 1113-22.

> Deals with long-run pricing strategies pertinent to certain real business situations.

Rutenberg, David P. "Three Pricing Policies for a Multiproduct Multi-National Company." MANAGEMENT SCIENCE 17 (April 1971): B451-B461.

> When the company is multinational, pricing becomes complicated by the issues of centralization and autonomy of national subsidiaries. Article examines three pricing policy schemes.

Schiff, J.S., and Schiff, Michael. "New Sales Management Tool: ROAM." HARVARD BUSINESS REVIEW 45 (July-August 1967): 59-66.

Discusses the concept and application of return on assets managed
which is said to be very important in introducing a new product
just as much as revenues and costs. Describes a training program
for marketers in the use of the concept.

Seglin, Leonard. "How to Price New Products." In THE PRICING STRATEGY,
edited by B. Taylor, and G. Wills, pp. 556–60. London: Staples Press, 1969.

Sohns, V.E. "Cost Analyses for New Products." AMERICAN OIL CHEMISTS
SOCIETY JOURNAL 48 (September 1971): 362A.

Stone, David John. "The Use of Input–Output Analysis As a Planning Tool for
Multi–Product Firms." Ph.D. dissertation, New York University, 1969. 213 p.
Ann Arbor, Mich.: University Microfilms. Order no. 70-03115.

Examines whether Leontief's input–output model can be used to assist the multiproduct, vertically integrated firm in arriving at short-
run product strategy decision.

Stork Photos, Inc. "New Product Profitability." In MARKETING: TEXT CASES
AND READINGS, edited by Harry L. Hansen, pp. 347–51. Homewood, Ill.:
R.D. Irwin, 1968.

Taylor, Bernard, and Wills, G. PRICING STRATEGY. London: Staples Press,
1969. 566 p.

Tull, Donald S. "The Relationship of Actual and Predicted Sales and Profits
in New Product Introductions." JOURNAL OF BUSINESS 40 (July 1967):
233–50.

Provides descriptive data on the questions concerning the relationships between predicted and actual sales and profits of new products introduced. Test sales and profit forecast hypotheses.

Tull, Donald S., and Rutemiller, Herbert C. "Note on the Relationship of
Actual and Predicted Sales and Profits in New Product Introductions." JOUR-
NAL OF BUSINESS 41 (July 1968): 385–87.

Gives the results of a regression analysis relating to forecast and
actual sales and profits of new products.

Udell, Jon G. "The Pricing Strategies of United States Industry." In PROCEED-
INGS: AMERICAN MARKETING ASSOCIATION COMBINED CONFERENCE,
edited by Thomas V. Greer, pp. 151–55. Chicago: American Marketing Association, 1973.

Survey methods used in pricing 485 successful products in an attempt to explain the major pricing strategies available for the
American executive.

Watson, Guy E. "How Much Will That New Product Cost?" MACHINE DE-
SIGN 45 (19 April 1973): 96-101.

Forecast product cost is based on historical data. In this method,
records are kept of the cost of previous products and components,
and are used to make cost forecasts on new but analogous items.
The other method discussed is the cost evaluation committee method.
This can be used only if the company is willing to risk development
money to build a model of the proposed new product.

Weiss, E.B. "Slash New Product Costs With Conceptual Testing." ADVERTIS-
ING AGE 40 (3 February 1969): 76.

Wilkinson, James D. "Profit Performance Concepts and the Product Manager."
MANAGEMENT SERVICES 5 (July-August 1968): 17-25.

Explains how a product manager measures financial performance of
new products. Tells how he can make use of concepts like return
on investment, discounted cash flow, payback, and average rate
of return.

Wilson, J.R.M. "Profitability as a Tool in Product Planning." ARTHUR YOUNG
JOURNAL 14 (Winter 1966): 12-16.

Woodside, Arch G. "Relation of Price to Perception of Quality of New Products." JOURNAL OF APPLIED PSYCHOLOGY 59 (February 1974): 116-18.

Discusses the results of an experiment where a new product, an
electric lunch box, was shown to six groups of twelve construction
workers, using an eleven-point rating scale on advantage, use,
and quality, plus a questionnaire selecting favorable and unfavorable words to describe the product. Results indicated that a linear
regression model significantly fitted the scale responses for the
treatment.

_____. "Retail Experiments in Pricing a New Product." JOURNAL OF RE-
TAILING 50 (Fall 1974): 56-65.

Study of a new electric lunch box. Author finds positive price-
quality and price-demand relationships consistent with economic
demand theory.

Wortuba, Thomas R., and Nelson, R.H. "Evaluating Price Alternatives for a
New Product." AKRON BUSINESS AND ECONOMIC REVIEW 4 (Summer
1973): 9-14.

Wright, M.G. "New Product Pricing Strategies." CERTIFIED ACCOUNTANT
(February 1973): 91-93.

Chapter 10

CASE STUDIES AND CASE HISTORIES

Adler, Lee. "Time Lag in New Product Development." JOURNAL OF MAR-
KETING 30 (January 1966): 17–21.

It takes much longer to develop new products than usually is
thought to be the case. Here the author analyzes forty-two case
histories to illustrate that contention. Both consumer and industrial goods are included.

"Allen-Bradley Company: Addition of New Products By a Manufacturer of Control Devices." In CASES IN MARKETING: DECISIONS, POLICIES STRATEGIES,
edited by Richard R. Still and Clyde E. Harris, pp. 92–94. Englewood Cliffs,
N.J.: Prentice-Hall, 1972.

"The Allgood Drug Company Develops a New Athlete's Food Remedy." In
MARKETING MANAGEMENT AND CASES, edited by William M. Weilbacher,
pp. 97–122. New York: Macmillan, 1970.

"American Telephone and Telegraph Co. Princess Telephone. Use of Sales
Test and Consumer Survey Before Marketing a New Product." In ADVANCED
CASES IN MARKETING MANAGEMENT, edited by Edward C. Bursk and
Stephen A. Greyser, pp. 21–27. Englewood Cliffs, N.J.: Prentice-Hall, 1968.

Angell, B. "Why do New Products Fail." VITAL SPEECHES 35 (15 November
1968): 91–96.

Discusses the reasons for so many new product failures. It is estimated that 90 percent of the new product introductions result in
failure each year. Several case studies of both successful and
failing products are presented.

"Bear Vinyl Foam Tape. Introduction of New Product." In MARKETING
PROBLEMS: SITUATIONS FOR ANALYSIS, edited by Ernest B. Uhr, pp. 47–78.
New York: Wiley, 1973.

"Beecham Ford and Drinks Division: Prefillings Development and Test Market

Problems." In CASE STUDIES IN MARKETING, edited by G.B. Giles. London: Macdonald and Evans, 1967.

"Behind the Design: Background Stories of Some of this Year's Design Council Awards Winners." ENGINEERING 217 (September 1977): 736-39.

> Summarizes object lessons learned from award winning design's background stories. Companies were also chosen to give the widest variety of case studies. All products were introduced with aim of making profits. Case studies also illustrate the commercial pressure as main spur to the designers.

Bingham, J.S., ed. BRITISH CASES IN MARKETING. London: Business Books, 1969. 183 p.

> Includes case histories to illustrate ways in which the risk of new product development might be reduced. The entire spectrum of marketing mix is examined for each of the firms.

Bird, K. "Key Factors in Successful New Foods." FOOD TECHNOLOGY 23 (September 1969): 1159-61.

> Stresses that successful new products must satisfy a demand, be technologically sound and economically feasible, and offer the innovator an opportunity for profit. Article presents three examples of new product innovations where the three criteria for a successful product are satisfied.

Briscoe, G., et al. "The Market Development of New Industrial Products." EUROPEAN JOURNAL OF MARKETING 6 (Spring 1972): 7-16.

> Contains studies concerning an aluminum company and a steel company to illustrate the types of problems which are frequently encountered in attempting to build up primary market demand of new industrial materials and products. Cases were developed through interviews with personnel at various levels in the organizational hierarchy.

Brown, Kevin V. "How to Make a New Product From an Old Product." PRODUCT MANAGEMENT 5 (December 1976): 26-31.

> Case study about a famous old product "Ovaltine" that found itself towards the end of its product life cycle. It was revived as a new product with application of marketing techniques.

Bylinsky, Gene. "How Intel Won its Bet on Memory Chips." FORTUNE 88 (November 1973): 142-47.

> Relates the case of a company with a new product and the development of a market where none previously existed.

"Cadbury Brothers, Ltd. Cakes: A Major Diversification." In CASE STUDIES IN MARKETING, edited by G.B. Giles. London: Macdonald and Evans, 1967.

Casey, J.P. "High Fructose Corn Syrup: A Case History of Innovation." RESEARCH MANAGEMENT 19 (September 1976): 27-32.

> Traces the sequence of events from basic discovery and conception of a new, revolutionary sweetener to its commercialization. Explains why it is such a time-consuming process. Also sets out eight points that were lessons learned from the above.

"Cessna Aircraft Company: Introduction of New Product." In MARKETING PROBLEMS: SITUATIONS FOR ANALYSIS, edited by Ernest B. Uhr, pp. 59-67. New York: Wiley, 1973.

Cohen, A.B. "New Venture Development at DuPont." LONG RANGE PLANNING 2 (June 1970): 7-10.

> Case study of the introduction of a new system for manufacturing electric circuitry at DuPont. Describes the system at the company for encouraging innovation.

Collins, M. "Product Testing." In EFFECTIVE USE OF MARKET RESEARCH, edited by J. Aucamp. London: Staples Press, 1971.

"Commodity Chemical Company: Marketing Strategies for New Products." In ADVANCED CASES IN MARKETING MANAGEMENT, edited by Edward C. Bursk and Stephen A. Greyser, pp. 156-65. Englewood Cliffs, N.J.: Prentice-Hall, 1968.

Cooklin, L. "Rumalade: A Cautionary Tale." In BRITISH CASES IN MARKETING, edited by J.S. Bingham. London: Business Books, 1969.

Coram, T., ed. CASES IN MARKETING AND MARKETING RESEARCH. London: Crosby, Lockwood, 1969.

Cunningham, M.T., and Hammond, M.A.A. "Product Strategy for Industrial Goods." JOURNAL OF MANAGEMENT STUDIES 6 (May 1969): 223-42.

> Examines the contribution of product planning to the improvement of the business performance of several engineering companies. Provides case history portraying the formulation and implementation of a product strategy by one company for dealing with declining profitability and market share.

Day, C. "How to Set the Stage for a New Product Success." SALES MANAGEMENT 94 (1 January 1965): 35-41; 94 (5 February 1965): 59-60.

> Contains case histories of new products which proved successful in

the market after having gone through application of improved test market techniques.

"Dayton Shirts, Inc.: New Products Promotion." In BASIC MARKETING, edited by Robert S. Raymond, pp. 46-47. Cleveland: World, 1967.

Dean, J.M., and Buck, R.C. "Two Case Studies on New Products for the Building Industry." IMRA JOURNAL (November 1966): 96.

> Market research survey for a new product in the field of polystyrene foam is studied. Second case history deals with marketing research in the field of pitch fiber pipes.

"Dick, Rice-Inventor: New Product Test Marketing." In BASIC PROBLEMS IN MARKETING MANAGEMENT, edited by Edwin C. Greif, pp. 103-5. Belmont, Calif.: Wadsworth, 1967.

"Dixie Instruments, Inc.: New Product Evaluation." In CASES IN MARKETING MANAGEMENT, edited by Edward C. Bursk, pp. 98-102. Englewood Cliffs, N.J.: Prentice-Hall, 1965.

"Dow Chemical Company: Effect of High Price On New Product." In BASIC MARKETING: A MANAGERIAL APPROACH, edited by Jerome E. McCarthy, pp. 699-700. Homewood, Ill.: R.D. Irwin, 1968.

"Dow Chemical Company: Introduction of a New Product." In MARKETING TEXT CASES AND READINGS, edited by Harry L. Hansen, pp. 397-404. Homewood, Ill.: R.D. Irwin, 1968.

"Duncan House: Consumers Preference Test Before Marketing a New Product." In MARKETING TEXT, CASES AND READINGS, edited by Harry L. Hansen, pp. 382-85. Homewood, Ill.: R.D. Irwin, 1968.

"Earthworm Tractor Company: A New Product Line." In CASES IN PRODUCT POLICY PRICING TACTICS AND COMPETITIVE STRATEGY, edited by Chester R. Wasson, pp. 235-39. St. Charles, Ill.: Challenge Books, 1972.

Ehrenberg, A.S.C., and Goodhardt, G.J. "Repeat Buying of a New Brand - A 10-point Case History." BRITISH JOURNAL OF MARKETING 1 (Autumn 1968): 200-05.

> Stresses the importance of past experience of a wide range of similar cases for viable interpretation of repeat - buying data for a new brand.

Engel, James F., et al., eds. CASES IN PROMOTIONAL STRATEGY. Homewood, Ill.: R.D. Irwin, 1971. 382 p.

" Facilities Corp. Technical Equipment and Office Machine Division: Problem with New Product Line of an Equipment Manufacturer." In CASES IN MARKETING DECISIONS, POLICIES, STRATEGIES, edited by Richard R. Still and Clyde E. Harris, Jr., pp. 80-84. Englewood Cliffs, N.J.: Prentice-Hall, 1972.

"Ford Motor Company, Special Products Division. Naming a New Product Line." In INTRODUCTION TO MARKETING MANAGEMENT, TEXT AND CASES, edited by James D. Scott and Martin R. Warshaw, pp. 226-31. Homewood, Ill.: R.D. Irwin, 1969.

"General Foods. Maxim Coffee. New Product Development." In MARKETING RESEARCH, TEXT AND CASES, edited by Harper W. Boyd, Jr. and Ralph Westfall, pp. 730-40. Homewood, Ill.: R.D. Irwin, 1972.

Gerard, William J. "An Adventure into Product and Market Development." PAPER, FILM AND FOIL CONVERTOR 42 (July 1968): 31-33.

> Case history method illustrates techniques of new product introduction in this article about polypropylene film for twist-wrapped candy. Author provides a step-by-step analysis of market research, project review, and product development. Report includes a proposed weekly timetable for new product introduction.

"Giantcliff Company: New Product Promotion." In ELEMENTS OF MARKETING, edited by Paul D. Converse, et al, pp. 681-82. 7th ed. Englewood Cliffs, N.J.: Prentice Hall, 1965.

Giles, George Bernard, ed. CASE STUDIES IN MARKETING. London: Macdonald and Evans, 1967. 248 p.

"Great Shapes Solve Product Design Problems." MODERN METALS 33 (September 1977): 34-38.

> Shows how resourceful new product design can cut manufacturing cost while retaining quality and enhancing product appearance.

"Harold F. Ritchie, Inc.: New Product Promotion." In INTRODUCTION TO MARKETING MANAGEMENT: TEST AND CASES, edited by Stewart H. Rewoldt, et al, pp. 507-11. Homewood, Ill.: R.D. Irwin, 1969.

Hayes, John F. "The UPC Success Story." In PROCEEDINGS: AMERICAN MARKETING ASSOCIATION COMBINED CONFERENCE, edited by Edward M. Mazze, p. 393. Chicago: American Marketing Association, 1975.

Hayhurst, R. "The Alpine Launch." In CASES IN MARKETING AND MARKETING RESEARCH, edited by T. Coram. London: Crosby Lockwood, 1969.

"Hazard Sales Company: New Product Distribution." In MARKETING TEXT, CASES AND READINGS, edited by Harry L. Hansen, pp. 196-200. Homewood, Ill.: R.D. Irwin, 1968.

"Hillcrest Products, Inc. New Product Promotion." In FUNDAMENTALS OF MARKETING, edited by William J. Stanton, pp. 558-59. 2d ed. New York: McGraw-Hill, 1967.

"Hillcrest Products, Inc. Pricing a New Product." In FUNDAMENTALS OF MARKETING, edited by William J. Stanton, pp. 484-85. 2d ed. New York: McGraw-Hill, 1967.

"Holmes Manufacturing Company. Marketing Strategy for New Product." In INTRODUCTION TO MARKETING MANAGEMENT, edited by Stewart H. Rewoldt, et al., pp. 207-13. Homewood, Ill.: R.D. Irwin, 1969.

"Home Products Universal's. Handsome Boy Super Copper Brightner -- Test Marketing." In MARKETING MANAGEMENT CASES, edited by William M. Weilbacher, pp. 16-31. New York: Macmillan, 1970.

"How a New Item is Born." PROGRESSIVE GROCER 46 (August 1967): 54-59.

> Behind-the-scenes look at the research testing and merchandising that went into the development of a new snack food. Case history is offered as an example of the food manufacturing industry's efforts to keep the supermarket selling scene a profitable one through new product development.

"Inland Steel Co. New Product Acceptance." In BASIC MARKETING: A MANAGERIAL APPROACH, edited by Jerome E. McCarthy, pp. 692-94. Homewood, Ill.: R.D. Irwin, 1968.

"Insul-Kool. New Product Marketing Strategy." In PRINCIPLES OF MARKETING: MANAGEMENT VIEW, edited by Richard Buskirk, pp. 814-17. New York: Holt, Rinehart and Winston, 1966.

"John Bache, Inc. New Product Pricing." In BASIC PROBLEMS IN MARKETING MANAGEMENT, edited by Edwin C. Greif, pp. 221-23. Belmont, Calif.: Wadsworth, 1967.

Jones, Harold Ralph. "Constraints to Product Development and Marketing of Medical Electronic Equipment Industry." Ph.D. dissertation, University of Michigan, 1968. 291 p. Ann Arbor: University Microfilms. Order no. 69-12147.

> Case study into the problems which impede the development and marketing of new medical electronic equipment. Chief problem

seemed to be the lack of a demand analysis and small degree of awareness by doctors of the product. Suggests how to deal with these problems.

"Kiddies Kitchen, Inc. Test Marketing." In MARKETING--TEXT, CASES AND READINGS, edited by Harry L. Hansen, pp. 340-45. Homewood, Ill.: R.D. Irwin, 1968.

Kleiman, Herbert S. "A Case Study of Innovation." BUSINESS HORIZONS 9 (Winter 1966): 63-70.

Through a study of the development of the integrated circuit, the author examines the government - industry relationship as a new product is innovated. Although not smooth, it is an independent relationship in which government acts as research and development patron, and industry is relied upon to produce results and to expand on the opportunity potential of the innovation.

Klein, Frederick C. "Taking the Plunge: Putting New Product On Market is Costly, Complicated and Risky." WALL STREET JOURNAL, 18 February 1971, 1.

Korman, Natheniel L. "Planning a New Venture: A Scientific Approach." In PROCEEDINGS: AMERICAN MARKETING ASSOCIATION SPRING CONFERENCE, edited by David L. Sparks, pp. 27-28. Chicago: American Marketing Association, 1970.

Case study of a new business venture planning.

Levit, Theodore. "The New Markets: Think Before You Leap." HARVARD BUSINESS REVIEW 47 (May-June 1969): 53-67.

Examines with the use of actual case histories the question of when and how to pursue a new product opportunity.

"Lipto Lighter Manufacturing Company. New Product Evaluation." In BASIC PROBLEMS IN MARKETING MANAGEMENT, edited by Edwin C. Greif, pp. 107-11. Belmont, Calif.: Wadsworth, 1967.

"Locke Company. New Product Development." In MARKETING RESEARCH TEXT AND CASES, edited by Harper W. Boyd, Jr. and Ralph Westfall, pp. 723-30. Homewood, Ill.: R.D. Irwin, 1972.

"McGregor Company. New Product Organization." In FUNDAMENTALS OF MARKETING, by William J. Stanton, pp. 243-46. 2d ed. New York: McGraw-Hill, 1967.

McNab, Bruce E. "To Be or Not To Be or the Imperative for Product Develop-

ment." In PROCEEDINGS: AMERICAN MARKETING ASSOCIATION COM-
BINED CONFERENCE, edited by Edward M. Mazze, pp. 379-87. Chicago:
American Marketing Association, 1975.

> Case study of importance of new product development for corporate
> survival and growth.

"Macto Co. New Product Bidding." In MARKETING--TEXT, CASES AND
READINGS, edited by Harry L. Hansen, pp. 784-89. Homewood, Ill.: R.D.
Irwin, 1968.

"Mal Mills Company. New Product Distribution." In BASIC PROBLEMS IN
MARKETING MANAGEMENT, edited by Edwin C. Greif, pp. 143-35. Belmont, Calif.: Wadsworth, 1967.

"The Margeann Chemical Company. New Product Planning." In INDUSTRIAL
MARKETING, edited by Ralph S. Alexander et al., pp. 638-41. 3d ed.
Homewood, Ill.: R.D. Irwin, 1967.

"Merrill, Inc. New Product Marketing Strategy." In INTRODUCTION TO
MARKETING MANAGEMENT: TEXT AND CASES, edited by Stewart H. Rewoldt,
et al., pp. 690-95. Homewood, Ill.: R.D. Irwin, 1969.

"Miladys Shop. New Product Selection Criteria." In RETAIL MANAGEMENT
PROBLEMS, edited by C.H. McGregory and Paul C. Chankonas, pp. 108-10.
4th ed. Homewood, Ill.: R.D. Irwin, 1970.

"Modern Shirt Company. Demand Sampling of New Product." In BASIC MAR-
KETING A MANAGERIAL APPROACH, edited by Jerome E. McCarthy, pp.
738-41. Homewood, Ill.: R.D. Irwin, 1968.

"Modern Shirt Company. New Product Planning." In BASIC MARKETING: A
MANAGERIAL APPROACH, edited by Jerome E. McCarthy, pp. 742-43. Homewood, Ill.: R.D. Irwin, 1968.

"Morefiber Wire Rope Company. Change in Sales Force New Product." In
BASIC MARKETING: A MANAGERIAL APPROACH, edited by Jerome E.
McCarthy, pp. 711-12. Homewood, Ill.: R.D. Irwin, 1968.

Morner, Aimee L. "A Product is Born." FORTUNE, February 1977, 125-33.

> Examines some obstacles to new product development, using an
> actual case study. These include personality clashes, labor prob-
> lems, interdepartmental communications gap, and technological
> road blocks.

"Motor Car Corp. Introduction of a New Product." In MARKETING PROB-

LEMS: SITUATIONS FOR ANALYSIS, edited by Ernst B. Uhr, pp. 68-84. New York: Wiley, 1973.

"National Foods Company. Opinion Polls of New Product Introduction." In BASIC PROBLEMS IN MARKETING MANAGEMENT, edited by Edwin C. Grief, pp. 117-19. Belmont, Calif.: Wadsworth, 1967.

"National Manufacturing Company. Reorganization of Marketing Department to Increase New Product Sales." In BASIC MARKETING: A MANAGERIAL AP- PROACH, edited by Jerome E. McCarthy, pp. 685-86. Homewood, Ill.: R. D. Irwin, 1968.

"New Products Aluminum Corp. Market Entry For New Products." In BASIC PROBLEMS IN MARKETING MANAGEMENT, edited by Edwin C. Greif, pp. 169-71. Belmont, Calif.: Wadsworth, 1967.

"The Ordway Company. New Product Diversification." In INDUSTRIAL MAR- KETING, edited by Ralph S. Alexander and Richard M. Hill, pp. 648-53. 3d ed. Homewood, Ill.: R.D. Irwin, 1967.

Parry, Eugene W. "New Product Management: Part II: A Case History." ELECTRICAL ENGINEER 28 (February 1969): 31-37.

Surveys a successful company's practice regarding new product planning and evaluation.

"The Perlick Company. New Product Competition." In BASIC MARKETING: A MANAGERIAL APPROACH, edited by Jerome E. McCarthy, pp. 697-99. Home- wood, Ill.: R.D. Irwin, 1968.

Perry, M., and Perry, A. "The Case of Avocado." EUROPEAN RESEARCH 2 (January 1974): 10-16, 36.

Case study using consumer research to plan the launching of an unfamiliar, new product in the market.

Pessemier, Edgar A. "A New Product Venture." BUSINESS HORIZONS 11 (August 1968): 5-19.

Contains case histories illustrating risk analysis of new products.

Peterson, R.W. "New Venture Management in a Large Company." HARVARD BUSINESS REVIEW 46 (May-June 1967): 68-76.

Describes the case study of the DuPont company's new product programs. Also discusses new venture organizations, idea genera- tion methods, and new product evaluation procedures.

"Picturephone Service: A Market Development Problem." In CASES IN PRODUCT POLICY, PRICING TACTICS AND COMPETITIVE STRATEGY, edited by Chestor R. Wasson, pp. 77-80. St. Charles, Ill.: Challenge Books, 1972.

"Pop-Tent. New Product Introduction." In INTRODUCTION TO MARKETING MANAGEMENT: TEXT AND CASES, edited by Stewart H. Rewoldt, et al., pp. 27-29. Homewood, Ill.: R.D. Irwin, 1969.

Pymont, Brian C., et al. "Towards the Elimination of Risk from Investment in New Products." EUROPEAN SOCIETY FOR OPINION SURVEYS AND MARKET RESEARCH (ESOMAR) CONGRESS, Venice, 1976, pp. 169-93.

Presents case histories illustrating the ability of micromarket testing to provide the basis of accurate volume estimates, to differentiate between price levels, and to provide a speed of response and degree of flexibility which would be beyond conventional test marketing.

"Rainbow Products, Inc. New Product Planning and Organization." In ADVANCED CASES IN MARKETING MANAGEMENT, edited by Edward C. Bursk and Stephen A. Greyser, pp. 177-84. Englewood Cliffs, N.J.: Prentice Hall, 1968.

"Raynell's Company. New Product Acceptance." In BASIC PROBLEMS IN MARKETING MANAGEMENT, edited by Edwin C. Greif, pp. 302-4. Belmont, Calif.: Wadsworth, 1967.

"Red Cedar Shingles Bureau. Trade Association Research Study." In PRINCIPLES OF MARKETING: THE MANAGEMENT VIEW, edited by Richard Buskirk, pp. 780-82. Rev. ed. New York: Holt, Rinehart and Winston, 1966.

Reynolds, William H. "The Edsel Ten Years Later: Faulty Execution of a Sound Marketing Plan." BUSINESS HORIZONS 10 (Fall 1967): 39-46.

Examines how and why a sound marketing plan and a promising new product failed to live up to expectations.

Robertson, Andrew. "Multinational Expertise is Not Enough: The Sobering Story of Corfan (Market Resistance)." MULTINATIONAL BUSINESS 4 (July 1975): 1-7.

"Rockemorgan Company. Development of Money Collecting Machine." In MARKETING MANAGEMENT CASES, edited by William M. Weilbacher, pp. 32-74. New York: Macmillan, 1970.

Rondeau, H.F. "1-3-9 Rule for Product Cost Estimation." MACHINE DESIGN 47 (21 August 1975): 50-53.

Explains the basic rules involved in coming up with an estimated cost of a new product which comes as close to reality as possible.

"Royds (London), Ltd. The Role of Research in a New Product Launch." In THE EFFECTIVE USE OF MARKET RESEARCH, edited by J. Aucamp. London: Staples Press, 1971.

"Samco, Inc. Marketing Strategy of a New Product." In MARKETING--TEXT, CASES AND READINGS, edited by Harry L. Hansen, pp. 345-46. Homewood, Ill.: R.D. Irwin, 1968.

Samuels, I. "The Launch of Kerrygold Butter." In BRITISH CASES IN MARKETING, edited by J.S. Bingham. London: Business Books, 1969.

Shoraka, Rahim. "The Determination of Market Potential for a New Food Product: A Case Study of Guava." Ph.D. dissertation, University of Hawaii, 1973.

Siekman, Philip. "The Plane That Could Teach Industry to Fly." FORTUNE, April 1971, 96-99.

Case study of how Cessna Aircraft introduced a new jet in the aircraft market and was successful.

"Smile Toothpaste Company: New Product Development." In BASIC MARKETING: A MANAGERIAL APPROACH, edited by Jerome E. McCarthy, pp. 100-101. Homewood, Ill.: R.D. Irwin, 1968.

Sobin, Sharon. "At Nuclepore, They Don't Work for G.E. Anymore." FORTUNE, December 1973, 144-56.

Case study of a large high-technology company developing a new filter product with only a small potential market.

"Tidewater Mills, Inc. Market Study--For New Production Introduction." CASES IN MARKETING MANAGEMENT, edited by Edward C. Bursk, pp. 94-98. Englewood Cliffs, N.J.: Prentice-Hall, 1965.

"Towland Corp. New Product Promotion." In CASES IN MARKETING MANAGEMENT, edited by Edward C. Bursk, pp. 68-70. Englewood Cliffs, N.J.: Prentice-Hall, 1965.

"Trolex Sales Company. New Product Pricing." In INTRODUCTION TO MARKETING MANAGEMENT: TEXT AND CASES, edited by Stewart H. Rewoldt, et al., pp. 579-85. Homewood, Ill.: R.D. Irwin, 1969.

Usher, J.N. "The Updating of Andrews." In BRITISH CASES IN MARKETING, edited by J.S. Bingham. London: Business Books, 1969.

"Van Wart Chemical, Inc. Mathematical Model for New Products." In MAR-KETING--TEXT, CASES AND READINGS, edited by Harry L. Hansen, pp. 404-18. Homewood, Ill.: R.D. Irwin, 1968.

"Ventures, Inc. Testing New Products." In MARKETING, TEXT CASES AND HEADINGS, edited by Harry L. Hansen, pp. 336-40. Homewood, Ill.: R.D. Irwin, 1968.

Wank, Martin. "Introducing New Technology Takes Perseverance, Patience." INDUSTRIAL MARKETING 62 (August 1977): 34-36.

> Describes how PolyGulf Associates developed a program to break "the skepticism barrier" in introducing its new soluble oil coal process to the technical engineering world.

Wasson, Chester R., ed. CASES IN PRODUCT POLICY, PRICING TACTICS AND COMPETITIVE STRATEGY. St. Charles, Ill.: Challenge Books, 1972. 267 p.

Webster, Frederick Arthur II. "A Theory of Product Diversification Strategy With Selected Case Histories." Ph.D. dissertation, University of California, Berkeley, 1965. 255 p. Ann Arbor: University Microfilms. Order no. 66-03717.

Wills, G. "The Reading Evening Post." In CASES IN MARKETING AND MARKETING RESEARCH, edited by T. Coram. London: Crosby Lockwood, 1969.

"The Wonder Foods Company and Market Potential for Picture Pretty Deluxe Cake Mixes. (New line Research)." In MARKETING MANAGEMENT CASES, edited by William M. Weilbacher, pp. 75-93. New York: Macmillan, 1970.

"Wonder Foods Company and the New Friendly Girl Market Test." In MAR-KETING MANAGEMENT CASES, edited by William M. Weilbacher, pp. 233-48. New York: Macmillan, 1970.

"Wonder Foods Company and New Friendly Girl Product Development (Motivational Research and Concept Testing)." In MARKETING MANAGEMENT CASES, edited by William M. Weilbacher, pp. 220-32. New York: Macmillan, 1970.

"Wonder Foods Company Develops a Flanker Product. (Market Analysis)." In MARKETING MANAGEMENT CASES, edited by William M. Weilbacher, pp. 124-57. New York: Macmillan, 1970.

"Worley-Sewell Company. The Addition of a New Line in a Clothing Company." In CASE IN MARKETING, edited by Richard R. Still and Clyde E. Harris, pp. 59-61. Englewood Cliffs, N.J.: Prentice-Hall, 1972.

Wright, A.T. "Quaker Puffed Wheat: Rebirth of a Brand." In BRITISH CASES IN MARKETING, edited by J.S. Bingham. London: Business Books, 1969.

"Wright Pen Company. New Product Pricing." In BASIC MARKETING, edited by Robert S. Raymond, pp. 270-72. Cleveland: World, 1967.

"Yard-Man, Inc. New Product Addition." In INTRODUCTION TO MARKETING MANAGEMENT: TEXT AND CASES, edited by Stewart H. Rewoldt, et al., pp. 218-25. Homewood, Ill.: R.D. Irwin, 1969.

"Yorktown Manufacturing Company. Adding a Secondary Product Line by a Copper Fabricator." In CASES IN MARKETING, edited by Richard R. Still and Clyde E. Harris, pp. 62-64. Englewood Cliffs, N.J.: Prentice-Hall, 1972.

Chapter 11

TESTING AND EVALUATION

Abed, M.I., and Yaple, J.L. "Estimating the Demand for New Products." BELL LAB RECORD 55 (June 1977): 154-58.

> Describes a method for the economic evaluation of the new product relative to the demand for its predecessors.

"Advertisers Take Harder Look at the Traditional Test Methods." ADVERTISING AGE 43 (16 October 1972): 3.

> Producers of packaged goods are starting to doubt the effectiveness of the standard test marketing procedure. They feel that more testing and research should be conducted before the product gets to the test marketing stage. Several case studies of successful and non-successful new food products are presented.

"Advice on Test Marketing." DUNS REVIEW 85 (May 1965): 74.

> Test marketing decisions should be made quickly during the test marketing phase, because it is expensive to keep a failing product on the market too long. The author feels that some failures are inevitable, and if no failures are found, the test marketing procedure is probably faulty.

"Amusement Parks Can Test Products." ADVERTISING AGE 45 (25 November 1974): 49.

> Claims that amusement parks can be used as test markets for new products. Paid admissions are higher than most other amusement or sporting events. New products can be marketed in the parks and, through the use of coupons, their success can be measured.

Angelus, Ted. "Experts Choice: Top Test Markets." MARKETING/COMMUNICATIONS 298 (May 1970): 29-38.

> Selecting test markets by whim is passe. The accelerated rate of new product introductions, cost of testing, and the cost of failure require a formal set of criteria for the selection of the most ef-

ficient markets. Thirty-four prime test markets, as selected by the criteria described in this article, are listed.

Axelrod, Joel N. "Reducing Advertising Failures by Concept Testing." JOURNAL OF MARKETING 38 (April 1974): 41-42.

Explains how concept testing can be used to identify and develop new product ideas.

Beattie, D.W. "Marketing a New Product." OPERATIONAL RESEARCH QUARTERLY 20 (December 1969): 429-35.

Explains how managers and researchers decide the question of whether to test market a new product by use of decision tree techniques.

Berdy, Edwin M. "Testing Test Market Predictions." JOURNAL OF MARKETING RESEARCH 29 (May 1965): 196-98.

Reply by Jack A. Gold can be found in the same journal (May 1965): 198-200. Discusses the view that current techniques of test market predictions are poor and stresses need for reevaluation.

Bloom, J.E. "Match the Concept and the Product." JOURNAL OF ADVERTISING RESEARCH 17 (October 1977): 25-27.

Describes the technique called product perceptor bipolar scales and its application in concept testing when different alternatives of the same concept are to be tested against the same product prototype.

Brenner, Vincent C. "Evaluation of Product Pricing Models." In ACCOUNTING FOR MANAGERIAL DECISION MAKING, edited by Don T. Decoster, pp. 177-95. Los Angeles: Melville, 1974.

Brown, David. "Test Marketing: A User's View." EUROPEAN SOCIETY FOR OPINION SURVEYS AND MARKET RESEARCH (ESOMAR) CONGRESS, Brussels, September 1966, p. 15.

Brown, Gordon, et al. "Monadic Testing of New Products - An Old Problem and Some Partial Solutions." JOURNAL OF THE MARKET RESEARCH SOCIETY 15 (April 1973): 112-31.

Describes pros and cons of blind paired comparison testing. Attempts to minimize the discrepancies between research results and test market results by resorting to monadic testing.

Cadbury, N.D. "When, Where and How to Test Market." HARVARD BUSINESS REVIEW 53 (May-June 1975): 96-105.

Guidelines on how to measure the results of test marketing, how to select the regions for the tests and how long to test. Also analyzes why new products fail, despite successful test market results.

Caffyn, J.M. CONCEPT TESTING. London: Market Research Society Course on Research for New Products, 1968.

Calabaro, Natalie. "Bayesian Theory in the Evaluation of New Product Ideas." JOURNAL OF THE ACADEMY OF MARKETING SCIENCE 1 (September 1973): 12-24.

Carter, Eugene E. "What are the Risks in Risk Analysis." HARVARD BUSINESS REVIEW 50 (July-August 1972): 72-82.

Examines some of the successful and unsuccessful applications of risk analysis of new products and old products.

Catry, Bernard, and Chevalier, Michael. "Market Share Strategy and the Product Life Cycle." JOURNAL OF MARKETING 38 (October 1974): 29-34.

Explains how both these concepts are used in evaluating investment alternatives.

Clarke, Ken, and Roe, M. "The Marketing Mix Test - Relating Expectations and Performance." MARKET RESEARCH SOCIETY CONFERENCE, March 1977, pp. 207-16.

Describes a marketing model for a new product launch based on the assumption of a three-stage process of awareness-trial-repeat purchase. It is first simulated under laboratory conditions evaluating responses with standard questionnaire techniques.

Clarke, T.J. "Product Testing in New Product Development." JOURNAL OF MARKET RESEARCH SOCIETY 9, no. 3 (1967): 135-46.

Claycamp, J. ESP: A NEW WAY TO PREDICT NEW PRODUCT PERFORMANCE BEFORE TEST MARKETING. New York: National Purchase Diary, 1976.

Cohen, Stanley I. "Dynamics of Quantifiable Brand Loyalty in Test Marketing." In PROCEEDINGS: AMERICAN MARKETING ASSOCIATION SUMMER CONFERENCE, edited by John S. Wright and Jack L. Goldstucker, pp. 401-19. Chicago: American Marketing Association, 1966.

Presents a consumer oriented model of loyalty that partitions the population into groups and assigns each group a probability of purchasing a product brand.

Commercial Development Association. EVALUATION OF NEW PROJECTS AND SUCCESSFUL TECHNIQUES TO IMPLEMENT THEM. Papers presented at the 1 November 1972 meeting of the Commercial Development Association held in Chicago. Ill. New York: 1973. 61 p.

"Computer in Test Marketing: Blazing New Dimensions." SALES MANAGEMENT 102 (1 March 1969): 38.

> Reports on the use of computers in test marketing situations. Various capabilities of a computer in this area are discussed as well as trends for the future. Several examples from companies using computers for test marketing procedures are reported.

"Controlled Lab Mini-Market Tests for New Products." FOOD PROCESSING 36 (January 1975): 32-34.

Coplin, R.A. "Industrial Test Marketing (Concept Testing)." SALES MANAGEMENT 93 (18 September 1964): 61-62.

> New industrial products can be test marketed just like consumer products. An outline of the testing procedure, as it relates to new product development, is described along with limitations of industrial test marketing.

Danzig, F. "New Products: Test Them Fast or Lose Edge." ADVERTISING AGE 39 (1 January 1968): 3.

> Deals with the rate of growth of competition when a product is released. Stresses that the innovator of a new product should get the product on the market as soon as possible to keep up with the competition.

David, Morton A. "Positioning the Product Conceptually." In PROCEEDINGS: AMERICAN MARKETING ASSOCIATION SPRING CONFERENCE, edited by David L. Sparks, p. 33. Chicago: American Marketing Association, 1970.

> Advocates early product testing of the new product idea. This advanced evaluation would indicate to the management the areas where the product is weak and how it can be improved.

Davis, E.J. "Test Marketing: An Examination of Sales Patterns." In CREATING AND MARKETING NEW PRODUCTS, edited by R. Hayhurst, pp. 335-49. London: Crosby Lockwood Staples, 1973.

Davis, Linden A. "New Product Forecasting Techniques May Make Test Markets Obsolete." MARKETING NEWS 9 (19 November 1976): 1.

> Discusses some techniques used in the prediction of new product development, including simulation laboratories, computer modelling, and heuristic methods.

Day, C. "Consumer Testing, Mighty Power Behind the Products." SALES MANAGEMENT 95 (2 July 1965): 20-22.

> Describes how consumer panels can eliminate new products which looked very promising to developers and marketers. The panels are relatively inexpensive and people are generally willing to serve on such panels.

Day, R.L. "Position Bias in Paired Tests." JOURNAL OF MARKETING RESEARCH 6 (February 1969): 98-100.

> Deals with the use of paired comparison tests as a form of product testing. Position bias is said to occur only when two products are quite similar.

_____. "Preference Tests and the Management of Product Features." JOURNAL OF MARKETING 32 (July 1968): 24-89.

> One of the decisions required to be made in the introduction of new product process is to evaluate the competitive effectiveness of product features. Article examines how managers arrive at this estimate.

"Day the Testing Stops Go-No-Go?" SALES MANAGEMENT 102 (1 March 1969): 35-36.

> Discusses the length of the test period necessary before a new product can be launched into the market and also the appropriate time to make a go-no-go decision.

DeKadt, Pieter P. "New Techniques in Evaluating Test Markets." In PROCEEDINGS: AMERICAN MARKETING ASSOCIATION SPRING-FALL CONFERENCE, edited by Fred C. Allvine, pp. 154-57. Chicago: American Marketing Association, 1971.

> Discusses some nontraditional methods of test marketing from the point of view of speed, accuracy, and low cost. These include sales wave research, simulated store technique, controlled stores, and consumer panels.

Duncan, J.K. "Test Marketing is Passe." ADVERTISING AGE 38 (20 February 1967): 18+.

> Deals with the problem of test marketing such as expense, delay, and insufficient data collection. Suggests instead the test whether a product can be easily promoted on television or not which would indicate product success.

Eassie, R.W.F. "Test Marketing." ADMAP 8 (November 1972): 362-67.

> Examines the future flow of new products and their characteristics, and considers where test marketing procedures fit into the develop-

ment programs of these new products, in terms of the length and cost of test markets, lack of secrecy, and the exposure of one's plans and product to the competition.

Edge, H.A., et al. "The Survival Probability Function: A Useful Concept in Evaluation of Innovation Projects." R & D MANAGEMENT 2 (1972): 91-96.

Enrick, Norbert Lloyd. "A Quick and Ready Approach to the Evaluation of Individual Product Potentials." INDUSTRIAL CANADA 69 (August 1968): 26-30.

Same article also in MARKETING INSIGHTS 3 (6 January 1969): 14-17.

Eskin, Gerald J. "A Case for Test Marketing Experiments." JOURNAL OF ADVERTISING RESEARCH 15 (April 1975): 27-33.

Reports a controlled-variable test conducted during the test marketing of a new convenience food product in which attempts were made to determine how two major marketing tools, advertising and price, affected product performance. Results indicate that the effectiveness of advertising as a sales-inducing factor depended on the price charged. They suggest low price, high advertising to building a market as an alternative to high price, and low advertising to build margin. Implications of the research for test-market planning are also examined.

Eskin, Gerald J., and Baron, Penny H. "Effects of Price and Advertising in Test - Market Experiments." JOURNAL OF MARKETING RESEARCH 14 (November 1977): 499-508.

Examines the effects of price and advertising expenditure on new product sales across four test-market experiments involving two levels of advertising expenditure across cities, and two or three price levels across stores within a city. Results supported a negative price main effect, a positive advertising main effect, and a negative price-advertising interaction.

EVALUATING NEW PRODUCT PROPOSALS. Report no. 604. New York: Conference Board, 1973. 108 p.

Discusses the criteria for evaluating new product projects, evidence required to justify their approval, commercialization, and the testing methods to obtain such evidence.

Ferris, George E. "Merchandising Tests." In PROCEEDINGS: AMERICAN MARKETING ASSOCIATION SUMMER CONFERENCE, edited by John S. Wright and Jack L. Goldstucker, pp. 428-32. Chicago: American Marketing Association, 1966.

Case study in the marketing of a low-profit item.

Floyd, T.E., and Stout, R.G. "Measuring Small Changes in a Market Variable." JOURNAL OF MARKETING RESEARCH 7 (February 1970): 114-16.

> Describes a controlled experiment and a conventional test market technique of evaluation to determine the impact on sales of two slightly different packages for the same product. The controlled test provided management with usable results at substantially less cost than the conventional method.

Ford, K., et al. "Management Guide: Test Marketing." PRINTERS INK 291 (August 1965): 21-95.

Frank, Newton. "The Extended Use Testing - The Neglected Area of Research." In PROCEEDINGS: AMERICAN MARKETING ASSOCIATION SPRING CONFERENCE, edited by David L. Sparks, pp. 5-6. Chicago: American Marketing Association, 1970.

> Explains how this technique would be useful in concentrating on winners and weeding out product losers.

Frech, E.B. "Score Card for New Products: How to Pick a Winner." MANAGEMENT REVIEW 66 (February 1977): 11.

> Describes how to use a product profile chart to help spot best bets through graphic multiplier evaluation.

Freimer, Marshall, and Simon, Leonard. "Evaluation Potential of New Product Alternatives." MANAGEMENT SCIENCE 13 (February 1967): B279-B292.

> Relates facts which must be taken into account in evaluating a new product through use of a rating scheme.

_____. "Screening New Product Ideas." In PROCEEDINGS: AMERICAN MARKETING ASSOCIATION FALL CONFERENCE, edited by Robert L. King, pp. 99-104. Chicago: American Marketing Association, 1968.

> Explains the use and advantages of sensitivity analysis for studying new product opportunities.

Frost, W.A.K. NEW PRODUCT CONCEPT RESEARCH: GETTING STARTED. London: Market Research Society Course on Concept Testing, 1968.

Gediman, L.M. "Management Guide to Testmarketing." PRINTERS INK 291 (27 August 1965): 63-64.

> Special issue. Discusses when, what and where, to test market, how much to spend for advertisement, role of research and values, and limitations of test marketing methods.

Gensch, D.H., and Golob, T.F. "Testing the Consistency of Attribute Meaning in Empirical Concept Testing." JOURNAL OF MARKETING RESEARCH 12 (August 1975): 348-54.

> Deals with the problems of accurately gauging the public's perception of a new product or service, and their preference for alternative designs of new product.

Gerenia, J.O. "Test Less, Learn More." MACHINE DESIGN 49 (8 September 1977): 110-15.

> Describes a method for optimizing performance of a new product with relatively few test runs. Provides a three dimensional picture which enables marketers to see the effects of system variable over the entire operating range.

Goldberg, Robert. "The Laboratory Test Market." MARKETING REVIEW 8 (September 1969): 10-13.

Gottlieb, Morris J., and Roshwalb, I. "The Present Value Concept in Evaluating New Products." In PROCEEDINGS: AMERICAN MARKETING ASSOCIATION SUMMER CONFERENCE, edited by John S. Wright and Jack L. Goldstucker, pp. 387-400. Chicago: American Marketing Association, 1966.

> Time value of dollar investment is used to compare profitability of new product opportunities.

Greenwald, H.M. "Product Concept Testing on Film." BUSINESS MANAGEMENT 35 (March 1969): 26-29.

> Some companies test a concept before pouring money into a new product. Here is a way to test the concept better and cheaper on film.

Haley, Russel I., and Gatly, Ronald. "Trouble with Concept Testing." JOURNAL OF MARKETING RESEARCH 8 (May 1971): 230.

> Concept testing is in deep trouble in new product research and advertising because researchers confuse the testing of concepts with the testing of particular executions of those concepts. An experiment which demonstrates the problem and suggests how it should be handled is reported.

Hamilton, H. Ronald. "Screening Business Development Opportunities." BUSINESS HORIZON 17 (August 1974): 13-24.

> Describes an evaluation system for new business opportunities before investing money into them.

Hanan and Son. "Market Test Game." SALES MANAGEMENT 103 (1 July 1969): 37-44.

Describes a simulated new product development and test marketing which allows managers to test without risking their skills in market analysis, product activity, and planning for market entry.

Hansen, W.P. "Quick Audit Methods of Determining Effects of Competitors, New Items." QUICK FROZEN FOODS 27 (April 1965): 41-42.

Hardin, D.K. "Changing Test Market Technology in the U.S.A." EUROPEAN SOCIETY FOR OPINION SURVEYS AND MARKET RESEARCH (ESOMAR) CONGRESS, Cannes, 10-14 September 1972, pp. 315-39.

Results of a survey of test marketing practice covering major American grocery, drug, and household product manufactures in terms of number of products test marketed, environment, number of markets, market selection criteria, marketing research, levels of success, and predictive ability of testing.

_____. "New Approach to Test Marketing." JOURNAL OF MARKETING 30 (October 1966): 28-31.

Discusses how traditional test market techniques are useless in predicting ultimate product success.

Hase, Paul F. "A New Products Management Process Using the Portfolio Concept." In PROCEEDINGS: AMERICAN MARKETING ASSOCIATION SPRING CONFERENCE, edited by David L. Sparks, p. 3. Chicago: American Marketing Association, 1970.

Suggests an adaptation of the portfolio concept for use by management in the frequent evaluation of alternative new product development projects.

Hertz, David B. "Investment Policies That Pay Off." HARVARD BUSINESS REVIEW 46 (January-February 1968): 96-108.

Assesses the effects of alternative investment decisions by a computerized analysis. This is then compared with traditional method of evaluating an investment opportunity.

Horden, D.K., and Marquardt, R. "Increasing Precision of Market Testing." JOURNAL OF MARKETING RESEARCH 4 (November 1967): 396-99.

Increasing use of objective criteria in marketing management calls on researchers to give more accurate data at acceptable cost levels. Article describes a method -- paired test stores-which increases accuracy in sales prediction data in test marketing.

Hoskins, W.A. "Role of Sensory Evaluation In New Product Development." FOOD TECHNOLOGY 25 (April 1971): 397-99.

"How It Paid to Put an Idea to the Test." BUSINESS WEEK, 14 October 1967, pp. 176-78.

Describes the lessons learned by General Electric from its market testing when it thought it had developed a surefire consumer product.

"How Test Runs Give Budget Answers." BROADCASTING 80 (1 February 1971): 52-56.

Huger, A. "Possibilities of Test Marketing." EUROPEAN SOCIETY FOR OPINION SURVEYS AND MARKET RESEARCH (ESOMAR) CONGRESS, Brussels, September 1966, 17 p.

Testmarketing is defined and the author believes that the majority of marketing problems can be solved without resorting to test market surveys. First section of the paper deals with the test marketing of existing products. Second section concerns test marketing new products.

Hutchinson, Alex C. "Planned Euthanasia for Old Projects." LONG RANGE PLANNING 4 (December 1971): 17-22.

Describes a technique for the financial evaluation of the desirability for closing manufacturing activities which are showing declining profitability.

"In A Tossing Sea of Risk and Wrecks: Testings Hold Privateers." SALES MANAGEMENT 102 (1 March 1969): 29-30.

Outlines a plan for minitesting involving usually small, isolated markets away from the urban area where controlled store experiments may be necessary. Plan is cheaper and quicker than conventional test marketing.

"Industrial Test Marketing: A Quickening Pace." SALES MANAGEMENT 102 (1 March 1969): 31-32.

Explains the factors involved in industrial test marketing and how it differs from testing in the consumer product area.

Iuso, B. "Concept Testing: An Appropriate Approach." JOURNAL OF MARKETING RESEARCH 12 (May 1975): 228-31.

Suggests a more professional treatment of the concept testing theory including preparation of appropriate idea stimuli, conduct of length, and sensitive consumer interactions and systematic assessment procedure.

Jagetia Lal, C., and Marien, Edward J. "Evaluating New Product Decision Processes." OMEGA: INTERNATIONAL JOURNAL OF MANAGEMENT SCIENCE 2 (June 1974): 379-88.

Development of a new product requires a sequence decision process, many stages of which may involve a choice of alternatives. Paper describes an efficient algorithm for solving this sequential decision process.

Johnson, Michael L. "Matching Products With Markets." INDUSTRY WEEK 191 (15 November 1976): 96-98.

Pretesting the new product is necessary to reduce failures. This is especially necessary because of today's higher cost demand. Customers are more value-conscious than ever before.

Kaponen, A. "Improve Test Marketing." SPONSOR 19 (1 November 1965): 25.

Several common errors in test marketing are cited. Urges companies to be sure their products live up to the advertising claims to insure repeat purchase.

Kelly, P.J. "How Media Men React to Test Market Efforts." PRINTERS INK 291 (27 August 1965): 81-82.

Reports on a survey of media men on their feelings towards test marketing. Some of the responses were that the media lacks awareness of test results. The biggest problem was a lack of a basic groundwork underlying test marketing.

Keshin, M. "Planners Role in Test Marketing." MEDIA/SCOPE 11 (December 1967): 14.

King, S.J. "How Useful is Proposition Testing?" ADVERTISING QUARTERLY 6 (Winter 1965-1966). 24 .

Kirk, N.S., and Ward, J.S. "Product Evaluation." DESIGN no. 204 (December 1965): 64-67.

Klassen, E.T. "Test of the Total Product." DUNS REVIEW 88 (November 1966): 139-40.

Klompmaker, Jay, et al. "Test Marketing In New Product Development." HARVARD BUSINESS REVIEW 54 (May-June 1976): 128-38.

Clarifies when a market test should be done, shows objective of test marketing and uses. Results of a survey of executives involved in product innovation.

Kraushar, Peter M. "New Products and Diversification." ADVERTISING AGE 45 (September 1970): 25-27.

Suggests that the amount of risk in the introduction of new products decides the question whether there is a need for test marketing before launch and, if so, how much.

Kroeger, A.R. "Test Marketing: The Concept and How it is Changing."
MEDIA/SCOPE 10 (December 1966): 63-66, also 11 (January 1967): 51-54.

Kubick, Robert R. "Test the Concept, Not the Product." BUSINESS MAN-
AGEMENT 32 (July 1967): 58-62.

Because the odds against a new product's survival are so high,
marketing men constantly seek ways to make sure that their product is the right product. Article discusses a method that is not
so well known: concept testing. This involves the testing of the
product concept rather than the product itself, and can apply to
both consumer and industrial products.

Lance, J.R. "Will That New Product Make It?" MACHINE DESIGN 48 (26
February 1976): 72-77.

Describes a model for evaluating product proposals quickly which
will provide an accurate, before-the-fact, look at cost and profit
under changing market conditions.

Land, Thomas H. "Test Market Measurements for Small Business." In PRO-
CEEDINGS: AMERICAN MARKETING ASSOCIATION SUMMER CONFERENCE,
edited by John S. Wright and Jack L. Goldstucker, pp. 420-27. Chicago:
American Marketing Association, 1966.

Examines methods of screening new products for potential success
which would reduce reliance on test markets.

LaPasso, Leonard J. "Reducing the Risks in New Product Planning." MACHINE
DESIGN 47 (24 July 1975): 42-45.

To prevent failure of new products, a thorough, systematized evaluation and planning procedure is necessary. Article discusses how
this can be done.

Laric, Michael V. "New Product Planning: The Case for Concept Pretesting:
A Methodology for Evaluating the Effect of a Concept's Execution on Respondent's Preference." Ph.D. dissertation, City University of New York, 1976.
218 p.

Lincoln, J.E. "Improving Test Marketing." SPONSOR 19 (3 May 1965):
32-35.

Lipstein, Benjamin. "The Design of Test Marketing Experiments." JOURNAL
OF ADVERTISING RESEARCH 5 (December 1965): 2-7.

Deals with the structure and development of test markets. Variations both within and outside the market need to be considered. List of external disturbances to test markets is also provided.

_____. "Test Marketing: A Perturbation in the Market Place." MANAGEMENT SCIENCE 14 (April 1968): B437-B448.

Develops a method of analysis to measure the market's stability prior to new product entry and the disequilibrium created by the entry. Method would enable management to reduce by half the time lost in test marketing.

Locander, William B., and Scammell, Richard W. "Screening New Product Ideas - A Two-Phase Approach." RESEARCH MANAGEMENT 19 (1976): 14-18.

Discusses a method that groups product ideas according to commonalities and then considers the traditional viability-profitability factors.

McCausland, J. "Staging a Prepared Frozen Product Prior to Test Marketing." QUICK FROZEN FOODS 32 (January 1970): 103-4.

McGuire, E. Patrick. EVALUATING NEW-PRODUCT PROPOSALS. New York: Conference Board, 1973. 108 p.

Because of the integral role of decision in the marketing life of the new product, management ever seeks to improve the quality of decision making. Practices of 203 manufacturing and service firms with active programs of product and service developments, as well as the experience of outside researchers, consultants, advertising practitioners, and university professors are described.

"Management Guide to Test Marketing." PRINTERS INK 291 (27 August 1965): 21-90, also 291 (26 August 1966): 10.

Discusses all aspects of test marketing in terms of its current complexity, media selection and package redesign. Also discusses DEMON techniques.

"Market Pretesting - A Quickening Pace." SALES MANAGEMENT 102 (1 March 1969): 33-34.

Explains concept testing and product testing methods which represent two standard steps in pretest marketing research in major consumer product companies.

MARKET TESTING CONSUMER PRODUCTS. New York: Conference Board, 1967. 196 p.

Symposium on concept testing, product testing, prototype testing, purchase simulation, and miniature market tests. Participants were noted marketing practitioners.

"Market Testing Overrated as a Sole Means of Evaluating Frozen Food Potential." QUICK FROZEN FOODS 34 (February 1972): 36-37.

"Masterson, W.W. "Fresh Concept for Test Marketing New Products." MARKETING/COMMUNICATIONS 296 (May 1968): 29.

_____. "Test Marketing: Pathway Through New Product Maze." PRINTERS INK 291 (27 August 1965): 69-70.

Meshulach, Avraham. "Product Selection Decisions in Small Electronic Companies." Ph.D. dissertation, Harvard University, 1967. 30 p.

Morley, John. "How to Run a Test Market." BUSINESS 96 (July 1966): 64-67.

Morrissey, Thomas F. "Decision Theory and Choice Criteria for New Product Selection." UNIVERSITY OF FLORIDA, COLLEGE OF BUSINESS ADMINISTRATION, BUSINESS AND ECONOMIC DIMENSIONS 5 (October 1969): 1-11.

> Methodical process of new product selection can raise a firm's average of successes in the market place. Article stresses that the qualitative terms that describe a new product in its conceptual stage must first be defined. These terms are expressed by a set of factors described in detail.

Mullins, Peter L. "Integrating Marketing and Financial Concepts in Product Line Evaluations." FINANCIAL EXECUTIVE 40 (May 1972): 32-38.

> Explains the advantages and disadvantages of a "turn and earn" concept for product line comparisons.

Nemec, Joseph R., and Herbat, Terry. "New Trends in Product Testing." BUSINESS HORIZON 18 (October 1975): 31-36.

> Explains the importance and the efficacy of product safety and labelling in product tests.

"The Odds in Test Marketing." NIELSEN RESEARCHER, no. 4, 1972, pp. 2-15.

> Examines the predictive validity of test marketing efforts taking the case of a grocery brand after it has been introduced. Also outlines the basic procedures in test marketing.

Odesky, Stanford H. "Handling the Neutral Vote in Paired Comparison Product Testing." JOURNAL OF MARKETING RESEARCH 4 (May 1967): 199-201.

In a paired comparison test, the number of "no preference" responses can definitely be influenced by the wording of the question. More important, allocation of such responses among the total test score can have serious effects. Article suggests a method for handling the neutral vote.

Parry, Eugene W. "New Product Management: How to Get More Products for Your Engineering Dollars." ELECTRICAL ENGINEER 28 (January 1969): 38-46.

Discusses the engineering aspects of screening, product design and development, testing, evaluation, and commercialization.

Payne, Donald E. "Jet Set, Pseudo Store, and New Product Testing." JOURNAL OF MARKETING RESEARCH 3 (November 1966): 372-76.

Simulated retail stores appear to offer promise for analysis of consumer purchasing decisions. Article reports the results of a test conducted in such a store to determine consumers' appeal of a manufacturers' proposed new portable television. This approach is feasible for relatively highpriced, infrequently purchased, products and appears to be a valid procedure for predicting subsequent market acceptance.

Penny, J.C. "Product Testing Methodology in Relation to Marketing Problems: A Review." JOURNAL OF MARKET RESEARCH SOCIETY 14 (January 1972): 1-29.

Puts forward the view that consumer discrimination and preference be taken as a guide in designing models for use in consumer product testing experiments.

"Pretesting: When is a Market Test Not a Test Market." SALES MANAGEMENT 108 (10 January 1972): 34.

Deals with technique used early in product development process before major effort is expended on a production design, promotion, marketing, and sales.

Pymont, B.C. "The Development and Application of a New Micro-Market Testing Technique." EUROPEAN SOCIETY FOR OPINION SURVEYS AND MARKET RESEARCH (ESOMAR) CONGRESS, Barcelona, 1970, pp. 201-21.

Describes the development and application of a new technique designed to expose a new product to test market type evaluation, in particular the crucial repeat-buying factor. The technique operates through a consumer panel of housewives which is serviced by a mobile retail system supported by its own self-contained advertising medium in the form of a brochure exclusive to panel members.

Rao, Vithala R., and Soutar, Geoffrey N. "Subjective Evaluations for Product Design." DECISION SCIENCES 6 (January 1975): 120–34.

Reitter, R.N. "Product Testing in Segmented Markets." JOURNAL OF MARKETING RESEARCH 6 (May 1969): 179–84.

Segmentation conflicts with aims of traditional preference testing. Article suggests modified differential scales to enable study of preference for alternative products and concepts among relevant market segments.

Roberto, Eduardo, and Pinson, Christian. "Compatibility Analysis for the Screening of New Products." EUROPEAN JOURNAL OF MARKETING 6 (Autumn 1972): 182–89.

Deals with the screening stage of new product development, i.e., where a quick analysis is required to determine which ideas are pertinent and merit more detailed study. The evaluation method developed is referred to as the lexographic technique and its application is illustrated by consideration of a hypothetical case where fine new product candidates were under review for possible inclusion in a company's current line.

Root, Harvey Paul. "The Analysis of New Products: A Comparative Study of the Evaluation of Product Innovations." Ph.D. dissertation, Purdue University, 1969. 245 p. Ann Arbor, Mich.: University Microfilms. Order no. 69-17247.

Examines the role of computer simulation models in the analysis of new product investment decisions.

Roscow, Y.S. "Can Success Spoil a Test Marketing Plan?" PRINTERS INK 295 (25 August 1967): 17–18.

Stresses need for marketing caution in cases where new product gains instant acceptance in the test market place.

Ross, I. "Handling the Neutral Vote in Product Testing." JOURNAL OF MARKETING RESEARCH 6 (May 1969): 221–22.

Reports an empirical test to determine which of two methods for allocating neutral responses, i.e., no preference, or no difference, or just right, for a product attribute evaluation which would approximate real preference, had they been forced to make a choice.

"Sales Management Asks Marketing Executives: How Do You Test Market a Product." SALES MANAGEMENT 97 (1 October 1966): 81–83.

Survey of opinions of marketing executives as to how they market tested new products before introduction.

Scanlon, Sally. Test Markets: Is the Chemistry Changing?" SALES MAN-
AGEMENT 110 (16 April 1973): 21-28.

> Traditional factors which go into the makeup of test areas included
> effective buying income, trade distribution, competition, and media.
> Article discusses some conditional factors which are increasingly
> taken into account by test marketers.

Schwartz, D.A. "Six Keys to Evaluating New Consumers Products." RE-
SEARCH/DEVELOPMENT 22 (February 1971): 22-23.

> Model which can be used to insure that engineering tests will
> provide a true picture of the worth of new product.

Scott, G.C. "Evaluation of Ideas for New Products." FOOD TECHNOLOGY
19 (October 1965): 1523-27.

Sellstedt, Bo. SELECTION OF PRODUCT DEVELOPMENT PROJECTS UNCER-
TAINTY. Stockholm University, Department of Business Administration. Monograph no. 6. Bonnier: Stockholm University, 1972. 230 p.

Sherak, Bud. "Control and Reduction of Error in Marketing Tests." In PRO-
CEEDINGS: .AMERICAN MARKETING ASSOCIATION SUMMER CONFERENCE,
edited by John S. Wright and Jack L. Goldstucker, pp. 433-39. Chicago:
American Marketing Association, 1966.

> Describes the operation of a controlled market testing facility and
> how to reduce variability and error in testing.

_____. "Testing New Product Ideas." EUROPEAN SOCIETY FOR OPINION
SURVEYS AND MARKET RESEARCH (ESOMAR) CONGRESS, Brussels, September
1966, 15 p.

Shinneman, William J. "Product Evaluation Using the Assigned Value Approach." MANAGEMENT ACCOUNTING 49 (May 1968): 35-40.

> Describes how to determine the profitability of the product which
> may be produced from another manufacturered within the company.

Shoemaker, Robert Worrall. "Decision Procedures Using Purchase Panel Data
for New Product Introductions." Ph.D. dissertation, Carnegie-Mellon University, 1972. 272 p. Ann Arbor, Mich.: University Microfilms. Order no.
72-29868.

> Using consumer panel derived from introductory period for five
> new products, this study attempts to develop and test the under-
> lying distribution models.

Silk, Alvin J., and Urban, Glen L. "Pre-Test-Market Evaluation of New
Packaged Goods: A Model and Measurement Methodology." JOURNAL OF
MARKETING RESEARCH 15 (May 1978): 171-91.

Presents a set of measurement procedures and models designed to produce estimates of the sales potential of a new packaged good before test marketing. Case application of the system also is discussed.

"Simulation Sharpens Product Pretesting." PRINTERS INK 295 (25 August 1967): 15-16.

Expresses the view that simulation pretests help make tests more accurate, but they are not a substitute for market tests.

Sittenfield, Hans. TEST MARKETING. New York: International Publications, 1969. 123 p.

Smulian, P.A. TESTING THE PRODUCT. London: Market Research Society Course on Research on New Products, 1968.

Sobel, Charles A., and Lysaker, Richard L. "New Developments in the Use of Experimental Designs in In-Store Testing." In PROCEEDINGS: AMERICAN MARKETING ASSOCIATION SUMMER CONFERENCE, edited by John S. Wright and Jack L. Goldstucker, pp. 450-60. Chicago: American Marketing Association, 1966.

Demonstrates the working of some in-store testing methods.

Springer, J. "Step-by-Step Entry into New Product Area Fends off Nasty Surprises." ADVERTISING AGE 42 (22 November 1971): 34.

Describes how to eliminate guesswork in new product evaluation even before the idea is put to a test market.

Stanton, Frank. "What is Wrong With Test Marketing." JOURNAL OF MARKETING 31 (April 1967): 43-47.

Article examines the desirability of the testing of marketing innovations by actually placing them in a limited number of test markets and then observing consumer reaction has become a way of life for most consumer packaged goods companies.

Tauber, Edward M. "Forecasting Sales Prior to Test Market." JOURNAL OF MARKETING 41 (January 1977): 80-84.

Reviews four systems for forecasting: concept and product tests for probabilistically predicting trial, and first repeat for continuous innovations but not measuring adoption and frequency of purchase, historical data regression models, laboratory test markets, and sales wave experiments.

_____. "What is Measured by Concept Testing." JOURNAL OF ADVERTISING RESEARCH 12 (December 1972): 35-37.

Discusses what is involved in a concept test including the product idea, communication, positioning, and design. Also surveys available literature.

_____. "Why Concept and Product Tests Fail to Predict New Product Results." JOURNAL OF MARKETING 39 (October 1975): 69-71.

High failure rate of new product introductions suggests the need for reevaluation of concept and product tests. Factors leading to failure include poor product, advertising, pricing, or distribution. Author calls for a method which would help predict ongoing sales for a test product.

Taylor, T.C. "Test Marketing: High Hopes for those Go/No-Go Decision." SALES MANAGEMENT 97 (15 September 1966): 75-82.

Explains and illustrates the application of computerized test marketing techniques.

"Test Marketing." INTERNATIONAL TRADE FORUM 5 (October 1969): 10-11.

"Test Marketing--Is It Worth It?" BUSINESS WEEK, 4 March 1972, pp. 72-77.

Advantages and disadvantages of test marketing are illustrated by using actual examples from the experience of large companies, such as General Foods. Also discusses alternatives to test marketing.

"Test Marketing--1976: Calling the Shots More Closely." SALES AND MARKETING MANAGEMENT 116 (May 1976): 43-48.

Testmarketing has become more important, the author claims, because it is the only tool that comes close to predicting a new product's return on investment (ROI). Article lists and discusses significant trends in market testing, including more sophisticated matching of test market sites to the needs of the particular product, and the company's market plan.

"Test Marketing--Think Small." SALES MANAGEMENT 101 (15 September 1968): 39-40.

"Test Marketing: Who's Got the Pulse of the Consumer." SALES MANAGEMENT 106 (1 March 1971): 19-26.

Describes some of the more popular and promising test adjuncts and, where applicable, their costs. More and more marketers are finding that test market results alone do not tell the whole story of a product's market potential. As a result, they are exploring supplementary channels of information, some formal, some not so formal.

Thornton, C. CONCEPT TESTING. England: University of Bradford, Management Center Course on Creating and Marketing New Products, 1969.

Vanderwicken, Peter. "P & G's Secret Ingredient." FORTUNE, July 1974, 75.

Describes the procedures followed in the Proctor and Gamble Company for concept testing new products.

Weiss, E.B. "Industry Needs System for Evaluating Product Innovation." ADVERTISING AGE 40 (29 September 1969): 104.

_____. "New Product Evaluation Needs Serious Revamping." ADVERTISING AGE 40 (15 December 1969): 59-60.

_____. "Test New Consumer Products First in Institutional Markets." INSTITUTIONS/VOLUME FEEDING MANAGEMENT 68 (1 April 1971): 14.

Wells, Donald A. "Test Marketing and the Computers." PRINTERS INK 293 (26 August 1966): 37.

Explains the DEMON systems approach to coping with myriad of variables involved with new product introduction. Article explains how this system works.

Wills, Gordon. "Cost Benefit Analysis of a Test Market." MANAGEMENT DESIGN 14 (Winter 1969): 17-21.

Explains the use of bayesian decision theory, network analysis and discounted cash flow concept in the evaluation of test marketing effectiveness.

Wind, Yoram. "A New Procedure for Concept Evaluation." JOURNAL OF MARKETING RESEARCH 37 (October 1973): 2-11.

Analyzes the technique of multivariate concept testing to identify market segments and competitive positioning of products.

Wisz, Geral G. "A Markovian Approach to Product Evaluation." Ph.D. dissertation, Johns Hopkins University, 1965. 144 p. Ann Arbor, Mich.: University Microfilms. Order no. 65-10439.

Most firms need to establish a list of priorities in the development of new products, based on potentiality for profit. Study investigates the possibility of applying a model based on Markov process to the problem of arriving at such priorities.

Yuspeh, Sonia. "Diagnosis: The Handmaiden of Prediction." JOURNAL OF MARKETING 39 (January 1975): 87-89.

Need for fully testing new product ideas early in their developmental stages has always been felt by marketing managers. Author suggests a method to measure at the same time a predisposition to buy and market potential. The idea of need-satisfaction concept testing is put forward. Author calls for gathering data in the following areas: dissatisfaction with existing products, purchase and use patterns, competitive brand substitutability, anticipated usage patterns, and the perceived strength and weakness of the product or concept.

Zeitner, Herbert. "When Should You Market Test: Five Guides Help You Decide." ADVERTISING AGE 48 (17 January 1977): 46.

Underlines the pitfalls of overreliance on or misuse of test marketing and its results. Problems as pointed out are: assuming a degree of reliability that is simply not realistic, problems of accuracy and validity, impractical levels of expenditure, problems of scale, loss of lead time and a strategic advantage. Author also gives guidelines to test marketing.

Ziegler, I. "How to Target New Target Media Plans." MEDIA/SCOPE 11 (September 1967): 146.

AUTHOR INDEX

This index includes all authors, editors, compilers, translators, and contributors cited in the text. References are to page numbers and alphabetization is letter by letter.

Author Index

Barnes, J. 100
Barnett, Norman L. 101, 150
Baron, Penny H. 198
Bass, F.M. 22, 52, 107
Bass, Lawrence Wade 135
Baumann, H.D. 28
Baumgarten, S.A. 75, 101
Beardsley, G. 52
Beattie, D.W. 194
Beattie, J.M. 28
Becker, S.W. 136
Beckman, Dale M. 75
Beliveau, Donald 101
Bell, D.E. 28
Bell, J.B. 125
Bell, W.E. 85
Bellas, Carl J. 53
Ben Daniel, David 2
Bennet, J.B. 2
Bennett, K.W. 28, 136, 150
Bensahel, J.G. 28
Benson, George 28
Berdy, Edwin M. 194
Bergeron, Pierre G. 3
Berkman, K.A. 143
Berliner, Joseph S. 170
Berman, S.I. 136
Bernado, Nicoletti 101
Bernhardt, Irwin 53
Berning, Carol A. Kohn 53
Berow, S. William 29
Berton, L. 136
Betts, D.J. 29
Bickford, J.J. 29
Bieda, John C. 126
Biller, Alan D. 136
Bingham, J.S. 180
Binkered, E.F. 29
Bird, K. 180
Bissell, Herbert D. 136
Bjorksten, Johan 150
Blake, Brian 101
Blattberg, R. 53
Blecke, Curtis J. 170
Blitch, Charles Parrish 170
Blood, Jerome W. 136
Bloom, J.E. 194
Bobbe, Richard A. 137
Bobis, A.H. 137
Bogaty, Herman 3

Boger, C.K. 150
Boliek, Paul E. 137
Bolz, Roger W. 29
Boone, Louis E. 102
Booze, Allen and Hamilton Inc. 30
Borden, Neil Hopper 102, 150
Bours, W.A. 137
Boykin, A.L. 150
Bradbury, R.F. 75
Braden, John H.C. 53
Bradley, H.A. 137
Bradspies, R.W. 40
Brand, Gruber 3
Braun, Michael A. 102, 122
Brenner, Vincent C. 194
Brickner, William Homer 170
Briscoe, G. 180
Britt, Steuart Henderson 151
Brooks, Robert W. 3
Brooksher, William R. 154
Brown, Alfred E. 137
Brown, Charles G. 3
Brown, David 194
Brown, G.H. 137
Brown, Gordon 194
Brown, James W. 148
Brown, Kevin V. 180
Bruce, Robert D. 126
Bruno, Albert V. 4
Bryk, Terry 102
Buck, R.C. 182
Buddenhagen, F.L. 30
Buell, Victor P. 30
Bujake, John E. 30, 75
Bull, John S. 30
Burger, Phillip Clinton 151
Burger, Phillipe 102
Burgman, Roland 103
Burnham, R.A. 75
Burns, Robert Obed 76
Bursk, E.C. 30
Butrick, Frank M. 4, 30
Buzzell, Robert D. 76, 170, 171
Bylinsky, Gene 180

C

Cadbury, N.D. 194
Caffyn, J.M. 103, 195
Calabaro, Natalie 195

Author Index

David, Morton A. 196
Davidson, J. Hugh 152
Davis, D.S. 78
Davis, E.J. 152, 196
Davis, John C. 138
Davis, Linden A. 196
Day, C. 181, 197
Day, George S. 6, 57, 104
Day, R.L. 127, 197
Dean, Burton Victor 138, 139
Dean, J.M. 182
Dean, Joel 171
Dean, Michael Lewis 104
Dearden, John 171
De Jong, P.L.F. 57
DeKadt, Pieter P. 197
DeNisco, S. 104
Desrosier, John N. 171
Desrosier, Norman W. 171
Dessauer, John H. 139
DeVries, Marvin G. 33
Dhalla, Nariman K. 152
Diehl, Rick W. 78
Digman, Lester A. 68
Dillon, T.F. 127
Doblin, J. 6
Dodds, Wellesley 57
Dodson, John W. 57
Dominguez, George S. 33
Donnelly, James H. 104, 105, 110
Dore, J.B. 152
Dorr, E.L. 17
Douglas, G. 6
Dov, A.G. Beged 139
Dowst, S. 57
Doyle, Peter 153
Drake, Nick J. 127
Duncan, J.K. 197
Duncan, P.L. 124
Dunkley, John C. 7
Dunn, Dan T. 33
Dunn, M.J. 153
Dunne, Patrick M. 7
Dusenbury, Warren 57
Dutton, R.E. 139

E

Eassie, R.W.F. 197
Eastlack, J.O. 7, 42, 153

Eckles, Robert W. 34
Edelman, Franz 171
Edge, H.A. 198
Edmondson, B.C. 56
Eggleston, David 34
Egloff, William F. 34
Ehrenberg, A.S.C. 58, 127, 182
Ehrenfeld, E. 54
Elnicki, R.A. 172
el-Enein, Gaber Abou 172
Engel, James F. 78, 83, 105, 182
England, L. 127
Enrick, Norbert Lloyd 198
Erdos, Paul L. 127
Eskin, Gerald J. 58, 198
Etzel, Michael J. 104
Evans, Richard H. 7, 105
Exton, William 78
Eyrith, G.I. 72

F

Fabris, Richard Harris 78
Fast, Norman D. 139
Fazia, Harry 139
Feldman, Laurence P. 79
Fendrich, C. Welles 34
Ferrell, Odies Collins 172
Ferris, George E. 198
Fiedler, J.A. 105
Field, G.A. 153
Field, J.G. 128
Fisher, Rupert 58
Fisk, George 106
Flanagan, Robert James 172
Fliegel, Frederick C. 79, 106
Floyd, T.E. 199
Fogg, C. Davis 7
Fond, A.B. 7
Ford, K. 199
Foss, B. 7
Foster, Douglas W. 8
Foster, Richard N. 36
Foster, W.K. 128
Fox, Harold W. 79, 106, 139, 153
Foy, G.E. 153
Frand, Ervin A. 153
Frank, L.K. 154
Frank, Newton 199
Frank, Ronald E. 8, 59

Author Index

Author Index

Leroy, Georges Paul 85
Lerviks, Alf-Erik 62
Lesley, Kenneth L. 41
Lessig, V.P. 114
Lester, William Bernard 114
Levine, Philip 62
Levit, Theodore 86, 157, 185
Libien, Myron A. 42
Liddy, L.E. 55
Liles, Patrick R. 86
Lincoln, J.E. 204
Linehan, Thomas A. 114
Linsky, Barry R. 14
Lipinsky, E.S. 48
Lipstein, Benjamin 62, 204
Little, Blair 14, 17, 63, 77, 86, 90, 126, 130
Little, J.D.C. 63
Locander, William B. 14, 205
Locke, H.B. 86
Lodish, L.M. 63
Long, Durwood 130
Long, James 8
Long, John B. 13
Longbottom, D.A. 63
Lorsch, Jay William 86
Lovell, M.R.C. 114
Loyd, A. 103
Luck, David J. 42
Luck, T.J. 42
Lynn, J.E. 14
Lysaker, Richard L. 210

M

McCarthy, J. 42
McCarthy, J.F. 142
McCausland, J. 205
McConnell, John Douglas 114
McDonald, D.J. 42, 174
MacDonald, Morgan B. 14, 157
McDonald, Philip R. 42
McFarlane, Iain 42
Mcginnis, M.A. 37
McGuire, Edward Patrick 14, 86, 142, 205
McKay, K.G. 86
McKay, Samuel F. 157
Mackenzie, George E. 158
Mackenzie, Kenneth D. 53

McKersie, R. 27
McNab, Bruce E. 185
McNeal, James U. 114
McNeill, Winfield L. 174
Mancuso, Joseph R. 115
Mansfield, Edwin 52, 87, 143
Margulies, W.P. 158
Marien, Edward J. 202
Marks, E.S. 63
Marks, Norton E. 87
Marquardt, R. 201
Marquis, Donald G. 87, 88
Marsden, B.A. 43
Martin, Albert Joseph 63
Martin, Warren S. 115
Martinez, Arthur 130
Marton, Katherine 143
Marvin, Philip Roger 15
Mason, Joseph Barry 74
Massey, Morris Edgar 115
Massy, William F. 56, 64, 87
Masterson, W.W. 206
Mathey, C.J. 15
Maw, J. Gordon 174
Mayeur, J.P. 130
Mazze, Edward M. 60
Mazzoni, Dominick J. 159
Meck, L.L. 159
Medcalf, Gordon 159
Megathlin, Donald E. 15
Meile, C.H. 174
Melville, Donald R. 43
Mellott, Douglas W. 21
Mendez, A. 87
Merims, Arthur M. 115
Mertes, John E. 115
Meshulach, Avraham 206
Metcalfe, J.S. 87
Michaels, P.W. 115
Midgley, David F. 87
Miles, John Karl 174
Miles, Robert H. 143
Miles, V. 130
Miller, H.M.S. 43
Miller, James R. 143
Miller, Myron M. 174
Millgram, Joseph B. 64
Mills, M.J. 159
Minkes, A.L. 143
Mintz, H.K. 115

Author Index

Peach, Leonard H. 145
Pearl, D.R. 18
Pearson, Arthur S. 18
Pedraglio, Gerard 44
Pegram, R.M. 161
Penny, J.C. 207
Perreault, C.M. 66
Perry, A. 187
Perry, M. 187
Pessemier, Edgar A. 18, 44, 66, 118, 131, 187
Peters, Bruce 90
Peters, J.I. 145
Peters, Michael 10
Peters, Michael Paul 118
Peterson, Robert Allen 118, 162
Peterson, R.W. 187
Petrini, Bart F. 44
Phelps, Ernest D. 44
Phines, W. 46
Piersol, Robert James 67
Pilditch, J. 44
Pinson, Christian 208
Pizam, A. 90
Plant, A.F. 45
Plummer, Joseph T. 131
Polli, R. 162
Poisson, W.H. 162
Popielarz, D.T. 118
Posner, Frederick 19
Pratt, Robert W. 132
Pressley, Milton 19
Primak, G.J. 45
Prince, George M. 90
Purnell, J.M. 65
Pymont, Brian C. 188, 207

Q

Quinlal, J.C. 119
Quinn, James Brian 67, 145

R

Raddant, R. 20
Rae, Alan J. 45
Ragnitz, K. 162
Randall, J.S. 45
Rao, Vithala R. 208
Rapaport, John 90

Raun, Donald L. 67
Raviolo, V. 20
Rawlings, T.C. 119
Reinmuth, J.E. 67
Reitter, R.N. 208
Rengilly, P.J. 66
Reynolds, Fred D. 78, 90
Reynolds, William H. 68, 91, 162, 188
Rhodes, Clifford 145
Richard, Lawrence Milton 119
Ricker, H.S. 163
Ricketts, Donald E. 68
Riegel, W.M. 46
Riggio, C.A. 46
Riley, D. 91
Ringbakk, Kjell-Arne 20
Robert, Edward 91
Roberto, Eduardo 208
Roberts, E.B. 91
Roberts, George A. 145
Roberts, Mary Low 119
Roberts, P. 132
Robertson, A. 91
Robertson, Andrew 163, 188
Robertson, Dan Hugh 91
Robertson, J.A. 68
Robertson, Thomas S. 68, 91, 92, 119, 120
Robinson, Bruce 175
Robinson, Richard Kent 132
Rockley, Lawrence E. 20
Rockwood, Persis Emmett 92
Rodgers, William N. 20
Roe, M. 195
Rogers, Everett M. 92, 93
Romeo, A.A. 93
Rondeau, Herbert F. 46, 188
Root, H. Paul 18, 20, 68, 93, 208
Roscow, Y.S. 208
Rosen, Charles E. 145
Rosen, E.M. 146
Rosenbloom, Richard S. 93
Roshwalb, Irving 120, 200
Ross, Ivan 53, 118, 208
Rossiter, John R. 92
Rotandi, Thomas 93
Rothberg, Robert R. 20, 21
Rothe, J.M. Harvey 46

Author Index

SUBJECT INDEX

This index contains subject areas of interest within the text. Numbers refer to page numbers, and alphabetization is letter by letter.

Subject Index